MULTICULTURAL EDUCATION SERIES

James A. Banks, Series Editor

continued

Teaching What *Really* Happened

How to Avoid the Tyranny of Textbooks and
Get Students *Excited* About Doing History

JAMES W. LOEWEN

TEACHERS COLLEGE PRESS

TEACHERS COLLEGE | COLUMBIA UNIVERSITY
NEW YORK AND LONDON

Illustration Credits: Scott Nearing, p. 6; Minnesota Historical Society, p. 16; James W. Loewen, pp. 55, 72 (top), 142, 202; Idaho State Historical Society, p. 69; *New York Times*, p. 72 (bottom); Glencoe McGraw-Hill, p. 106; *U.S. News and World Report*, p. 156; Library of Congress, p. 172; National Museum of American History, p. 199

Published by Teachers College Press, 1234 Amsterdam Avenue, New York, NY 10027

Library of Congress Cataloging-in-Publication Data

Loewen, James W.
    Teaching what *really* happened : how to avoid the tyranny of textbooks and get
        students *excited* about doing history / James W. Loewen.
        p. cm. — (Multicultural education series)
    Includes bibliographical references and index.
    ISBN 978-0-8077-4991-3 (pbk. : alk. paper)
    ISBN 978-0-8077-4992-0 (hardcover : alk. paper)
        1. United States—History—Textbooks. 2. United States—History—Study
    and teaching. 3. United States—Historiography. I. Title.
    E175.85.L65   2009
    973—dc22   2009015336

ISBN 978-0-8077-4991-3 (paper)
ISBN 978-0-8077-4992-0 (hardcover)

Printed on acid-free paper
Manufactured in the United States of America

22 21 20 19 18 17   12 11 10 9 8 7 6

Contents

Series Foreword

THE NATION'S DEEPENING ETHNIC TEXTURE, interracial tension and conflict, and the increasing percentage of students who speak a first language other than English (Suárez-Orozco, Suárez-Orozco, & Todorova, 2008) make multicultural education imperative. The U.S. Census (2008) projects that ethnic minorities will increase from one-third of the nation's population in 2006 to 50% in 2042 (Roberts, 2008). Ethnic minorities made up 100 million of the total U.S. population of just over 300 million in 2006.

American classrooms are experiencing the largest influx of immigrant students since the beginning of the 20th century. About a million immigrants are making the United States their home each year (Martin & Midgley, 1999). Almost four million (3,780,019) legal immigrants settled in the U.S. between 2000 and 2004. Only 15% came from nations in Europe. Most (66%) came from nations in Asia, from Mexico, and from nations in Latin America, Central America, and the Caribbean (U.S. Department of Homeland Security, 2004). A large but undetermined number of undocumented immigrants also enter the U.S. each year. In 2007, *The New York Times* estimated that there were 12 million illegal immigrants in the United States (Monday, June 4, 2007, p. A22). The influence of an increasingly ethnically diverse population on U.S. schools, colleges, and universities is and will continue to be enormous.

Schools in the U.S. are characterized by rich ethnic, cultural, language, and religious diversity. U.S. schools are more diverse today than they have been since the early 1900s when a flood of immigrants entered the country from Southern, Central, and Eastern Europe. In the 30-year period between 1973 and 2004, the percentage of students of color in U.S. public schools increased from 22 to 43%. If current trends continue, students of color might equal or exceed the percentage of White students in U.S. public schools within one or two decades. Students of color already exceed the number of Whites students in six states: California, Hawaii, Louisiana, Mississippi, New Mexico, and Texas (Dillon, 2006).

Language and religious diversity is also increasing among the U.S. student population. In 2000, about 20% of the school-age population spoke a language at home other than English (U.S. Census Bureau, 2003). The Progressive Policy Institute (2008) estimated that 50 million Americans (out of 300 million) spoke a language at home other than English in 2008. Harvard professor Diana L. Eck (2001) calls the United States the "most religiously diverse nation on earth" (p. 4). Islam is now the fastest-growing religion in the U.S., as well as in several European nations such as France, the United Kingdom, and the Netherlands (Banks, 2009; Cesari, 2004). Most teachers now in the classroom and in teacher-education programs are likely to have students from diverse ethnic, racial, language, and religious groups in their classrooms during their careers. This is true for both inner-city and suburban teachers in the U.S. as well as in many other Western nations (Banks, 2009).

An important goal of multicultural education is to improve race relations and to help all students acquire the knowledge, attitudes, and skills needed to participate in cross-cultural interactions and in personal, social, and civic action that will help make our nation more democratic and just. Multicultural education is consequently as important for middle-class White suburban students as it is for students of color who live in the inner city. Multicultural education fosters the public good and the overarching goals of the commonwealth.

The major purpose of the *Multicultural Education Series* is to provide preservice educators, practicing educators, graduate students, scholars, and policy makers with an interrelated and comprehensive set of books that summarizes and analyzes important research, theory, and practice related to the education of ethnic, racial, cultural, and language groups in the United States and the education of mainstream students about diversity. The books in the *Series* provide research, theoretical, and practical knowledge about the behaviors and learning characteristics of students of color, language minority students, and low-income students. They also provide knowledge about ways to improve academic achievement and race relations in educational settings.

The definition of "multicultural education" in the *Handbook of Research on Multicultural Education* (Banks & Banks, 2004) is used in the *Series*: Multicultural education is "a field of study designed to increase educational equity for all students that incorporates, for this purpose, content, concepts, principles, theories, and paradigms from history, the social and behavioral sciences, and particularly from ethnic studies and women's studies" (p. xii). In the *Series*, as in the *Handbook*, multicultural education is considered a "metadiscipline."

The dimensions of multicultural education, developed by Banks (2004) and described in the *Handbook of Research on Multicultural Education*, provide the conceptual framework for the development of the publications in the *Series*. They are: *content integration, the knowledge construction process, prejudice reduction, an equity pedagogy,* and *an empowering school culture and social structure*. To implement multicultural education effectively, teachers and administrators must attend to each of the five dimensions of multicultural education. They should use content from diverse groups when teaching concepts and skills, help students to understand how knowledge in the various disciplines is constructed, help students to develop positive intergroup attitudes and behaviors, and modify their teaching strategies so that students from different racial, cultural, language, and social-class groups will experience equal educational opportunities. The total environment and culture of the school must also be transformed so that students from diverse groups will experience equal status in the culture and life of the school.

Although the five dimensions of multicultural education are highly interrelated, each requires deliberate attention and focus. Each publication in the *Series* focuses on one or more of the dimensions, although each book deals with all of them to some extent because of the highly interrelated characteristics of the dimensions.

This interesting, informative, and deftly crafted book is enriched by Loewen's extensive and transformative knowledge of history and the social sciences, a lifetime of innovative teaching, and a deep commitment to social justice and human rights. Loewen's keen intellect, breadth of knowledge, understanding and empathy for the daily life and challenges of classroom teachers, and desire to educate students to be informed citizens is evident and compelling on every page of this gracefully written and incisive book.

Educating effective and thoughtful citizens who can take actions to make their local communities, the nation, and the world more just and humane is a significant aim of this enlightening book. Loewen's candid and revealing descriptions of institutional racism in U.S. society and in textbooks are not presented to make students cynical or disempowered, but to help them acquire the knowledge, skills, and commitments needed to attain agency and to act to create a better world.

Readers of this book will not only deepen their knowledge of U.S. history because of the hidden and fascinating facts about the nation's history that Loewen presents; they will also learn valuable lessons about the nature of history, social science, and the construction of knowledge. Loewen illustrates, for example, how accounts of the past created by today's historians often reveal as much about our own times as about people who lived in the past. He also demonstrates how "learning more accurate history gives students tools with which they can change our culture to make it more just and more factual." Throughout this book, Loewen explicates topics and teaching activities that will help students to become reflective and active citizens. All teachers—including those in history, the social sciences, the humanities, the language arts, and the sciences—will find this book revealing and engrossing. High school students will also find this book informative, interesting, and engaging.

I am especially pleased to welcome this book to the *Multicultural Education Series* because of my personal and professional admiration and respect for Jim Loewen, which is a consequence of his actions to promote racial equality and social justice during his lifetime and career. I first became acquainted with Jim's work when he coauthored an innovative and bold Mississippi history textbook, *Mississippi: Conflict and Change* (Loewen & Sallis, 1974), which evoked an enormous controversy because it shattered the silences of the oppressive racial history in Mississippi. The controversy ended in a legal victory for Jim and his co-author because of the truth and accuracy of their book. *Lies My Teacher Told Me: Everything Your American History Textbook Got Wrong* (Loewen, 1995), as well as *Sundown Towns: A Hidden Dimension of American Racism* (2005), continue to break silences and change our perspectives on history. Jim walks the talk in his books, in his workshops for teachers, and in his inspiring and popular public lectures. This timely, needed, and erudite book exemplifies his transformative and creative work at its best.

—James A. Banks

REFERENCES

Banks, J. A. (2004). Multicultural education: Historical development, dimensions, and practice. In J. A. Banks & C. A. M. Banks (Eds.), *Handbook of research on multicultural education* (2nd ed., pp. 3–29). San Francisco: Jossey-Bass.

Banks, J. A. (Ed.). (2009). *The Routledge international companion to multicultural education*. New York and London: Routledge.

Banks, J. A., & Banks, C. A. M. (Eds.). (2004). *Handbook of research on multicultural education* (2nd ed.). San Francisco: Jossey-Bass.

Cesari, J. (2004). *When Islam and democracy meet: Muslims in Europe and the United States*. New York: Pelgrave Macmillan.

Dillon, S. (2006, August 27). In schools across U.S., the melting pot overflows. *The New York Times*, vol. CLV [155] (no. 53,684), pp. A7 & 16.

Eck, D. L. (2001). *A new religious America: How a "Christian country" has become the world's most religiously diverse nation*. New York: HarperSanFrancisco.

Loewen, J. W. (1995). *Lies my teacher told me: Everything your American history textbook got wrong*. New York: The New Press.

Loewen, J. W. (2005). *Sundown towns: A hidden dimension of American racism*. New York: The New Press.

Loewen, J. W., & Sallis, C. (Eds.). (1974). *Mississippi: Conflict and change*. New York: Random House.

Martin, P., & Midgley, E. (1999). Immigration to the United States. *Population Bulletin, 54*(2), 1–44. Washington, DC: Population Reference Bureau.

Progressive Policy Institute. (2008). *50 million Americans speak languages other than English at home*. Retrieved September 2, 2008 from http://www.ppionline.org/ppi_ci.cfm?knlgAreaID=108&subsecID=900003&contentID=254619

Roberts, S. (2008, August 14). A generation away, minorities may become the majority in U.S. *The New York Times*, vol. CLVII [175] (no. 54,402), pp. A1 & A18.

Suárez-Orozco, C., Suárez-Orozco, M. M., & Todorova, I. (2008). *Learning a new land: Immigrant students in American society*. Cambridge, MA: Harvard University Press.

U.S. Census Bureau. (2003, October). *Language use and English-speaking ability: 2000*. Retrieved September 2, 2008 from http://www.census.gov/prod/2003pubs/c2kbr-29.pdf

U.S. Census Bureau. (2008, August 14). *Statistical abstract of the United States*. Retrieved August 20, 2008 from http://www.census.gov/prod/2006pubs/07statab/pop.pdf

U.S. Department of Homeland Security. (2004). *Yearbook of immigration statistics, 2004*. Washington, DC: Office of Immigration Statistics: Author. Retrieved September 6, 2006 from www.uscis.gov/graphics/shared/statistics/yearbook/Yearbook2004.pdf

ALSO BY JAMES W. LOEWEN

Lies My Teacher Told Me:
Everything Your American History Textbook Got Wrong

Lies Across America: What Our Historic Sites Get Wrong

Sundown Towns

Lies My Teacher Told Me About Christopher Columbus

Social Science in the Courtroom

Mississippi: Conflict and Change (with Charles Sallis et al.)

The Mississippi Chinese: Between Black and White

Rethinking Our Past (audio lectures)

Acknowledgments

FOR HELPFUL COMMENTS, I thank Mary Cavalier, Irene Laroche, Nick Loewen, Susan Luchs, Jackie Migliori, Jeff Schneider, Laura Updyke, series editor Jim Banks, and editor Brian Ellerbeck.

For illustrations, I thank Scott Nearing, the Minnesota Historical Society, the Idaho State Historical Society, the *New York Times*, Glencoe McGraw-Hill, *U.S. News and World Report*, the Library of Congress, and the National Museum of American History.

WHAT'S WRONG WITH THE PICTURE ON THE COVER?

In 1851, working in Germany, Emanuel Leutze completed "George Washington Crossing the Delaware," now on permanent display in the Metropolitan Museum of Art in New York City. A copy adorns the White House and an electronic copy is on site at Washington Crossing State Park in New Jersey. Currier & Ives produced thousands of copies; in 1976 the U.S. Postal Service made a five-stamp set of it; and throughout the decades it has been widely mocked by other artists, including Grant Wood, James R. Huntsberger, and Robert Colescott. Political cartoonists still use the image.

The original sacrificed accuracy for art. Washington would never have stood up in such a small boat, even if he did want to look heroic. The boat is far too small for the number of people in it. Moreover, it's not right in other ways. The real boats, called Durham boats, were designed for carrying cargo and had no seats. The troops had to stand, but the sides of the boat came well above their waists, so they were in no danger of falling overboard. Both ends were pointed. The original flag was wrong: Congress would not authorize such a flag for months. The man facing astern at Washington's knee is Prince Whipple, a black patriot, but he was not present. (Other African Americans were likely in the boat, however, probably including the man steering in the stern.) The weather was terrible, changing from rain to sleet. No icebergs dotted the river—the Delaware freezes as a sheet. (Germany's Rhine, which flowed past Leutze's studio, does have icebergs.) Finally, the crossing was mostly made at night. Washington almost certainly crossed at night. Even the moon was obscured by clouds and sleet.

The creative art department at Teachers College Press made it even worse historically, and I helped them do it! Additional errors and anachronisms include the jet plane, the outboard motor (although it would have made the trip easier), the sea serpent, and the "Confederate flag" (actually the battle flag of the Army of Northern Virginia). John Brown stands just in front of the flag. George Washington has morphed into Christopher Columbus. Spearing the serpent is Rosa Parks. Rowing below the flag is none other than Pocahontas, in her English finery.

Besides being fun, this image illustrates that once we start lying to children—teaching things that did not happen—there is no logical stopping point. If it is useful to teach that the Dutch bought Manhattan for $24 worth of beads, then why not show Columbus crossing the Delaware, helped by Pocahontas and an outboard motor? Where do we draw the line? If, on the other hand, the picture seems absurd, then maybe we should also question—and get students to investigate—the usual myths as retold in our U.S. history textbooks.

History as Weapon

ISTORY AND SOCIAL STUDIES,[1] as usually taught before college, can hinder rather than help build students' understanding of how the world works. Indeed, my bestseller, *Lies My Teacher Told Me*, opens with the claim that American history as taught in grades 4 through 12 is in crisis and typically makes us stupider.

Of course, it's easy to make such a bold statement. At some point since 1980 just about *every* field in education has been declared "in crisis."[2] The reception of *Lies My Teacher Told Me*, however, implies that many readers, including many teachers of American history in grades 4 through 12, agree with my assessment. In 2007, *Lies* passed a million copies sold and was selling at a higher rate than ever, even though it had been on the market, unchanged, for twelve years.[3] Teachers have been special fans, leading to overflow workshops at venues like the National Council for the Social Studies and the National Association for Multicultural Education. So maybe I'm right. Maybe history/social studies *is* in crisis.

Certainly we can do better.

Since *Lies My Teacher Told Me* came out in 1995, I have traveled the country, giving workshops for school districts and teacher groups on how to teach history and social studies better. Some of the ideas I present in these workshops came from other K–12 teachers I have met over the years. Others derive from my own teaching experience and from my years of thinking about what Americans get wrong about the past. This book collects the best shticks from those workshops for the benefit of teachers and future teachers I will never meet.

Teachers who already teach beyond and occasionally against their U.S. history textbooks will find that this book will help them explain their approach to other teachers who still teach traditionally. For those who have not yet dared to break away from the security of just teaching the textbook, this book will provide specific ways to do so—ways that have worked for other teachers. It may also help them explain their new approach to principals and more traditional parents.

Before plunging into *how* to teach history better, however, we need to spend a few pages considering *why*. This introduction begins with a cautionary tale from Mississippi, showing how history was used there as a weapon to mislead students and keep them ignorant about the American past. Moving north to Vermont, I show that ignorance about the past is hardly limited to Mississippi. Mississippi merely exemplified the problem in exaggerated form, as Mississippi embodied many national problems in exaggerated form in the late 1960s and '70s. The introduction goes on to dissect the usual reasons that teachers and textbooks give to persuade students that history is worth knowing. I suggest other more important reasons why history is important, both to the individual and society. The introduction then closes with a brief overview of the book.

A LESSON FROM MISSISSIPPI

I first realized how history distorts our understanding of society in the middle of my first year of full-time teaching, at Tougaloo College in Mississippi. I had started teaching at Tougaloo, a predominantly black institution, in the fall of 1968, after finishing my doctorate in sociology at Harvard University. That first year, in addition to my sociology courses, I was assigned to teach a section of the Freshman Social Science Seminar. The history department had designed this seminar to replace the old "Western Civ" course—History of Western Civilization—then required by most colleges in America, including most black colleges. The FSSS introduced students to sociology, anthropology, political science, economics, and so on, in the context of African American history—appropriate enough, 99% of our students being African Americans.

African American history uses the same chronology as American history, of course, so the second semester began right after the Civil War, with Reconstruction. I had a new group of students that first day of the spring semester in January 1969, and I didn't want to do all the talking on the first day of class. So I asked my seminar, "What was Reconstruction? What images come to your mind about that era?"

The result was one of those life-changing "Aha!" experiences—or, more accurately, an "Oh, no!" experience. Sixteen of my seventeen students told me, "Reconstruction was that time, right after the Civil War, when African Americans took over the governing of the Southern states, including Mississippi, but they were too soon out of slavery, so they messed up, and reigned corruptly, and whites had to take back control of the state governments."

I sat stunned. So many major misconceptions of facts glared from that statement that it was hard to know where to begin a rebuttal. African Americans never took over the Southern states. All Southern states had white governors and all but one had white legislative majorities throughout Reconstruction. Moreover, the Reconstruction governments did not "mess up." Mississippi in particular enjoyed less corrupt government during Reconstruction than at any point later in the century. Across the South, governments during Reconstruction passed the best state constitutions the Southern states have ever had, including their current ones. They started public school systems for both races. Mississippi had never had a statewide system for whites before the Civil War, only scattered schools in the larger towns, and of course it had been a felony to teach blacks, even free blacks, to read and write during slavery times. The Reconstruction governments tried out various other ideas, some of which proved quite popular. Therefore, "whites" did not take back control of the state governments. Rather, *some* whites—Democrats, the party of overt white supremacy throughout the nineteenth century—ended this springtime of freedom before full democracy could blossom. Spearheaded by the Ku Klux Klan, they used terrorism and fraud to wrest control from the biracial Republican coalitions that had governed during Reconstruction.

How could my students believe such false history? I determined to find out. I visited high schools, sat in on history classes, and read the textbooks students were assigned. Tougaloo was a good college—perhaps the best in the state. My students had learned what they had been taught. Bear in mind that they had been attending all-black high schools with all-black teaching staffs—massive school desegregation would not take place in Mississippi until January 1970, a year later. In school after school, I saw black teachers teaching black students white-biased pseudo-history because they were just following the book—and the textbooks were written from a white supremacist viewpoint.

The yearlong Mississippi History course was the worst offender. It was required of all 5th- and 9th-graders, in public and private schools, owing to a state law passed after the 1954 U.S. Supreme Court decision in *Brown v. Board of Education*, intended to desegregate the public schools. This Mississippi statute was part of a package of obstructionist measures designed to thwart the Court and maintain "our Southern way of life," which every Mississippian knew meant segregation and white supremacy. The one textbook approved for the 9th-grade course, *Mississippi: Yesterday and Today* by John K. Bettersworth, said exactly what my students had learned. Other than "messing up" during Reconstruction, this book omitted African Americans whenever they did anything notable. Among its 60 images of people, for instance, just 2 included African Americans.[4]

I knew John Bettersworth. In my junior year in college, I attended Mississippi State University, where he taught history. He knew better. Indeed, when he reviewed several books on Reconstruction in the *New York Times Book Review*, he made clear that he knew that the interracial Republican coalition that governed Mississippi during Reconstruction had done a good job under difficult circumstances. But in his 9th-grade textbook, Bettersworth wrote what he imagined the Mississippi State Textbook Board wanted to read. He knew full well that historians did not (and still do not) review high school textbooks, so his professional reputation would not be sullied by his unprofessional conduct.[5]

Dr. Bettersworth could not have believed that his textbook was an innocent way to make a few thousand dollars without hurting anyone. At Mississippi State, he encountered the graduates of Mississippi high schools by the hundreds, and he knew how racist some of them could be—partly because they believed the BS (Bad Sociology) about African Americans in his textbook.

Perhaps as a passive form of resistance against their racist textbooks, many Mississippi teachers—white as well as black—spent hours of class time making students memorize the names of the state's 82 counties, their county seats, and the date each was organized as a county. Or, perhaps more likely, they did this because it had been done to them. Regardless, these 250 twigs of information were useless and soon forgotten.[6] Meanwhile, students learned nothing about the past from this book that would help them deal with the wrenching changes Mississippi was going through in the 1960s and '70s.

Black students were particularly disadvantaged. What must it do to them, I wondered that January afternoon, to believe that the one time their group stood center-stage in the American past, they "messed up"? It couldn't be good for them. If it had happened, of course, that would be another matter. In that case, it would have to be faced: why did "we" screw up? What must we learn from it? But nothing of the sort had taken place. It was, again, Bad Sociology.

For more than a year, I tried to interest historians in Mississippi in writing a more accurate textbook of state history. Finally, despairing of getting anyone else to do so, I put together a group of students and faculty from Tougaloo and also from Millsaps College, the nearby white school, got a grant, and we wrote it. The result, *Mississippi: Conflict and Change*, won the Lillian Smith Award for best Southern nonfiction the year it came out. Nevertheless, the Mississippi State Textbook Board rejected it as unsuitable. In most subjects, the board selected three to five textbooks. In

Mississippi history, they chose just one. Only two were available, which might be characterized "ours" and "theirs." By a two-to-five vote, the board rejected ours, accepting only theirs. Two blacks and five whites sat on the board.

Our book was not biased toward African Americans. Six of its eight authors were white, as were 80% of the historical characters who made it into our index. An index 20% nonwhite looks pretty black, however, to people who are used to textbooks wherein just 2% of the people referred to are nonwhite. Moreover, in contrast to the white supremacist fabrications offered in "their book," our book showed how Mississippi's social structure shaped the lives of its citizens. So, after exhausting our administrative remedies, we—coeditor Charles Sallis and I, accompanied by three school systems that wanted to use our book—eventually sued the textbook board in federal court. The case, *Loewen et al. v. Turnipseed et al.*, came to trial in 1980, Judge Orma Smith presiding. Smith was an 83-year-old white Mississippian who believed in the 1st amendment—students' right to controversial information—and was bringing himself to believe in the 14th amendment—blacks' right to equal treatment.[7]

For a week we presented experts from around the state and around the nation who testified that by any reasonable criteria, including those put forth by the state itself, our book was better than their book. Among other topics, they found *Conflict and Change* more accurate in its treatment of prehistory and archaeology, Native Americans, slavery, Reconstruction, Mississippi literature, the Civil Rights era, and the recent past.

Then came the state's turn. The trial's dramatic moment came when the Deputy Attorney General of Mississippi asked John Turnipseed, one of the board members who had rejected our book, why he had done so. Turnipseed asked the court to turn to page 178, on which was a photograph of a lynching. "Now you know, some 9th-graders are pretty big," he noted, "especially black male 9th-graders. And we worried, or at least I worried, that teachers—especially white lady teachers—would be unable to control their classes with material like this in the book."

As lynching photos go, ours was actually mild, if such an adjective can be applied to these horrific scenes. About two dozen white people posed for the camera behind the body of an African American man, silhouetted in a fire that was burning him. The victim's features could not be discerned, and no grisly details—such as whites hacking off body parts as souvenirs—were shown or described. Nevertheless, our book was going to cause a race riot in the classroom.

We had pretested our book—along with Bettersworth's—in an overwhelmingly white classroom and an overwhelmingly black classroom. Both had preferred ours by huge margins. So we had material to counter

This is the lynching photo to which Turnipseed objected. A lynching is a public murder, done with considerable support from the community. Often, as here, the mob posed for the camera. They showed no fear of being identified because they knew no white jury would convict them.

this argument when our turn came for rebuttal. We never had to use it, however, because at that point Judge Smith took over the questioning.

"But that happened, didn't it?" he asked. "Didn't Mississippi have more lynchings than any other state?"

"Well, yes," Turnipseed admitted. "But that all happened so long ago. Why dwell on it now?"

"Well, it *is* a *history* book!" the judge retorted. And we nudged each other, realizing we were going to win this case. Eventually, in a decision the American Library Association ranks as one of its "notable First Amendment court cases," the judge ordered Mississippi to adopt our book for the standard six-year period and supply it to any school system, public or private, that requested it, like any other adopted book.[8]

Although we won the lawsuit, that experience proved to me that history can be a *weapon*, and it had been used against my students. This book helps teachers arm students with critical reading and thinking skills—historiography, for example—so they will not be defenseless. Indeed, they can even learn to do history themselves.

A LESSON FROM VERMONT

After eight years, I moved to the University of Vermont. Again, I found myself teaching first-year undergraduates, this time in huge classes in Introductory Sociology. I enjoyed these freshman classes, not least because they opened a wonderful window on the world of high school. The view was mighty discouraging at times. My UVM students—as the University of Vermont is known—showed me that teaching and learning "BS history" in high school was and is a national problem. These students were also ignorant of even the basic facts of our past, as were my Mississippi students, despite the hours spent in most high schools memorizing them.

In 1989, their ignorance astounded me in a course I taught intended for advanced undergraduates in education, history, and sociology. On the first day of class I gave my students a quiz. It contained some comical items (some posted at my website, http://sundown.afro.illinois.edu/), but also perfectly straightforward questions like this one: "The War in Vietnam was fought between _____ and _____." To my astonishment, 22% of my students replied "North and South Korea!"

Now, please don't infer that something special—and specially wrong— has eroded history education in Vermont. The University of Vermont is a national institution; only 40% of its students come from within the state. Moreover, repeated national studies show that high school students learn history exceptionally badly. In 2003, for instance, the National Assessment of Educational Progress granted "advanced" status in U.S. history to only 1% of high school seniors. College graduates did little better. In 2000, the American Council of Trustees and Alumni commissioned the Center for Survey Research at the University of Connecticut to administer a 34-item "high school level American history test" to 556 seniors at 55 top colleges and universities. "Nearly 80% . . . received a D or F," according to a summary. More than a third didn't know that the Constitution established the three-way division of power in the U.S. government; 99%, on the other hand, could identify "Beavis and Butt-Head" as adolescent television cartoon characters.[9] College courses failed to fill in the gaps in their knowledge, partly because many college students never take a history course, it having been so boring in high school.[10]

University of Vermont students were particularly bad, however, in learning and applying the basic concepts of sociology. Indeed, they were so bad at it that I coined a new term for the syndrome that they exhibited: soclexia. This learning disorder makes it very difficult for its victims to grasp the basic idea of sociology. It may be genetic; certainly it strikes certain racial and economic groups more than others. Children from white (and Asian American) upper-class and upper-middle-class families are especially vulnerable.[11]

What is the basic idea of sociology? It is this: *Social structure pushes people around, influences their careers, and even affects how they think.* I was unprepared for the level of soclexia I experienced in Vermont. My Tougaloo students readily understood that social structure pushed people around. Not one of their parents was an architect, for example, because no school in the Deep South in their parents' generation both taught architecture and admitted African Americans. So my Tougaloo students knew how social structure might influence careers. Then, too, neighbors of theirs—white children—had been their friends when they were four and five years old, but by the time they were fourteen and fifteen a barrier had gone up between them. My black undergraduates could see that this racial bias was hardly innate; rather, it showed that social structure affects how people think. Hence they were open to the sociological perspective.

My UVM students, in contrast, were very different. To be sure, they could memorize. If I asked them on a quiz, "What is the basic idea of sociology?" they would reply, "Social structure pushes people around, influences their careers, even affects how they think." But when I asked them to apply that idea to their own lives or to the next topic we dealt with in introductory sociology, most were clueless.

To understand their soclexia, it helps to know that during the years I taught there (1975–1996), UVM usually ranked #1 as the most expensive state university in America, both in-state and out of state. Hence, it drew extraordinarily rich students. In 1996, the last year I collected data (and no one else ever did), the median family income for out-of-state students at the University of Vermont (and most students came from out of state) was $123,500 (about $160,000 in 2008 dollars). In that year, the national median family income was $42,300 (about $55,000 in 2008 dollars). Only 5.5% of all families made $123,500 or more. Yet half of all out-of-state families at the University of Vermont came from this elite income group. The mean family income of UVM students was higher still.[12]

Despite being so rich, my students believed that they—not their parents' social positions—were responsible for their own success—which consisted mostly of their having been admitted to the University of Vermont. *They* pushed social structure around, most felt, and if some people were poor, that was their own damn fault—they simply hadn't pushed social structure around *enough*. Most of my students had no understanding that for children of their social class background, gaining admission to college was not an outstanding personal accomplishment but merely meeting expectations—going along with the flow.

I tried to show them that their understanding of the social world was itself a product of social structure—indeed, was entirely predictable from their membership in the upper-middle and lower-upper classes. In short, their view that social structure made no difference was the ideology "appropriate" to their position in social structure. It is precisely these classes that hold the idea that class makes no difference.

Their class position was not the sole cause of their soclexia. Their high school education contributed as well. Not their high school coursework in sociology—few high schools offer sociology, even as an elective. But there is one course that everyone takes and that purports to be about our society—American history. Unfortunately, American history as presented in high school textbooks (and by teachers who rely on them) not only leaves out social class entirely, it also avoids any analysis of what causes what in our society, past or present. Thus, American history is a key breeding ground of soclexia.

Indeed, in my experience, the more history a student has taken in high school, the *less* able s/he is to think sociologically. Some college history professors agree. A friend who taught the U.S. history survey at Vermont nicknamed its two semesters "Iconoclasm I and II," because he had to break the icons—the false images of the past that students carried with them from their high school history courses—to make room for more accurate information. He actually preferred students from other countries, who knew no American history at all or, as is often the case, knew it more accurately and more analytically than do American high school graduates.

In no other discipline do college professors prefer students with *less* preparation! On the contrary, the math department is delighted when high school graduates have taken a fifth year of math. After giving them a test to ensure that they have retained what they learned, the department places such students in advanced instead of introductory calculus. Shakespeare professors are similarly happy to teach students who have already read *Lear* in high school, along with the more usual *Romeo and Juliet*. While they may not place such a person in "Advanced Shakespeare" and may teach *Lear* differently, nevertheless, the student has read the play and thought about it and will be a pleasure to teach.

Not so in history.

I responded to my students' ignorance of American history just as I had in Mississippi: I visited nearby high schools to watch teachers in American history classrooms and studied the textbooks they used. I found that most of them relied far too much on these textbooks. This was not a local Vermont problem. Research shows that students spend more class time with their textbooks in history—reading the books in class, discussing them, answering the 60 questions at the end of each chapter—than in any other subject in the curriculum. This finding staggered me. I had thought the winner (or rather, loser) would be something very different—perhaps geometry. After all, students can hardly interview their parents about geometry. They can hardly use the web, or the library, the census, and so on, to learn about geometry. But all these resources, and many more besides, are perfectly relevant to the study of history.

When I studied the textbooks that so dominated these courses, my concern deepened. Although American history is full of gripping and important stories, these books were dull. Their basic storyline was: the United States started out great and has been getting better ever since! Only without the exclamation point. They failed to let voices from the past speak; instead, they told everything themselves, in a boring monotone.

Few of the teachers I watched supplemented the textbooks, despite their soporific impact. In many cases, I came to learn, teachers didn't go beyond the book because they didn't know how. History has more teachers teaching out of field than any other subject. According to a national survey, 13% never took a single college history course; only 40% had majored in history or a history-relevant discipline like American Studies, sociology, or political science.[13] Such a travesty cannot be imagined in math, science, or English. Such woefully underprepared teachers use textbooks as crutches. I do not mean to slur all history teachers, not at all. Many teach history because they love it and think it is important. Unfortunately, some teachers who would love to go beyond the textbook with their students feel they cannot, because their students have to take "standardized" multiple-choice tests at the end of the year based on the factoids with which textbooks abound.

As a result of this textbook-centric approach, many high school students come to hate history. In survey after national survey, when they list their favorite subject, history always comes in last. Students consider it "irrelevant," "borr-r-ring." When they can, they avoid it. Not every class, not every district, of course. Hopefully, yours is the exception. But across the nation, history/social studies does not fare well. As it is usually taught, I believe students are right to dislike it.

Students from out-groups hate history with a special passion and do especially poorly in it. But even affluent young white males are bored by most American history courses in high school.

WHY HISTORY IS IMPORTANT TO STUDENTS

Yet history is crucial. It should be taught in high school, partly because five-sixths of all Americans never take a course in American history after they leave high school. What our citizens learn there forms the core of what they know of our past.

The first thing that students do *not* learn about American history is why studying it is important. Teachers must go beyond the old saw by the philosopher George Santayana, "Those who cannot remember the past are condemned to repeat it."[14] This cliché won't do. Indeed, it is a mystification. The phrase itself is wrong, implying that knowing about the past somehow automatically makes us smarter. Consider the equal and opposite saying by the philosopher Georg Hegel, "People and governments have never learned anything from history."[15] Moreover, Santayana's saying sweeps conflict under the rug. My Tougaloo students—and their white counterparts at Ole Miss—were not repeating Mississippi's history of white supremacy because they could not remember the past. They were repeating it because they *did* remember the past—as it had been misrepresented to them in school. To put this another way, who wrote the history students are asked to recall, and who did not—and for what purpose—can make a world of difference to how it influences the present.

There are much better reasons for learning about history. Once we come to some agreement—not necessarily total—as to why the field is important, that agreement can inform how we should go about teaching it. I submit that the course is gravely important, because its purpose is to help students prepare to do their job *as Americans*. Students may grow up to be school bus drivers, computer programmers, or CEOs, but what is their job as Americans? Surely it is to bring into being the America of the future.

What does that task entail? Some vision of a good society is required: a society that allows and encourages its members to be all they can be.[16] A society enough in harmony with the planet that it can maintain itself over the long run. A society enough at peace with other countries that it does not live in fear of attack. Students might go beyond these basics, perhaps to some vision of the "beloved community." Their job as Americans—and ours—then consists of figuring out what policies help us move toward that community. What should the United States do about global warming? What should our policy be toward gay marriage? Regarding the next issue—the debate that is sure to engulf us next year, whatever it may be—what position should we take, and what concrete steps to implement it?

Every issue, every suggestion, every element of the America of the future entails an assertion of causation. "We must do X to achieve goal Y." Of course history is full of causation—and arguments about causation.

Even when an event seems to be new, the causes of the acts and feelings are deeply embedded in the past. Thus, to understand an event—an election, an act of terror, a policy decision about the environment, whatever—we must start in the past.

Unfortunately, high school textbooks in American history present the past as one damn thing after another. Few of the facts are memorable, because they are not shown as related. Therefore, most high school graduates have no inkling of causation in history. Consequently, they cannot use the past to illuminate the present—cannot think coherently about social life.

Why are textbooks compendiums of fact rather than arguments about causation? I don't think it's due to an upper-class conspiracy to keep us stupid, although it might be. One problem is precisely that there *are* arguments about causation. There are far fewer arguments about facts. So let's just stick with the facts. Another problem is that causation continues to the present, and arguments about the present are by definition controversial. Moreover, as the second edition of *Lies My Teacher Told Me* shows, high school history textbooks often aren't really written by the people whose names are on their title pages, especially after their first editions. The gnomes in the bowels of the publishing companies who write them aren't hired to interpret the past or sort out causation in the past and don't have the credentials for that task.

For all these reasons, textbooks downplay what causes what. Nevertheless, learning what causes what is crucial for our job as Americans.

So is critical thinking. Again, history textbooks—and courses centered on "learning" history textbooks—downplay critical thinking. Almost never does a textbook suggest more than one possible answer and invite students to assess evidence for each. Instead, they tell the right answers, over and over, in their sleep-inducing godlike monotone. We shall see (Chapter 5) that sometimes no one knows the right answer, yet history textbooks present one anyway!

A crucial ingredient of critical thinking is historiography. Earlier, talking about Mississippi, we noted that who wrote history, who did not, and for what purpose can make all the difference. That assertion comes from historiography—the study of the writing of history—and every high school graduate should know both the term and how to "do" it. (See Chapter 3.)

Perhaps the most basic reason why students need to take history/social studies is this: history is power. That I saw firsthand in Mississippi. History can be a weapon. Students who do *not* know their own history or how to think critically about historical assertions will be ignorant and helpless before someone who does claim to know it. Students need to be able to fight back. This line of thought is a strong motivator, especially for "have-not" students,[17] but all students enjoy "wielding" history.

There are still other reasons to learn history. The past supplies models for our behavior, for example. From the sagas of Lewis and Clark, Laura Ingalls Wilder, Helen Keller, Rachel Carson, and a thousand others, students can draw inspiration, courage, and sometimes still-relevant causes. We're not talking hero worship here, however, and all of the individuals named above have their imperfections. Present them whole. Instead of suggesting heroes as models, suggest heroic actions. Typically people perform heroically at a key moment, not so heroically at other moments. Students need to do accurate history, coupled with historiography, to sort out in which ways their role models are worth following. Recognizing both the good and not so good element within historical individuals can also make it easier to accept that societies also contain the good and not so good.[18]

History can (and should) also make us less ethnocentric. Ethnocentrism is the belief that one's own culture is the best and that other societies and cultures should be ranked highly only to the degree that they resemble ours. Every successful society manifests ethnocentrism. Swedes, for example, think their nation is the best, and with reason: Sweden has a slightly higher standard of living than the United States, and on at least one survey of happiness Swedes scored happier than the American average. But Swedes can never convince themselves that theirs is the dominant culture, dominant military, or dominant economy. Americans can—and without even being ethnocentric. After all, our GNP is the largest, Americans spend more on our military than all other nations combined, and for years athletes in countries around the world have high-fived each other after a really good dive, or dunk, or bobsled run. They didn't learn that from their home culture, or from Sweden, but from us, the dominant culture on the planet.[19] It is but a small step to conclude that ours is the *best* country on the planet. Hence, the United States leads the world in ethnocentrism.

Unfortunately, ethnocentrism is, among other things, a form of ignorance. An ethnocentric person finds it hard to learn from another culture, already knowing it to be inferior. Ethnocentrism also has a Siamese twin, arrogance; the combination has repeatedly hampered U.S. foreign policy.

History *can* make us less ethnocentric, but as usually taught in middle and high school, it has the opposite effect. That's because our textbooks are shot through with the ideology called "American exceptionalism." In 2007, Wikipedia offered a fine definition:

> the perception that the United States differs qualitatively from other developed nations, because of its unique origins, national credo, historical evolution, or distinctive political and religious institutions.[20]

Wikipedia went on to note that superiority, not just difference, is almost always implied, although not necessarily.

Of course, every national story is unique. Consider Portugal: no other nation "discovered" half the globe, as Portugal's tourism board puts it. Or Namibia: no other nation in the twentieth century had three-fourths of its largest ethnic group (the Hereros) wiped out by a foreign power (Germany). But by American exceptionalism, authors of U.S. history textbooks mean not just unique, but uniquely wonderful. Consider the first paragraph of *A History of the United States* by Daniel Boorstin and Brooks Mather Kelley:

> American history is the story of a magic transformation. How did people from everywhere join the American family? How did men and women from a tired Old World, where people thought they knew what to expect, become wide-eyed explorers of a New World?[21]

Surely that passage is meant to impart that the United States is truly special—and in a positive way. Presumably Boorstin and Kelley want students to be wide-eyed themselves as they learn more about the "magic transformation" that is American history.

I suggest that teachers want students to be clear-eyed, not wide-eyed, as they learn American history. American exceptionalism promotes ethnocentrism. Still worse, it fosters bad history. To get across the claim that Americans have always been exceptionally good, authors leave out the bad parts. Woodrow Wilson involved us in a secret war against the U.S.S.R., for example. Let's leave that out. Americans committed war crimes as a matter of policy in our war against the Philippines. Let's suppress that. Ultimately, writing a past sanitized of wrongdoing means developing a book or a course that is both unbelievable and boring.

Our national past is not so bad that teachers must protect students from it. "We do not need a bodyguard of lies," points out historian Paul Gagnon. "We can afford to present ourselves in the totality of our acts."[22] Textbook authors seem not to share Gagnon's confidence. But sugarcoating the past does not work anyway. It does not convince students that the U.S. has done no wrong; it only persuades them that American history is not a course worth taking seriously.

Thus far we have noted four reasons why history is an important course.

- History helps students be better citizens by enabling them to understand what causes what in society.
- History helps students become critical thinkers. Doing historiography (and learning that word) is part of that process.

- History helps students muster countervailing power against those who would persuade them of false ideologies. This is the "history as weapon" point.
- History helps students become less ethnocentric.

All four relate to history's effects upon students, which make sense, since this is a book for teachers. But history—what we say about the past—also has effects upon our society as a whole.

WHY HISTORY IS IMPORTANT TO SOCIETY

There is a reciprocal relationship between justice in the present and honesty about the past. When the United States has achieved justice in the present regarding some past act, then Americans can face it and talk about it more openly, because we have made it right. It has become a success story. Conversely, when we find a topic that our textbooks hide or distort, probably that signifies a continuing injustice in the present. Telling the truth about the past can help us make it right from here on.

This insight hit me between the eyes as I compared American history textbooks of the 1960s and 1990s in their handling of the incarceration of Japanese Americans during World War II. In 1961, Thomas Bailey's *The American Pageant*, for example, made no mention of the internment. Five years later, it got a paragraph, telling that "this brutal precaution turned out to be unnecessary," for their loyalty "proved to be admirable." The paragraph ends, "Partial financial adjustment after the war did something to recompense these uprooted citizens. . . ."

In 1988, Congress passed the Civil Liberties Act, apologizing for the "grave injustice" and paying $20,000 to each survivor of the camps. This amount hardly sufficed to recompense more than three years of life and labor lost behind barbed wire, as well as the loss of homes and businesses, but it was more than a token. Around that time, textbooks expanded their coverage of the incident. By 2006, *Pageant* had more than doubled its paragraph, added an ironic photograph of two Japanese Americans in Boy Scout uniforms posting a notice that read "To Aliens of Enemy Nationalities," and included a boxed quote from a young Japanese American woman that told her angry reaction to the order. It also devoted the next two pages to the Japanese as "Makers of America," providing a summary of the group's entire history in the United States, including a photograph of deportees getting into a truck and another of Manzanar Camp, with lengthy captions. The last sentence in the main text treats our 1988 apology and payment of $20,000.[23]

Because textbooks began to increase their treatment of the incarceration before 1988, historian Mark Selden suggests they may have helped to cause the 1988 apology and reparations payment. I suspect the textbooks merely reflected the change in the spirit of the times. But either way, there seems to have been an interrelationship between truth about the incarceration and justice toward its victims.

Evidence shows that our society is ready to look at many past atrocities without flinching. In 2000, for example, the exhibit of lynching photos, *Without Sanctuary*, broke all attendance records at the New York Historical Society.[24] To be sure, lynchings are over. Americans don't do that anymore.[25] So the lack of lynchings has become a success story and the topic is thus easier to face. Nevertheless, many visitors to the museum were surprised to learn that lynchings were not the work of a few hooded men late at night. The open daytime photos showing a white community proud to be photographed in the act startled them. Most Americans have not seen such images. Not one high school textbook on American history includes a lynching photo. Presented here is an example of the lynching photographs that are available but never included in U.S. history textbooks. Surely publishers' caution is mistaken. After all, in 2003 Duluth faced this event, dedicating a memorial to the victims after decades of silence.

On June 15, 1920, a mob took Elias Clayton, Elmer Jackson, and Isaac McGhie, three black circus workers, from the Duluth, Minnesota, jail and lynched them.

Images like the Duluth mob can help students understand that racism in the United States has not typically been the province of the few, but of the many; not just the South, but also the North. Today, too, the discrimination facing African Americans (and to a degree, other groups, such as Native Americans and Mexican Americans) does not come from a handful of extremist outcasts late at night. Leaving out lynchings, sundown towns,[26] and other acts of collective discrimination impoverishes students and hurts their ability to understand the present, not just the past.

History is important—even crucial. Helping students understand what happened in the past empowers them to use history as a weapon to argue for better policies in the present. Our society needs engaged citizens, including students. The rest of this book will suggest ways to teach this important topic importantly.

It begins with four general chapters about teaching history/social studies. First, teachers must free themselves from the straitjacket of the textbook—the message of Chapter 1. Then they need to address why the achievement gap between white students and black, Anglos and Native Americans, rich compared to poor, is larger in history than in any other discipline. Chapter 2 shows that teacher expectations play a role, which means, on the positive side, that changed expectations can narrow the gap. Historiography is the most important single gift that a history course can give to a student. Chapter 3 explains it and suggests ways to help students grasp and use the idea. Chapter 4 shows how to help students *do* history, not merely learn it.

The final six chapters treat six specific topics, arranged chronologically from prehistory through secession to the Nadir of race relations. Each has proven to be problematic. Teachers in my workshops have told me that they worry about these areas and have shown me that they do not teach them well. Yet these six topics have important implications for our time, so each should be taught. With added information and new ways to introduce them, these topics can become high points rather than pitfalls of the course.

I've found that learning new things about our American past is exciting, for me as well as for students and other teachers. So will you.

FOCUSED BIBLIOGRAPHY

I know how busy most teachers are, so each chapter will list only sources that are crucial for teachers to read. The following five books (choose either book by Percoco) are key preparation for any social studies or U.S. history teacher.

Either James A. Percoco's *A Passion for the Past* (Portsmouth, NH: Heinemann, 1998) or *Divided We Stand* (Portsmouth, NH: Heinemann, 2001) supplies a daunting list of innovations for history classes, from visiting cemeteries to getting students talking about controversial historic photographs. It's daunting because Percoco lays out so *many* ideas; but if a teacher chooses just two or three and makes them work, his book will have done its job.

In *Beyond the Textbook*, David Kobrin (NYC: Heinemann, 1996) suggests only a handful of innovations, but he explores each in depth, showing pitfalls to avoid.

Note Bill Bigelow's how-to accounts of several innovative classroom exercises in Wayne Au, Bigelow, and Stan Karp, eds., *Rethinking Our Classrooms* (Milwaukee: Rethinking Schools, 2007).

After the Fact, by two college professors, James Davidson and Mark Lytle (NYC: McGraw-Hill, 1992), intended for college history majors, covers about twenty topics, providing examples of how treat a topic at some length.

Do read Loewen, *Lies My Teacher Told Me* (NYC: Simon & Schuster, 2007).

CHAPTER 1

The Tyranny of Coverage

E VERY PROBLEM THE INTRODUCTION DESCRIBED stems from relying upon the huge U.S. history textbook. It boasts 1,150 pages, several hundred "main ideas," and thousands of "terms and names" to memorize.[1] Teachers can't run an interesting American history course if they try to cover that textbook. Nor can they do any of the things this book will suggest. Teachers must be selective. This chapter tells how to choose what to teach.

FORESTS, TREES, AND TWIGS

In a world history class, this does not seem revolutionary. World history teachers already grasp the fact that they could not hope to cover the history of the world without picking and choosing. Otherwise, they would have to devote perhaps 13 minutes to the history of Malaysia, 7 to Singapore, and a whopping 28 for Thailand—impossible! But in U.S. history, teachers still feel a compulsion to teach 4,444 twigs (8,888 if it's an "Advanced Placement" course), rather than a much smaller number of trees and only a handful of forests. Sometimes they feel compelled to do so by statewide "standardized" twig tests. Unfortunately, the more teachers cover, the less kids remember. Fragmenting history into unconnected "facts" practically guarantees that students will not be able to relate many of these terms to their own lives. As a professor who specializes in teaching first-year courses, I can guarantee that by the time they enter college, most students who were taught U.S. history the usual way have forgotten everything— except that World War I preceded World War II.

Our goal must be to help students *uncover* the past rather than cover it. Instead of "teaching the book," teachers must develop a list of 30–50 topics *they* want to teach in their U.S. history course. Every topic should excite or at least interest them. What meaning might it have to students' lives?

These topics will be the trees. They organize the twigs that students are to recall. More important, they organize the entire school year. After creating your list, sleep on it, then add any forgotten topics the next day. Then (and only then), check a good college textbook in U.S. history to see if you have made an egregious omission.[2] If so, add it, but only if you judge it important and are excited to teach it.

No list can be completely idiosyncratic. If it omits the making and use of the Constitution, it's an incompetent list. If it does not include the Civil War and its impact, it is an incompetent list. But must it include, for instance, the removal of the five so-called civilized tribes from the Southeast—the Trail of Tears of the Choctaws, Cherokees, Chickasaws, Creeks, and Seminoles? My list would. But a Minnesota teacher revealed to me that hers wouldn't—she'd rather teach the Dakota War or Sioux Uprising of 1862–63, which happened right in her part of Minnesota. She had a point. But at some point every list must include the taking of the land from its first possessors, or it cannot be competent. Teachers of APUSH—the Advanced Placement in U.S. History—will want to include the era that ETS's test will cover in its DBQ (Document-Based Question).

I made up my own list of 30–50 trees and wound up with just 36, so I know it can be done. I'll not publish my list, because doing so might deter some teachers from coming up with their own. But I will list a few topics that did *not* make it: the European explorers after Columbus (Ponce de Leon, Cabot, etc.), the formation and controversy over the national bank, the Plains Indian wars, the Progressive movement, and the Clinton presidency. I'm not excited about teaching any of them. I'm not sure what I think high school graduates must know about them, years later, that they couldn't look up for themselves.

Recall the old cartoon showing a lad defending his D in history to his parents: "When you took it, there wasn't as much history to learn!" He has a point. In the 1940s, the Civil War came in the second semester of U.S. history courses. Today Reconstruction often gets shoehorned into the first semester, because teachers now must cover the Cold War, the Korean War, McCarthyism, the Vietnam War, the energy crisis, Clinton's impeachment, two wars in Iraq, and more. Fifty years from now, contemplate the addition of four or five additional chapters totaling 200 more pages. Impossible. Backs will break, to say nothing of minds. Teachers must leave things out.

The greater danger lies in stuffing everything back in. For example, the Plains Indian wars could be shoehorned into "imperialism," which *is* on my 30–50 list, or "manifest destiny," which is not. But the teacher who does so merely reinvents the chapter titles of a typical overstuffed U.S. history textbook. *The American Pageant*, for example, organizes its thousands of twigs of information into 42 chapters, a number that does fall between 30 and 50. Such chapters—compendiums of topics—are *not* what we're talking about here.

A teacher can tell her students, "There was a Progressive movement. It happened around 1910. Chapter 28 treats it. A well-educated high school graduate needs to know about it. I suggest you read chapter 28." Then, she need not teach it . . . unless the Progressive movement excites her and makes her list of 30–50.

Every problem the introduction described stems from relying upon the huge U.S. history textbook. Educational researchers point out that U.S. schooling covers too many topics in all subject areas. Curricular consultant Lynn Erickson suggests that covering too many topics helps explain why U.S. students perform worse than students in most other modern nations in science and math. In history, she notes, the problem is especially acute. R. J. Marzano and J. S. Kendall surveyed the national and state standards that have proliferated in every discipline over the past two decades. Their conclusion is obvious from their title: "Awash in a sea of standards." Again, history and civics are by far the worst offenders, each with more than 400 "benchmarks" that students are supposed to be able to know or do.[3]

Everything suggested in this book—or any other book about how to teach history effectively—hinges upon solving the problem of how to use the huge U.S. history textbook. Teaching 30 to 50 trees is the solution.[4]

WINNOWING TREES

How do teachers decide whether to include a given topic? One way is to ask what students need to know about it 20 years from now, when they are in the workforce. If they need to know a lot of twigs, can't they look them up then? Admittedly, twigs are important. Knowing that the U.S. removed Native Americans from the Southeastern states in about 1830, not 1930, provides a historical context that helps a student understand both centuries. Students need to include twigs in the projects they do, the debates they hold, the papers they write. In states with statewide multiple-choice exams in history/social studies, teachers will want to include the topics, skills, and yes, twigs that the exam stresses. But twig memorization must not be the focus. Students will learn twigs for the best of reasons—because they need them to understand and complete the fascinating tasks on which they are working.

Key questions to raise when winnowing nonessential topics are: Why do I want my students to know all this? What should they be able to *do* with the information, assuming they recall it once they leave school? Teachers can ask friends, family members, or colleagues—maybe the math teacher!—what they remember and what they think everyone should know about the tree under consideration.

In a recent workshop, a teacher confessed that she did not understand the importance of the controversy about the national bank during Andrew Jackson's administration. "Do I have to teach it?" she asked. The answer is no. Indeed, she *should not* teach it, precisely because she does not understand its importance. The textbook she used, Boorstin and Kelley, devotes three full pages and two illustrations to the matter. Asking students to skip those pages can seem awkward (although students rarely complain about *not* having to read something). But she does not know what she wants students to do with the information—and for the record, neither do I.

I am not advising anyone to omit the bank issue. Another teacher may understand its importance better than I do, and better than my teacher. The bank issue can be linked to the principles of Keynesian economics that underlie the occasional decisions by the Federal Reserve Board to lower interest rates to avoid a recession. The nation has wound up with a mixed system of private banks, perhaps like those favored by Jackson, and public coordination, as favored by Nicholas Biddle and the Whigs. Perhaps this system combines the best of both worlds, or perhaps the rights of the common citizen are subordinated to those of the plutocracy, as Jackson implied. I write this paragraph in the midst of the mortgage lending crisis of 2008, when the federal government is taking steps to shore up huge private corporations like Fannie Mae and Freddie Mac. Teachers who understand this issue, are excited to teach it, see its relevance to the present, and think all students should understand it, should include the national bank. Teachers who don't should not.

One way to assess the significance of a topic is to consider the continuing major themes of U.S. history to which it may relate. I came up with ten:

- how cultures change through diffusion and syncretism
- taking the land
- the individual versus the state
- the quest for equity (slavery and its end, women's suffrage, etc.)
- sectionalism
- immigration and Americanization
- social class; democracy vs. plutocracy
- technological developments and the environment
- relations with other nations
- historiography, how we know things

Perhaps these are the forests. Each is central to the discipline of history, at least of the United States. Each refers to crucial issues in the development of our country. There are concepts and facts connected with each of these themes that I hope high school graduates can tell me, when I encounter them three years later in a college class. Another person's list might be somewhat different. It might usefully be shorter. I suggest it should not be longer. (Moses had a point: we do have ten fingers.)

Teachers might share their list of themes with students at the beginning of the year. They can all fit on a single sheet of poster paper, taped to the wall inconspicuously. From time to time, a given tree can be shown to tie in explicitly with one of these continuing themes. Chapter 6 will use diffusion and syncretism to explain the rise of Europe, for example. In turn, the key result of Columbus's voyages—"the Columbian exchange"—also exemplifies both terms. Forcing students to memorize the list or recall which themes apply to which topics throughout the year would be dreary. Instead, teachers can create "aha moments" by asking students, after they are well into a topic, "Does this topic relate to any of the themes on the poster?"[5]

DEEP THINKING

Years hence, as citizens, students need to be able to investigate deep issues. At the least, they need to be able to accept or debunk the cause-and-effect propositions that others suggest in answer to such issues. Tomorrow's issues, of course, we can predict only imperfectly today. Teachers prepare students to think about them by helping them learn to think about issues and causal statements in our past. High school textbooks in U.S. history do this poorly.

Consider this question: Why did slavery take greater hold in the South than the North? Slavery certainly existed in the North, after all. Indeed, the first colony to legalize slavery was not Virginia but Massachusetts. In 1720, of New York City's population of 7,000, 1,600 were African Americans, mostly slaves. Wall Street was the marketplace where slaveowners could hire them out by the day or week.[6] But slavery grew more important in the South and ended in most of the North after the Revolutionary War. Why? Let us research this question using a currently popular textbook by Boorstin and Kelley. Under "slavery," its index does not list "causes" or any other likely subtitle. Turning to the first mention, we find the familiar account of the arrival of a Dutch ship in Jamestown in 1619, off-loading twenty blacks, "probably not slaves but indentured servants." Fifteen pages later, Boorstin and Kelley tell that 400,000 blacks lived in the colonies in 1765, "scattered from Massachusetts Bay to Georgia." Only 40,000 lived north of Maryland.

The first question the book ignores is, What happened in Virginia (and other colonies) to cause Africans to lose the status of indentured servants and become enslaved? Instead of answering that question using evidence from Virginia, the authors turn to the assertion:

> To grow tobacco economically a planter needed a large estate and a sizable work force. It was easy to find the land, but hard to find the workers. Many indentured servants, once free, would go off and start their own farms. Why should they work for someone else?

In short, Boorstin and Kelley imply that planters had to import slaves.

This "analysis" begs the question. Of course it is "economical" to grow tobacco with slave labor. Doing *anything* with unpaid labor is likely to prove profitable. It is also true that tobacco culture requires work. Until recently, people transplanted tobacco seedlings, cut off the leaves from the bottom as they ripened, tied them in bunches, and hung them to dry—all by hand. On a small farm, one person can do all these things, however, and just as efficiently as 100 can do them on a plantation. Slavery itself made white workers, including formerly indentured servants, hard to recruit. Few immigrants to the United States chose to come to the South, where they would have had to compete with unpaid laborers.

Next, authors do not address the question of why so few slaves wound up north of the Mason-Dixon Line. Even if tobacco production somehow calls for slaves—which it does not—many farmers in Connecticut and western Massachusetts grew tobacco. Indeed, they still do—and never have with slaves. This our textbook authors simply don't know. "There was little tobacco," they assure us; "New England found its wealth in the sea." They also never address the issue of why the cod industry could not have relied on slave labor.

"Ask students to contrast the northern and southern economies," suggests the teacher's edition of *Holt American Nation*. That looks like a large and deep question, but all they want students to do is to "mention the southern economy's reliance on slave labor, the southern lag in industrialization, and the predominance of crops such as tobacco and cotton." Asking students that question verges on being anti-intellectual, because it encourages students to participate in premature closure. Instead of actually addressing the topic, it merely requests the parroting of memorized information, and we have already seen that some of the information is questionable. As to why, authors rely mainly on topography and climate to "explain" the absence of slavery in northern climes. "Because of its different climate and agricultural practices, the Upper South did not rely as heavily on slave labor as the Lower South," according to *Holt*. Virginia, Kentucky, and Maryland were the main states in the Upper South. Tobacco was their main crop (not including slaves for sale). *Holt* believes that tobacco automatically seems to require "reliance on slave labor." So this answer makes no sense. Also, if the authors of *Holt* gave but a glance at Connecticut, they would see tobacco being raised by free labor. Nevertheless, let's "learn" it.

I don't want to leave the question hanging. We begin to get a handle as to why slavery did not blossom in the North when we note that the only place where it did flourish was on the huge patroon estates established by the Dutch in the Hudson River valley. Rather than certain configurations of geography (or weather) calling forth plantations, it seems that plantations called forth slavery. Where the value system did not favor the vast hierarchy that is plantation social structure, and where working-class and lower-middle-class whites held proportionate political power, plantations did not thrive. There slavery did not penetrate. Conversely, where slavery thrived, working-class whites did not immigrate in great numbers, having no incentive to compete against unpaid labor.

The question of "Why did slavery take greater hold in the South than the North?" turns out to have appropriate depth. It's not shallow. It's not a matter for mindless regurgitation and is not a "yes-no" question. It's not too deep, so it won't require weeks to plumb to the bottom of it. I would have students think about it, because after students leave high school, I want them to understand that geographic or economic determinism is usually too simple. The role of various determinants including ideas is a central question in history, sociology, and political science. Causation is also worth thinking about in the normal course of citizenship. Often ideas make a difference. I think they did here. From first English settlement, the New England newcomers were more egalitarian than the Virginians.

There are other arenas in which these points can be discussed. Not every teacher needs to get students to ponder the geographic determination of slavery. But consider this generic deep question, to be asked near the end of any unit: What are the implications of this topic for us today? What does it matter?

Every tree needs to be amenable to consideration of that question. If not, maybe it should be chopped off the list of topics.

RELEVANCE TO THE PRESENT

Every tree must have consequences. What is its ongoing importance, its relevance to the present? It's easy to see how the recent past relates to the present. As I was writing this chapter in 2007–2008, for example, President George W. Bush pointed to the relevance of the Vietnam War to the present by comparing that war to his war in Iraq, then in its fifth year.[7] The present importance of more distant events—say, the War of 1812—can be harder to spot. Here is another point where the continuing themes play a role. Each still resonates as an issue today—that's why they are continuing.

Two continuing themes on my list—taking the land and sectionalism—may seem to have ended long ago. Not really. Europeans (with help from Africans) took most of what is now the United States by 1890. Ramifications of the taking process, however, still plague our society. Non-Natives have found it hard to admit that "we" took the land. Of course, "we" didn't—not one of us was alive in 1890. But white Americans unfortunately seem to identify with their forebears, in a process Chapter 8 calls "racial nationalism." Therefore, they would rather see them as innocents. As a result, Americans distort our past. Chapter 7 explains how this ideological need prompts many textbook authors to project low population estimates onto the pre-Columbian past. Thus, students learn bad history today about something that happened long ago.

Many specific issues remain between Native and non-Native governments and peoples. From northern Maine to Washington state, many whites do not accept that the treaties by which the U.S. forced Native Americans to yield most of their lands did (and still do) grant them hunting and fishing rights. In the West, reservations were granted water rights in perpetuity, but their water has been the backbone of nearby ranching and mining operations, leading to continuing conflict. The largest and longest-running lawsuit in U.S. history is the continuing Native American case against the Bureau of Indian Affairs, which has "lost" or mismanaged several billion dollars it was overseeing on behalf of tribes across the country. From Florida to Alaska, tribes have opened or proposed to open casinos, despite state opposition, making use of their quasi-sovereignty to deal directly with the federal government. Also from Florida to Alaska, high schools and colleges (and the NFL's Washington Redskins) have been asked to stop making mascots of Native tribes.

These specific controversies pale in significance next to the general ideological issue that the taking still embodies in our culture: How can non-Indians have treated these people so unfairly for so long? Since—like anyone—we Americans want to consider ourselves good people, we need to cover up the bad treatment. Chapter 7 explores one of the myths Americans tell each other. Such falsehoods constitute ongoing slander against Native Americans, being told today, in the present, in too many elementary school classrooms across the U.S.

Sectionalism hardly ended with the Civil War. During Reconstruction, of course, the North occupied the South. The two sections came to their greatest accord between 1890 and 1940 (the Nadir of race relations, the topic of Chapter 10), but serious sectional differences remain today. Compare the maps presented here. The South voted differently from the North in 1860 and 2004. To a lesser degree, the West still remains a distinctive section whose interests differ from the East.

1860 Presidential Election

Shown in white are states carried by Breckinridge, Douglas, and Bell, candidates for president in 1860 (against Lincoln), and territories.

2004 Presidential Election

Shown in white are contiguous U.S. states carried by George W. Bush, Republican candidate for president in 2004.

My other continuing themes are clearly ongoing. They can help teachers see the present relevance of a past topic. So can talking with colleagues—in history and beyond. If all else fails, a teacher who wants to teach a topic but can see no contemporary relevance for it might admit that to her students from the start. At the end of the unit, maybe they will come up with ways they deem it relevant.

SKILLS

Each tree in the master list must tie to at least one of the skills that the teacher, district, and state want students to develop. In my experience, the "behavioral objectives," "competencies," or "benchmarks" for student achievement set by state boards of education and subscribed to by local school boards are splendid. Rarely do they conflict with what a good teacher wants students to be able to do. (The multiple-choice tests that some states mandate for measuring student performance are another matter.)

Let me suggest that students should be able to:

- read effectively, finding the main ideas in a text (or movie, etc.)
- read critically, assessing whether those ideas are supported by evidence and placing a source in context with other sources and other knowledge
- understand the difference between primary and secondary sources, realizing the importance and role of each
- apply the principles of historiography to a source, locating the speaker and audience in social structure and time, and assessing the impact of that time and location upon the questions raised and the answers supplied
- write a coherent essay, creating an effective introduction, organizing a "storyline," justifying assertions with evidence, coming to a conclusion, and referencing sources correctly
- write effectively in other formats, such as drafting a letter to a public official or textbook editor, composing a list, writing a newspaper article, or creating a website
- speak effectively, perhaps including debate or mock-court formats
- read a map, grasping compass directions and knowing enough geographic twigs to use the map effectively
- understand, critique, and create tables of data
- cause change in society

These ten skills are essential to functioning as an effective adult in today's society.

State guidelines may not be as blunt as "cause change in society," but they still validate such a skill. Mississippi, for example, lists as a benchmark, "The student will understand the ideals, principles, and practices of citizenship in preparation for participation in a democratic society." That'll do. Even better is the key paragraph Mississippi supplies in describing what history or social studies should be in high school:

> Upper grade level social studies education should focus on depth of content in order to foster critical thinking skills. Appropriate breadth of social studies topics, varied resource materials (e.g., literature selections, primary documents, technology, audio visuals, guest speakers, etc.), along with critical analysis of the materials and production of social studies related projects must be used to promote active learners. Powerful social studies education at the upper grade levels will have a significant and meaningful impact on the development of positive democratic citizens.

That paragraph cannot be used to justify an American history course based primarily on "learning" the textbook. Such verbiage can only help teachers as they move beyond a textbook-centered approach. Each topic on the list of 30–50 trees can be tied to at least one skill, behavioral objective, or benchmark derived from paragraphs like this and from the course guidelines put out by the state or local school district.

The textbook will not disappear from class. But no longer will it move the class from topic to topic. Instead, the teacher will move the class to the next topic. Transitions prove to be no problem. As I look down my list, I realize that chronology and logic cause my first item ("How did people get here?", incorporating issues in archaeology and other disciplines) to lead inexorably to the second ("Native American societies"), and so on.[8] As students investigate how people got here, the textbook should be their first tool. Quickly they will realize that it is worse than Wikipedia—which has footnotes, after all—and far inferior to a good journalistic summary of recent research.[9] On other topics, such as "Women's rights, culminating in suffrage," the textbook can supply useful context about Woodrow Wilson's administration, for instance. For some topics, the textbook chapter might even suffice. Lecturing, too, still has its place, especially in a context where students need the information for some project or purpose of their own. Usually, however, a debate, mock trial, interview, term paper, small group project, and so on, will engage students much more intensely than just reading a textbook chapter and listening to lectures on it.

Since not all students learn the same way, a range of activities provides different ways to learn and different ways to shine. When students show they can do good work in one mode—maybe a graphic portrayal[10] or a well-conducted interview—that helps teachers to expect more from them in other settings. "Yes, you can write a good paper, Ernie. Do you remember that graphic you did? That was brilliant!" High expectations (and self-expectations) play a key role in learning, as the next chapter will show.

GETTING THE PRINCIPAL ON BOARD

Teachers who rely on the textbook imagine all kinds of bad things will be visited upon them by administrators, parents, and even students if they deviate. Hence, they relax into the security of self-censorship and reliance on the textbook. Usually they worry needlessly. In practice most teachers have substantial freedom. As they move away from relying on the textbook, their courses become more interesting, so their students grow more interested. Students rarely disrupt a class they relish. Parents rarely come in and chastise teachers because their children like a class.

Nevertheless, it's crucial to bring on board the principal and, in schools large enough to have departments, the department chair. They are teachers' first line of defense against parental complaints. Besides, they are professional educators who may have good advice. As soon as teachers realize that the old textbook-centric method doesn't really work, they should talk with their superiors about the problems. If they have been brought in from the start, principals cannot infer that the teacher is a naïve neophyte or rabble-rousing radical.

Teachers then gain their superiors' cooperation by showing them careful preparation. Before the school year begins, teachers develop lesson plans tying each of their 30–50 topics to at least one skill, as discussed above. These plans also lay out a schedule for the year. What will go on in class from day to day, the main tasks students will do, the basis of their grades—all these need to be clear. Of course, there is room to be flexible, but it is crucial not to fall behind. Teachers can then compose a preface that amounts to an argument for their new approach. The first pages of *Lies My Teacher Told Me* provide ammunition. They suggest four reasons why the traditional textbook-centric course does not work:

1. Students find it boring. Across the United States, history is the field least liked by students. Because this new approach will intrigue students, they will not find it boring.
2. Students don't learn much, especially when tested a year or more later. Because this new approach will prompt students to do good work, they will score well on statewide tests, at least to the extent that these tests measure critical reading, writing, and other important skills.

3. In history, large gaps separate the performance of whites and nonwhites, males and females, and rich and poor—larger than in any other field. Because it taps a variety of skills, this new approach will help a variety of students, including some formerly low-performing students, to do well.
4. College professors don't respect or reward students who recall 6,000 textbook twigs from high school. Some even prefer that their charges have had less of such history. This new approach—emphasizing primary versus secondary sources, historiography, etc.—will stand students in better stead in college history courses. Indeed, students who can read critically, write coherently, create tables, and so on, will do well in most college courses, not just history.

Let me be first to admit that each of the four charges above is an overgeneralization. Students find a substantial proportion—maybe 30%?—of U.S. history courses fascinating and learn a lot from them. Such courses may especially influence "have-not" students, getting them to *do* history, in the process doing their best high school work. College professors hardly put down *those* high school history courses. As best-selling historian Howard Zinn suggested some years ago at a public forum in Boston, "Maybe you should have called your book *Lies 70% of My Teachers Told Me.*" But those are the history and social studies courses that are already *not* textbook-centric. As teachers make their courses less reliant on the textbook, they can use the above four criticisms to justify their new strategy.

Next, teachers can share their plans, including their rationale, with their principal and department chair. Since principals are busy, they will want about five minutes of discussion about it, but those five minutes will be well spent. Teachers can invite their superiors' input on whether the new methods will interest and involve students. Of course, teachers must also assess administrators' strengths and quirks to make strategic presentations.

As the year goes by, teachers may be surprised to find that they have little need for their principal's backup, because they will engender few parental complaints. That's because the students will like and feel challenged by the new approach.

In some districts, schools have autonomy to choose textbooks. If yours is in that happy situation, consider adopting a shorter one. The catalog of Social Studies School Service carries several 300-page paperback textbooks on U.S. history, including some for potential citizens who are taking the INS citizenship exam. Since full-sized textbooks now retail for as much as $108 and cost $70 even when ordered in quantity, they often cost $12 per year when amortized over six students and six years. For about the same cost, students could *own* their own paperback textbook. Then they have the autonomy to take notes in the margins, carry on a "dia-logue" with the author, and insert flags to organize the chapter for better understanding. And then they take the book with them when they gradu-ate. Best of all, using a 300-page paperback almost obliges the teacher to supplement and to get students doing a variety of special projects like those advocated here.

COPING WITH REASONS TO TEACH "AS USUAL"

Reasons that *seem* sound have led many teachers to try to cover every-thing. These forces push teachers toward staying in the traditional textbook-dominated rut. This section provides some resources for dealing with them.

First is fear of the unknown. It seems easier just to "teach the book," especially since the book comes with ancillaries from the publisher like lesson plans, lecture outlines, and videos. Deep down, however, teachers of U.S. history know that relying on the textbook is poor pedagogy. Very few brag about how their textbook structures their course or how they take most of their exam questions from the CD the publisher included with the teacher's edition. Moreover, even though the first year seems a scary leap of faith, teachers will improve. Some topics will fizzle the first time, but not the next. No such learning curve is intrinsic to just teaching the book.

Second, so-called "standardized" tests can intimidate teachers from in-novating. From the MCAS in Massachusetts to Virginia's SOLs to the CSTs in California, state after state has turned to multiple-choice tests to mea-sure student progress. Teachers can reasonably infer that their principal, school district, state, and nation want them to drill pupils in twig history. Surely memorized details are *not* what Americans need, however. After all, after they graduate, students can always find most twigs on the web when they need them.

Some APUSH teachers particularly feel the need to emphasize text-book knowledge. They don't want to disadvantage their students by leav-ing out a twig that gets asked on the APUSH test. Their concern, while understandable, leads them to the wrong conclusion. The A.P. test in U.S. history isn't bad. In addition to the usual multiple-choice items, it features a "Document-Based Question" (DBQ) and other essay questions. The DBQ supplies students with a handful of sources related to a given era or issue, then asks them to write an essay using some of these documents to answer a question. Every May, ETS assembles a collection of mostly superior high school history teachers to evaluate the results. Many APUSH teachers have found that the way to get young people to retain twice as much history is not by teaching twice as many twigs, but by making their courses twice as interesting. When a history course has aroused students to think about matters that interest them, then they will connect the twigs with trunks and branches of issues. Then the details will stick in their minds for years, perhaps forever.[11]

Please note: I am not actually against twigs. I think students *should* know in which half-century the Civil War was fought, or that Lyndon Johnson got the Voting Rights Act through Congress in about 1965. Without some details, students have no context for thinking about the next historical claim they encounter. Teachers should require appropriate information, including twigs, within the assigned tasks that tie into their 30–50 topics and within the essay items on their tests. The way to get students to recall more twigs is not by trying to teach more twigs. That simply doesn't work. It even bores teachers. The head of the history department in an elite Washington, D.C., prep school told me he never assigned himself the Advanced Placement course, since he found it so boring. Why? Because he felt he had to teach twice as many details as he did in the regular course, so students would do well on the exam.

On the other hand, if the new method—whatever it is—excites the teacher, it will doubtless excite his or her students. Hence, it will work, even if by "work" we mean twig retention. My emails tell me so. An American history teacher in New Mexico wrote:

> At the beginning of the semester, I made [my students] a wager that, even though they were not going to be tested on the historical facts, they would nevertheless remember more of the facts than they would have from an ordinary textbook. One hundred percent of the students vouched that this was true for each of them.[12]

And here is corroboration from the students' side, in Kennebunk, Maine:

> I took AP US History last year. . . . Our textbook was the infamous *The American Pageant*. It quickly became an ongoing joke that whenever we learned about a new person, the class would ask his height, weight, and how many boats he had (recurring themes in the text). . . . Though this was her first year teaching AP History, our teacher, Ms. Rebecca L. Moy, quickly realized that the text was nothing short of ridiculous. Throughout the year, Ms. Moy photocopied sections of various books as supplements to the text. We'd read a chapter in the text and then be required to read a chapter of *The American Political Tradition*, your *Lies My Teacher Told Me*, and various books by Richard LaFeber. At the end of the year, . . . we were assigned projects. Each person in

the class had a question or a topic we had to present to the class. My topics were "The Vietnam Anti-War Movement and the Government's Response," and "The Iran-Contra Affair. . . ." When it came time to take the AP test, no one received a lower grade than a 4.[13]

The huge history textbook itself can deter teachers from teaching creatively. It seems to call out to be "covered," even if not to be read. It must be important. Moreover, it is filled with innumerable lists—main ideas, key terms, people to remember, dates, skill activities, review identifications. These make the course look rigorous and factual, so teachers and students can imagine they are learning history. The problem is, however, that they aren't. On the contrary, it's the opposite of history, in a way. It's remembering details but not using them to support (or not support) an interpretation. It's learning (as in memorizing) but not thinking. It's reading but not questioning. Instead of beginning with a question—hopefully a burning question—students begin with the answers, which they are supposed to memorize.

Inadequacies in their own education deter some teachers from abandoning or challenging their textbooks. In college, many did not major in history or in a history-related discipline, as we saw in the Introduction. One in seven never had a single course in American history in college.[14] Unsure of what is important, not knowing what it means to do history, such teachers are not ready to set their students free to do history or even to let them critique their textbooks.

Related to feelings of inadequacy is teachers' worry that they may lose control of their classroom if students sense that they can be challenged. Every semester I face this problem myself. The first time I am confronted intellectually, the first student objection to a point I just made, hits me right in the gut, or more accurately, in the ego. I feel threatened that my student may know more than I do about the point. I have to say to myself silently, "Wait! Don't feel intimidated that your student knows more. Feel grateful! This is your chance to learn something." Moreover, even if s/he turns out to be mistaken or misguided, teachers want to reward, not punish, class participation.

If I have to remind myself not to feel threatened, after dealing with college undergraduates, it can be much more threatening to face correction or even mere amplification from a high school or middle school student. Isn't the teacher supposed to know more than these children? Teachers do not have to know everything, however. Teachers who don't know the answer to a question can admit it, and say they'll come back with it tomorrow. Then their own quest to find out becomes a model for their students. Better yet, teachers can turn the question over to the class as a whole. What do they think is the answer? Will one of them vouchsafe to research the topic overnight?[15]

It's great when students go beyond their teachers. As soon as they are set free to do history (as Chapter 4 encourages), students will immediately learn more than their teacher about their topic, even if the teacher boasts a Ph.D. in history. Their expertise rebounds to their teacher's credit. She has not "lowered" herself to her students' level. The teacher is always in charge. She gives the grades, and she always expects excellent work.

Some teachers worry that without a textbook to be "learned," students will simply squabble. Indeed, teachers must allow students academic freedom. Model this by presenting multiple viewpoints to them. When they differ among themselves, encourage them to present their own viewpoints. Issues sometimes presented as matters of fact—for example, that the first people walked to the Americas over the Bering land bridge—are still unresolved, as Chapter 5 will show. Always remember, however, that while people have the right to their own opinion, they do not have the right to their own facts. They must back up their opinion with evidence—facts upon which all can agree. We shall see in chapters to come that some topics that have been presented as matters of opinion—the reason why the South seceded, for example—are matters of fact. All accounts are not equally valid. Just as geography teachers would disserve their students by letting them claim that the Earth was flat, history teachers must not allow them to disregard hard evidence for a given position, when such evidence exists.

However, if some students believe that Columbus's net impact upon Native Americans was for the better, bringing them the horse culture, Christianity, and so forth—while others hold that the arrival of Europeans and Africans led to centuries of depopulation and misery—the teacher's job is not to tell one group that they are wrong. Teachers do not lose control of their classes, nor do they lose students' respect, when they tolerate more than one point of view. On the contrary, teachers retain control and merit their students' respect when they grant them freedom to disagree, including freedom to disagree with the teacher, so long as they back up their opinions with good work.

Related to the fear of losing control of the classroom is worry that students won't emerge from the class as good citizens. Too many teachers of U.S. history believe they need to present a course that gets their students to think well about their country. They want to produce good citizens, by which they mean nationalists, people who take pride in their country. Such thinking complements the red, white, and blue covers of most history textbooks. But it blurs an important distinction between patriotism and nationalism. Defining "the duty of a true patriot," Frederick Douglass wrote: "He is a lover of his country who rebukes and does not excuse its sins."[16] Surely teachers want to produce patriots, not nationalists.

Usually this notion that teachers must protect students from the truth is thoughtlessly fearful. A parent recently gave me an example. Her daughter's 4th-grade teacher had asked each student to write a mini-biography of a "famous historical figure" and deliver it to the class on Parents Day. The girl chose Helen Keller. When she included the fact that Keller was a socialist in her biography, her teacher tried to stop her, telling her that she could not present her report to the class unless she removed that information. Parental intervention saved the day, but we need to consider: What did the teacher fear? That students might become socialists if they learned Keller was one? That students might dislike Keller if they learned she became socialist? That parents might criticize the teacher for allowing such a "radical" report? Surely all this is foolish. The parent suggested it was just "a knee-jerk reaction." The critical point is this: Once teachers step forth down this slippery slope of allowing such concerns to dictate what can and cannot be learned about the past, regardless of what actually happened, they are done for. Teaching what happened is our bedrock. When challenged by student, parent, or administrator, noting that students are learning what in fact happened is a powerful first defense.

Our past is not so horrific that if teachers let students see what happened, they will become bad Americans. Surely we are teaching the course so that they might become good Americans—citizens able to think about the past and make intelligent decisions about the future. To do this, what students need is not feel-good history. Neither, of course, do they need guilt-ridden feel-bad history. They need to know what happened, what caused it, and what it in turn causes, even today.

YOU ARE NOT ALONE

As teachers wean their courses from the textbook, they need to know that they are setting forth down a well-trod path. Thousands of teachers have taken this journey, and newcomers can learn from their innovations as well as from their mistakes. The tiny annotated bibliographies at the end of each chapter in this book contain ideas from such successful teachers. The end of this chapter lists several websites that can help. Local colleagues may have recommendations—specific questions, movies, projects—that have worked for them.

One way teachers can meet others who want to teach differently is at various summer and weekend seminars set up to help history teachers go beyond their textbooks. Some are supported by the Teaching American

History program, at ed.gov/programs/teachinghistory/index.html. If your school district has not participated, maybe you can spur it to. Nearby schools of education and history museums may offer these seminars. The Gilder Lehrman Institute, at gilderlehrman.org, offers seminars, lesson plans, documents online, and other aids. Educational Testing Service runs seminars for teachers of APUSH. Often these events come with all expenses paid.

Several national organizations offer the chance to meet other innovative U.S. history teachers face-to-face. The National Council for the Social Studies, ncss.org, is reasonably inexpensive; most state chapters are cheaper still. The Organization of American Historians, oah.org, is mainly a group of college professors but tries hard to appeal to high school teachers as well. Visit it the next time it meets nearby. The National Association for Multicultural Education (NAME), nameorg.org, covers much more than history/social studies and emphasizes issues of racial and sexual equity. The National Council for History Education, nche.net, holds semiannual conferences that draw middle and high school teachers who are serious about teaching history and social studies well.

Teachers can also meet in cyberspace. There are several free discussion groups on the web for teachers of U.S. history. The Humanities Net, h-net.org, hosts more than 100 discussion lists, mostly about history. Specifically for high school U.S. history teachers is h-high-s. Every K–12 teacher of U.S. history should sign up for h-high-s and consider signing up for other lists, such as H-South, H-CivWar, H-Women, or maybe a state list like H-Ohio. On an active list like h-high-s, teachers may receive several emails a day, asking for help teaching a given topic, responding with help to a prior query, telling about a new movie with historical implications, or reviewing a book. H-Net's book reviews are a particular strength. Not only do they evaluate and critique the book; they also supply an exegesis of it, helping teachers stay current on historical topics they would never have time to research. Even more valuable are the archives. Over time, teachers have asked for help teaching everything from archaeology to the Iraq War. Other teachers have replied with ideas.

Educational Testing Service hosts a discussion list for teachers of APUSH, the Advanced Placement test in U.S. History, but anyone can participate. The discussion is moderated with a heavy hand, so various kinds of comments cannot appear, but the discussants do include many intelligent and enthusiastic U.S. history teachers. Sign on at lyris.collegeboard.com/read/all_forums.

Other history teachers have put up very useful websites for their colleagues to mine for ideas and images. See historyteacher.net, for example. Addresses change, but teachers can find them by typing terms like

"American history" or "U.S. history" and "powerpoints," "lecture notes," or "class notes" into a search engine. My own website, http://sundown. afro.illinois.edu/, has illustrations for U.S. history courses, along with a quiz that students will enjoyably fail.

BRINGING STUDENTS ALONG

How do teachers get students on their side when questioning textbooks? A California high school graduate told me how his U.S. history teacher announced on the first day of class that "this textbook is bunk" and pitched his copy of the huge textbook assigned to his class the length of the room, where it hit the rear wall and crashed to the floor. There it remained for months. "This will be our textbook," he then proclaimed, holding aloft a copy of *Lies My Teacher Told Me*. While I enjoyed the story, I do not suggest such pedagogy. First, a course in U.S. history should allow multiple voices, not just his and mine; my book works better in tandem with a textbook than as a substitute. Second, this teacher was obviously no neophyte. He had already worked out with school authorities to provide or have students purchase *Lies My Teacher Told Me*. He had already proven to be a popular and effective history teacher who knew most students would be on his side from the start, owing to his reputation in the school.

Announcing that the textbook has problems may not be the best approach. Even if students do take on faith that their teacher is right and their book will be wrong, that is just one more example of a top-down educational directive, not different in kind from "learning" the textbook. Moreover, some students will think the teacher is merely being egotistical. "Why should we believe you rather than the four Ph.D.s who wrote this book?" will be their response, stated or unstated.

A 6th-grade U.S. history teacher in Illinois learned this early in the fall semester, when she said to her class that most American presidents before Lincoln were slaveowners. They were outraged—not at the fact, but at the teacher. "No they weren't, Ms. Walker," was their response, "or it would be in the book!" They pointed out that their textbook provided four pages about George Washington, six about Thomas Jefferson (including his life in Paris and at Monticello), two on Madison, four on Andrew Jackson, and so forth—and never mentioned their slaveholding. Ms. Walker, quick on her feet, did not stand her ground but used their response as a learning opportunity. "Maybe I'm wrong," she replied. "How can we find out?" Soon enough two students had signed up for each president with the overnight assignment of learning about their slaveowning practice. The task was easy. The next morning the students reassembled, still upset—

but now their outrage was directed against their book, not their teacher. With a little guidance, they ended up writing a class letter to the publisher, denouncing their textbook for omitting important information. Now they had become critical readers, ready to question, not just accept the next thing they read in its pages.

Rather than telling students that the textbook has problems, teachers can show them. Here's how one teacher does it. In a corner of her room she has a rectangular laundry basket full of old textbooks on U.S. history. This didn't cost much: they are the cheapest items in used bookstores.[17] Her oldest dates from the 1920s. For less than $50, teachers can amass two, three, or even four dozen textbooks dating from before 1900 to a few years ago. "When things get slow," she told me, she has her students "go get a book." She does this for President Herbert Hoover, for example. One student learns that Hoover cared a lot about poor people. He had been in charge of U.S. relief in Belgium after World War I and in Mississippi after the flood of 1927 and was lauded as a true humanitarian. Meanwhile, another student reading a different textbook finds that Hoover, a self-made millionaire, called out the army to evict poor people who were marching on Washington in 1932. Andrew Mellon, his millionaire secretary of the treasury, suggested the government should let the Depression run its course. "Let the slump liquidate itself. Liquidate labor, liquidate stocks, liquidate the farmers, liquidate real estate," he said. "It will purge the rottenness out of the system." A third student reads that Hoover indeed cared deeply about the poor, but his Republican ideology straitjacketed him into concluding that government should play only a minor role; private business and charitable organizations should and could carry the day. Yet a fourth book proclaims that Hoover's administration was more active in response to the economic woes than any previous one and claims that much of FDR's New Deal originally came from Hoover's policies.

What is the class to do? Obviously, it makes no sense to "learn" what one book says; the others are so different. To resolve the matter, students must find out for themselves. They must do history.[18]

In most districts, teachers cannot abandon textbooks altogether. They probably should not even where they're allowed to. So long as teachers do not let them dominate their classrooms, textbooks can be important aids. But that is all they can be: aids. Teachers need to help their students see that they can learn more about a given topic than the textbook author knows. Encourage students to mark up their own books with questions and challenges. Freedom to do so is another reason to favor the purchased 300-page paperback over the rented 1,150-page hardbound history textbook. But even rented books only gain in intellectual value when their margins contain intelligent questions and arguments, so long as the original text remains unmarked. Teachers who cannot bring themselves (or perhaps their librarian or principal) to accept the propriety of writing in rented books can give each student a couple of Post-it notes when assigning a new chapter. Their task is to come up with at least one challenge and one question about the material. Doing so empowers students. No longer are they passive readers. Now they are in implicit dialogue with the author. And now they are reading critically, bringing other knowledge to bear, thinking right in front of the teacher and each other.

Another way to get students to read their textbooks critically is to ask them to critique a topic as a group (or individual) project. For one of the 30–50 trees, students can be asked to read the account of the topic in their textbook and then work together to produce a thorough critique of it. Ultimately this gets shared with the publisher. It's especially worthwhile to do this early in the school year, to encourage students to read critically from then on. For that reason, and because most textbook accounts of it are so inadequate, this "critique a topic" approach might well be applied to the first settling of the Americas—usually presented as "walking across Beringia." Many textbooks also handle other early topics particularly poorly, such as the diverse societies Native Americans formed before (and after) the arrival of Europeans and Africans. Each student can select an American Indian group and write its history in compact form. Then they can compare what the textbook says about the group and about Native Americans in general.

Here is yet another way to bring students along, so they become participants in rather than combatants of the 30–50 major topics approach. Early in the school year, when first explaining the approach, invite students to develop their list of, say, the ten most important events or topics that must be included in a competent U.S. history course. First, have each person come up with his/her own list. (This may prove hard for some students. If a student can only come up with two, fine, unless they're only pretending they can't do it.) Then, for their favorite item, ask them to come up with a lesson plan by which the class will learn about it.[19] The teacher collects all the suggestions, of course. Some ideas may prompt modification of her list or help her teach some of the topics. The exercise ends by putting students into groups of two to four, depending on class size. Each group merges its individual lists into one, deciding as a group which to keep. Finally, each group presents its list to the class, and the class determines its final choices. Put the result in a "time capsule"—a shoebox covered with aluminum foil. At the very end of the year, repeat the exercise. Compare the lists. Did the items actually covered convince students they should have been on their list? Which items on their list do students feel were well learned?

Kindly allow me to close with one final argument against business as usual. A teacher communicates with students for no more than 160 hours in a school year. This is less than 2% of their waking lives in a given year. Teachers want to make a difference in students' lives. Teachers want them to grow intellectually during the year. Teachers also want students to realize their own dreams, or take a significant step toward doing so. In the case of U.S. history—or civic life, more broadly—teachers may need to help students understand that they can have dreams to realize. Every minute that they spend "going over" the textbook in the usual dreary way is a minute that will not make them better at doing history, to say nothing of transforming their lives. To make an impact, teachers have to engage students' energies and abilities. Business as usual—going over the textbook—rarely does that.

FOCUSED BIBLIOGRAPHY

Readers who remain unconvinced that our usual overemphasis on twig history is counterproductive should read Sam Wineburg, "Crazy for History," *Journal of American History* 90 #4 (2004), 1401–14 (also at history cooperative.org/journals/jah/90.4/wineburg.html).

Every middle school or high school U.S. history classroom needs a selection of high school history textbooks other than the textbook provided to every student. Some should be old. Then "the textbook" cannot be considered gospel.

A host of websites can help keep teachers and students from overrelying on textbooks. A metasite, Best of History, besthistorysites.net, lists some. Two government sites, the Library of Congress (loc.gov) and National Archives (archives.gov), have thousands of photographs, documents, and other aids.

History Matters, historymatters.gmu.edu, is aimed at teachers of the U.S. history survey course and contains many resources, including a discussion forum, a place where other teachers have posted lesson plans, and a list of more than a thousand history websites, reviewed and annotated. Teachers should also sign up for History News Network (hnn.us/), connected with GMU, which twice weekly delivers via email a batch of stories showing history in the news.

Avram Barlowe, *Teaching American History: An Inquiry Approach* (NYC: Teachers College P, 2004), contains suggestions for getting students to go beyond textbook accounts of the Revolutionary War period.

CHAPTER 2

Expecting Excellence

W HENEVER TEACHERS COMMUNICATE with their students, they are conveying expectations to them. What are those expectations? In every subject, from kindergarten through 12th grade, there are gaps in performance between "haves" and "have-nots" (white students compared to blacks, Latinos, and Native Americans; rich compared to poor). Students of color do somewhat worse than white students in mathematics. The same is true for children of poor parents, compared to those from affluent families. In English, the gap widens. It grows largest by far in history. African American, Native American, and Latino students view history with a special dislike. They also learn it especially poorly.[1]

Why is this? Surely history is not harder than trigonometry! Than Faulkner!

One reason for these gaps stems from teacher expectations. Most children of affluent white families give off an aura of competence and confidence that prompts most teachers to infer that they can do the work. Usually they can do it.[2] But so can others—kids from poorer families, nonwhite children, recent immigrants who are not so proficient in English. Before these nonelite students can do well, however, they have to believe they can. Sometimes, before that can happen, their teacher has to believe they can.

RACIAL AND SOCIOECONOMIC
CHARACTERISTICS AFFECT TEACHER EXPECTATIONS

Several social processes conspire to cause many teachers to conclude that most nonelite students *cannot* do outstanding work. First among these is how the children present themselves. Sociologists Dale Harvey and Gerald Slatin showed photographs of children to teachers. Nine children were white, nine black. A prior panel of teachers had judged three photos of each race lower class, three middle class, and three upper class, solely on the basis of their appearance.[3] Then they asked some 96 elementary school teachers to agree or disagree with eight statements about these 18 photographs, such as, "Read a good many books independently" or "Has been diagnosed as emotionally unstable." Like these examples, some of the statements were positive, some negative.[4] They took care to give the teachers the option to say that they could not predict which children might perform in a certain way based solely on a photo. Harvey and Slatin also asked the teachers to rank the children's IQs as high, medium, or low.[5]

Initially, Harvey and Slatin were concerned "that teachers would be reluctant to make either positive or negative judgments about children on the basis of their photographs alone." They need not have worried. Based solely on one picture of each person, teachers eagerly applied the eight positive and negative statements to the children, although they showed some reluctance to apply negative statements to white kids, even "lower-class" white kids. Without objecting, they classified student IQs as high, medium, or low. Experienced teachers were even more willing to categorize children on the basis of a photograph than were new teachers.[6]

We call this the "file folder phenomenon." We all do it, all the time. Someone asks a question after a public lecture, then perseveres with a followup, and we crane our necks to get a view of her—to learn her race, age, perhaps her ethnic group, and to divine what we can from her appearance. Until we get to know someone, they *are* their categories: female, 40ish, possibly Latino, frumpy, to continue our example. All too often, we never get beyond the categories. The teachers in this research never got to know the students they ranked—perhaps a good thing, because when the rankings were tabulated, the results were heartbreaking. Without exception, children whose photographs had previously been judged "lower class" were ranked less inclined to do anything good—like read a book independently—and more inclined to do something bad—like get in trouble with the law. IQ (as guessed by teachers) also correlated strongly and positively with social class. Race mattered, too. Regardless of social class, "white children were more often expected to succeed and black children were more often expected to fail."[7]

These teachers were not unusual. Nor were they bad people, consciously working to maintain America's racial and socioeconomic hierarchy in the next generation. The researchers had asked them to participate in a study of "the ability of people to make accurate estimates of the characteristics and performance capabilities of others on the basis of first impressions." They complied. Like all of us, they had a sense for the "right order," the way things should be, or at least the way they usually are. Unfortunately, the way things usually are is unfair to poor people; unfair to racial minorities (especially African Americans); unfair to children who don't read, write, and speak well in English; and in some subject areas, unfair to females or to males. The process can be circular. Anthropologist

John Ogbu found that some black students in Shaker Heights, Ohio, cited general societal unfairness and specific teachers' biases to rationalize bad grades, even when they failed to do their work well. In turn, poor performance convinces some teachers to expect less next year from students who look like those who performed badly this year.[8]

If mere photos can have such an impact, we should not be surprised to learn that the way children speak can make a big difference in what teachers expect from them. Between 1890 and 1940—the Nadir of race relations—segregation increased in the North as well as the South. Black English grew apart from white English, because blacks increasingly lived apart from whites. Today most African Americans sound identifiably "black" on the telephone. Their accent, dialect, and even the timbre of their voices differ from those of whites. This difference is not genetic; historian Barbara J. Fields points out that no such thing as "black English" exists in England. There, West Indian immigrants' children learn the English of their class and region. But in America, as a result of the Nadir, "black English" has intensified.[9] In turn, this black English then persuades many teachers to expect less from those who speak it.[10]

Careful research by David Figlio shows that teachers also make judgments based merely on children's first names. Figlio studied thousands of Florida birth certificates to identify "black" names like Dwayne and "white" names like Drew. He also identified names like "Damarcus" or "Da'Quan" as more likely to be given to working-class children, based on such socioeconomic characteristics as "no father present" and "mother did not complete high school." Then he compared the academic performance of children from the same family.[11] Even after controlling for variables that might influence performance—such as low birth weight— he found that those with "black" or "lower-class" first names did worse in school than their siblings. He inferred that teacher expectations were largely responsible, because teachers were simultaneously *less* likely to recommend children with black or "lower-class" names for gifted and talented programs and *more* likely to recommend them for promotion to the next grade. That is, at every level of academic achievement (measured by achievement test scores), from low to high, teachers nominated proportionally fewer black students than white students to gifted and talented programs. At the same time, teachers were more likely to promote black and poor students than white affluent students to the next grade, at every level of achievement. Figlio explained these seemingly paradoxical results by invoking expectations. Because they expected less from black and poor children, teachers didn't bother forcing them to repeat a grade and were also unlikely to recommend them to gifted and talented programs.[12]

Figlio concluded that white teachers were more likely to stereotype based on names; other studies have found white employers much less likely to hire or even interview job applicants with black-sounding names. Other research shows that Hispanic and African American teachers also often participate in expecting more from Euro American children. The black community has long been plagued by expectations that differ owing to color and ethnicity. I wrote my doctoral dissertation on a then little-known group, Chinese Americans in Mississippi. As a third party in a social system built for two, they proved sociologically fascinating, as they tested the norms of racial segregation. The minority within this minority, Chinese African Americans, also proved interesting. Today "everyone knows" that Asian Americans are good in school—most of 'em, anyway—the "model minority." This stereotype abides not only within white subculture, but also among African Americans. One Chinese African American undergraduate told me how he had benefitted in high school: "The teacher calls on you more often, expecting more from you. So you study harder." When these mixed-race students graduated from high school, almost all went on to college, and not to the usual choices— the state schools, where African Americans tended to go—but to private colleges or Northern universities.[13]

Before school desegregation, many teachers in black high schools expected more from light-skinned African Americans than from dark-skinned students. These expectations mirrored social class distinctions deriving from slavery times, when whites treated house slaves, often the product of sexual relations between a male owner and female slave, better, compared to darker field hands. As a graduate student in August 1965, I had an "aha moment" on this point. I was spending the summer directing the Social Science Lab at Tougaloo College, a predominantly black school near Jackson, Mississippi. At that time, Tougaloo offered a two-week "pre-freshman program" to its entering students, designed to get them reading, writing, and thinking closer to a college level. Most had just graduated from all-black high schools in Mississippi, the least-funded schools in America, and some of the worst. Students in graduate and law programs at Harvard and Brown universities had devised the program; some regular Tougaloo faculty members also participated. On the first day of the second session, the young undergraduates-to-be and their teachers milled around in a "mixer" in a large hall, trying to make small talk. So did I.

Twenty minutes into this awkward affair, I looked around the hall and had my "aha moment." Every single graduate student and faculty member—white or black, myself included—was talking with light-skinned students. Darker-skinned African Americans stood in small groups talking with each other. I spent the rest of the hour talking with the darkest students I could find. Of course, my little gesture—one person, in one setting, for 40 minutes—meant nothing. I could only hope that the darker-skinned African Americans were as oblivious to the pattern as I had been. This was hardly likely. Dark-skinned singer Big Bill Broonzy, born in the Mississippi Delta in 1893, incorporated three famous lines about the pattern in a blues song he wrote long before 1965.

> If you're white, you're all right.
> If you're brown, stick around.
> But if you're black, get back! Get back! Get back!

Lighter-skinned African Americans were sometimes even admitted to parties, fraternities and sororities, and even certain colleges only if their skin color was lighter than a brown paper bag.[14] The word "brighter" in black parlance at that time referred not only to intelligence but also to skin tone.

Within three years of my aha moment, the "Black Is Beautiful" movement arose, partly to combat this strain in black culture. It did alleviate the problem somewhat. The matter is more general, however. Sally Zepeda found that teachers in a Midwestern urban elementary school called on white students more often to answer "higher-order thinking questions," while asking nonwhites and ESL students easier questions that simply reflected the reading. Other researchers have shown that teachers give students whom they consider "stronger" more than twice as much time to answer questions before restating them or moving on to other students. Rhona Weinstein showed years ago that students are very aware of different teacher expectations for different students.[15]

A change of teacher behavior can mitigate this problem: teachers can regard silence as their friend. If teachers simply wait two or three seconds for a student to respond, usually s/he will respond, and often in more depth. Waiting is particularly important when the question does not ask for mere recall. Waiting can be hard; there is a lot to cover, and the teacher worries that the rest of the class will grow bored. Usually they won't, though. Silence focuses class attention, adding drama, especially if the teacher is part of it, waiting breathlessly for the student's important answer. This simple change in teacher behavior has been shown to produce higher achievement from all students, fewer disciplinary comments, and better and deeper questions from teachers. Silence can also be the teacher's ally when asking questions of the entire class. Again, absent a quick reply, a natural tendency is to rephrase the question or give a hint as to the answer. Wait. Be still. If the only hands raised belong to "the usual suspects," the teacher can ask, "Do none of the rest of you have a thought about this matter? This issue has implications for us, today. This is important." Then wait some more.

How quickly teachers' initial expectations can become fixed! I experienced this myself in 1st grade in Decatur, Illinois. Before September was halfway through, my teacher Miss Stone had divided us into three reading groups. The best were called the "bluebirds." They had already learned to read from their parents. Next came "redbirds." Slowest in this all-white class of 30 students were, of course, the "blackbirds." Some of them lived on the "wrong side" of Highway 48. Social class and first impression largely generated the initial placements. Whatever ability students developed or displayed as reading was taught played no role whatsoever, for no child moved from one group to another during the rest of the school year.

RESEARCH ON TEACHER EXPECTATIONS

There is a huge literature on teacher expectations. Among other things, it shows that many teachers not only expect better things from affluent white children, they also communicate that expectation to the children and thus help create the superior performance that they expect. In itself, that process seems unobjectionable—most of us got where we are today because someone believed in us and communicated that belief to us. It's the flip side that does the damage. Most researchers in this area find, as did Figlio, that low expectations also become a self-fulfilling prophecy. Some students internalize the view that they are not very competent. Others resist this inference but choose to slide by with little effort, after they realize that teachers don't demand much from them. Over time, both paths lead to the same outcome: students who in fact have little knowledge and ability.

Research by Robert Rosenthal and Lenore Jacobson at an elementary school in San Francisco in the late 1960s sparked the entire expectancy literature. Rosenthal taught social psychology at Harvard, where he devised an experiment to see if he could generate teacher expectations and measure their effect on students. He and his team came to the school in late May, flaunting their Harvard credentials, and gave all K–5 students an IQ test—not the usual Stanford-Binet, but an IQ test nonetheless. However, they did not call it an IQ test. They touted it as a new "Harvard Test of Inflected Acquisition" and claimed it could predict which students were about to spurt—show a considerable increase in school performance. Just before school opened the next fall, they returned and met with the teachers of these students, now in grades 1–6. They talked about their research, reminded the teachers of the test they had given at the end of the previous school year, and told each teacher that a handful of their students—listed by name—had scored exceptionally well. They could expect a burst in performance from those students. (In fact, the students had been chosen at random; no test in existence then or now can predict spurting.) The teachers then proceeded to teach for the school year. From time to time Rosenthal and his staff visited and observed. At the end of the year, they gave the IQ test again, along with other measures of students' performance, and interviewed each teacher about his or her class.

In the 1st and 2nd grades, the experiment worked spectacularly. The students who were expected to spurt did spurt—an average gain of 28 points in IQ among the 1st graders and 17 among 2nd graders. Was this because teachers spent more time with those who were expected to spurt? Taught them better? The researchers considered this unlikely, because the other students, too, gained, showing that teachers had hardly neglected them. Rather, the large increases came about because the teachers subtly expected more from the named students, and the children met their teachers' expectations. Since the children had been selected randomly, no characteristic of theirs could possibly have played a role. They had about the same mixture with regard to class background, race, sex, even height, as those not selected to spurt.

This result became so famous that it has been called "the Rosenthal effect," though it is now usually known as "the expectancy effect." Even laboratory rats running a maze run it better when researchers expect them to, so psychology students now take care not to know which rat had which background when they put them in mazes for their final runs.[16]

The experiment also caused substantial gains in the performance of students about whom nothing was said. First graders gained an average of 12 points, second graders 8 points, and students in higher grades showed similar increases in their IQs. According to IQ theory, no large gains should occur, because IQ supposedly stays steady over time and may even be mainly genetic. Furthermore, psychologists norm the test so that the usual gains associated with a year's maturation and education cause no change in IQ. The children in this study—even those in the control group—showed larger gains, resulting in increased IQ scores. The researchers concluded this was another example of the familiar Hawthorne effect, named after the industrial company where social scientists first systematically observed it. This is the effect on those studied that results simply from doing the study. The children may have felt important, since researchers had traveled clear across the country to study them. Their teachers may have taught extra well, since they were being observed. Harvard's prestige may somehow have rubbed off.

Whatever caused the control group children to excel, to me Rosenthal's second most important finding—after the expectancy effect itself—was the teachers' assessment of those in the control group who spurted the most. Teachers often rated them unfavorably. Remember, these are students who did particularly *well*. Nevertheless, their teachers did not like them. They were the "wrong" students—those from whom nothing special had been expected. They didn't get the same subtle rewards for good work as the students who were *supposed* to do good work received. Other researchers have reported that when African American children excelled, their teachers liked them less, while when white children excelled, their teachers liked them more.[17] Again, these teachers were not intentionally racist; some were black. They simply had a subconscious sense for the way things should be and didn't appreciate students who upset that order. Subconsciously, they acted to restore the order.

"STANDARDIZED" TESTS AFFECT TEACHER EXPECTATIONS

If mere photographs and the mention of student names at the start of the school year can prompt such different teacher expectations, followed by different educational results, it should not surprise us to learn that "standardized" test results—many of which purport to measure aptitude—can influence how teachers view students and how they rate and reward their work. The hopefully apocryphal tale of the substitute elementary teacher makes this point. Rushed into service after the sudden illness of the regular teacher in October, he managed the class well and caused his principal no problems. In June, as he was cleaning out his desk, the principal came to his room to commend his performance. "I'm sorry we never really had time to chat until now," she said. "I was so busy last fall that I never even had time to give you a proper orientation." "That's OK," the teacher responded. "Mrs. Tyler had left me a sheet with the children's IQ scores, and I found that most helpful. As I looked back over the year, the children really behaved according to their potential." "IQ scores?" the principal asked. "We don't *have* IQ scores! Let me see that sheet." He handed it to her. "My God, those are your children's locker numbers!"

Unlike the expectations given to teachers in San Francisco, "standardized" test scores aren't random, nor do they match locker numbers. They correlate strongly with student characteristics, especially race, sex (girls scoring worse than boys on math), and social class. This problem with "standardized" tests slapped me upside my head when I left graduate study at Harvard University and took up full-time duties as a sociology professor at Tougaloo College. At Harvard I had enjoyed considerable teaching responsibilities, including running the sophomore seminar in sociology, key to a successful major, for some twenty undergraduates.

One of my charges could not do the work. Back then, when "gentlemen" like George W. Bush and John Kerry attended Yale and Harvard, some undergraduates *would* not do the work. But this lad was trying hard, yet still had difficulty. In those days, faculty members could freely examine student records, so I looked up his. He came from a wealthy background. His father and grandfather had graduated from Harvard; he had attended Phillips Exeter Academy, an elite New England prep school. Surely he had taken at least one coaching course for the SAT,[18] and he had taken the SAT and PSAT several times. His best scores were 500 on the verbal and 550 on the math, on the SAT's 200–800 scale. Scores so low were unusual at Harvard, and I realized his poor performance in my seminar was not his fault.

My first year at Tougaloo, my students impressed me. The best ones equaled my best protégés at Harvard, and the middle group was able, too. Only the lowest quartile would have been unable to do the work at Harvard. Owing to a grant the department head had gotten from the Field Foundation, every senior major took the Graduate Record Examination. Not only is it produced by the same corporation (Educational Testing Service, or ETS) that produces the SAT; its verbal and math tests are drawn from the same bank of items. The results were fascinating. Their GRE scores ranked Tougaloo students in a reasonable order, one reflective of their classroom performance, especially taking into consideration a handful of academic underachievers. But their scores were dramatically lower than those of Harvard students. The best student received maybe a 570. The worst scored 200 (which you get for signing your name) to 220. An average Tougaloo student scored from 340 to 440 or so.

I had to realize that a 500/550 at Harvard was very different from a 500/550 at Tougaloo. Tougaloo graduates with scores around 500 went on to prestigious law schools and graduate programs in sociology and completed them with fine academic records. One Tougaloo student who scored about 500/550 as a senior found my introductory course in sociology too slow-moving for her as a sophomore and made a deal with me: after mastering what I was teaching, she read sociological essays by Karl Marx and then wrote a riveting essay on false class consciousness. The regular course material that was too easy for her included some of the same readings that had caused my Harvard student, with similar scores, to despair of majoring in sociology. Upon reflection, this made sense. My Tougaloo student's scores put her near the top of her milieu, while my Harvard student's scores put him near the bottom of his.

The more I learn about SAT items, the more understandable all this seems. Verbal SAT items rely on common knowledge. To a degree, so do math items. But what is common knowledge to one group may not be commonly known by another. Therefore, the tests are biased when used to compare students from different backgrounds.

I recalled an item biased against me from a test I took to get into graduate school, the Miller Analogies Test. According to the test-maker, "The MAT is a high-level mental ability test. . . . Performance on the MAT is designed to reflect candidates' analytical thinking, an ability that is critical for success in both graduate school and professional life."[19] I recall the item imperfectly but have captured its essence in the following reconstruction:

_____ is to sake as opera is to _____.

a.   Pete's . . . many
b.   hit . . . run
c.   swordplay . . . Chianti
d.   attend . . . forego
e.   her . . . star

"For Pete's sake," I groaned—"'sake' is like a pronoun. A pronoun is a place holder, a chameleon word that takes on the attributes of the word it stands in the place of, and you cannot easily make an analogy with a place holder." I have no idea what I put for an answer, but I'm sure I got it wrong. Upon leaving the exam, I asked a fellow student, who taught me that I had mispronounced and misunderstood the word. It was not "SAYK" as in "Pete's sake," but two syllables: "SAH-kee." I still looked blank, until he explained that "sake" is a type of wine. I had never heard the word. For that matter, I neither knew what "Chianti" was nor how to pronounce it. In my defense, the year was 1964, I had lived only in the Midwest, and sake was not on the list of alcoholic beverages wholesaled by the state of Minnesota, where I attended school.

Who was likely to know "sake"? Upscale residents of the West and perhaps East coasts. They would also know "Chianti." For them, the question was easy: a vaguely Japanese activity is to Japanese wine as a vaguely Italian activity is to Italian wine. A test of "high-level mental ability"? Hardly. To the rest of us, the level of our mental ability mattered not. We did not know the vocabulary. We were guessing in the dark.

STATISTICAL PROCESSES CAUSE
CULTURAL BIAS IN "STANDARDIZED" TESTS

The problem of bias affects all standardized tests, from Stanford Binet IQ tests to the Metropolitans to the Miller Analogy Test. It also affects achievement tests, like the multiple-choice exams many states now prescribe for high school graduation. The SAT is national, while most multiple-choice achievement tests differ in each state, so I shall focus on bias in the SAT. But the same problems beset all "standardized" tests. For two obvious reasons, students from groups that are sociologically distant from white upper-middle-class students in Princeton, New Jersey, won't do well. First, such students haven't had equal opportunity to learn the culture and vocabulary of upper-middle-class students in Princeton. Second, the material such students *do* know will never get tested on a real SAT.

For several years, I invented SAT-type items that favored various groups—the working class, females, males, blacks, whites, and so forth. I learned how to construct an entire test on which blacks outscored whites, students from working-class backgrounds outscored elite students, or females outscored males in math. Adding a few of my questions while removing those ETS questions that showed the largest disparities in the traditional directions resulted in tests on which group means were about equal.

If I could do this, why couldn't ETS? The answer has to do with how the tests are built. Inadvertently the test-construction process excludes items on which minority students outperform white and some Asian students, math items on which girls outperform boys, and items that students from the working class get right more often than more elite students. Before an item becomes part of the SAT, ETS tests it by putting it on the "experimental section" of the test. Students taking the SAT act as guinea pigs for new questions, the results of which do not count toward their test scores. ETS seeks items that "behave" statistically. An item behaves when those who get it right have more ability than those who get it wrong.

At first glance, this makes sense. Indeed, shouldn't people with ability get *any* item right more often than those with less ability? Items on which people with *less* ability do better would seem perverse indeed. Unfortunately, however, ETS uses no independent measure of ability. Even though the SAT is intended to predict first-semester college grades, researchers do not actually gather grades from past test-takers during their first semester in college.[20] If they did, they could assess which items on the experimental test correlated with better grades in college. Nor do researchers bother to correlate item results with students' high school grade point averages (GPAs). Instead, they take a shortcut: they use overall test score as their measure of ability.

Like most other "standardized" tests given widely in the U.S., researchers originally validated the SAT on affluent white students. Affluent white students have always done better on it than have African Americans, Hispanics, Native Americans, Filipino Americans, or working-class whites. Consider a hypothetical item on the experimental test that favors minority students. For example, it was widely bandied about in the 1970s that ETS tried an experimental item using "dashiki"—perhaps an analogy, "dashiki is to shirt as . . ."—on the SAT. Such an item resembles the "sake" item discussed earlier, except the vocabulary knowledge is opposite. That is, white suburban students were *less* likely to know "dashiki," a handmade African shirt popular at times in black culture. African American students, along with Latinos and inner-city whites familiar with black culture, were *more* likely to get the item right.[21] Thus the item "misbehaved" and never appeared on an actual SAT exam. In statistical terms, the item had a negative point-biserial correlation coefficient or item-to-scale correlation coefficient. Statistically speaking, the "wrong people" got it right. No one at ETS *wanted* nonwhites to score lower. No intentionality was involved. The process is purely statistical.

This problem goes far deeper than the question of whose specialized vocabulary and knowledge will be tapped, the elite's ("sake") or the ghetto's ("dashiki"). Some items that favor African Americans contain no specialized vocabulary. Consider "environment." When white students hear the word, most think first of the natural environment—ecology, pollution, the balance of nature, and the like. Nothing wrong with that—everyone knows that meaning of the word "environment." According to research at ETS, when minority students hear the word, most think first of the social environment—"what kind of environment does that child come from?" Again, nothing wrong with that—everyone knows that meaning of "environment." In the pressure-cooker conditions under which students take "standardized" tests, the first meaning that flashes into their minds when they encounter a word influences whether they pick a "distracter" (wrong answer) or get the item right. It follows like night after day that a potential item based upon the second meaning of "environment" could never make it to the SAT. Statistically speaking, the "wrong people" would get it right on the experimental test.[22]

Just as some items favor African Americans and those who know black culture, and hence do not get selected, other items favor Hispanics and Filipinos, and hence do not get selected. ETS researchers have shown how English words with Spanish cognates, like "pallid" (*palido* in Spanish), favor Hispanics and Filipinos. Words without such cognates, like "ashen," do not. Thus, Hispanics did much better than white students on an antonym item asking for the opposite of "pallid"; Anglos did better on an antonym asking for the opposite of "ashen." Both items had the same five alternatives; the desired opposite for both was "vividly colored." "Pallid" and "ashen" occur with roughly equal frequency in English.[23] Therefore, both items equally test "verbal reasoning," or whatever the SAT is alleged to test. As the proportion of test-takers from Hispanic backgrounds increases, however,

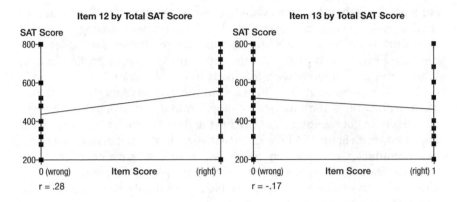

Item 12 by Total SAT Score

Item 13 by Total SAT Score

r = .28

r = -.17

The graph to the left shows the behavior that earns an item a place on a "standardized" test, in this case an SAT. Each test-taker either gets it wrong (0 on the horizontal axis) or right (1). The vertical axis shows each person's score on the rest of the test. Those who got the item wrong have mostly lower scores than those who got it right. The "regression line" summarizing the relationship slopes upward and to the right, showing a positive correlation, or r. For this item, r = .28. On the whole, the "more able" students got it right.

The graph to the right shows a test item that fails this statistical test. Items using *dashiki* or *environment* in each word's social meaning wind up like this. On the whole, the "more able" students—defined by their overall score on the other items—got it wrong. It has a negative point-biserial correlation coefficient: r = −.17.

items like "pallid" will become rarer on real SATs because, again, the wrong people—Hispanics with lower overall test scores—get them right.

For the same reason, no item on which girls outscore boys is likely to make it to the mathematics part of the SAT. The wrong people—girls, who have lower overall test scores on the math test—would get it right. I found that simply setting a math item in a girls' camp caused girls to outperform boys on it by a narrow margin. ETS set the same item in a boys' camp; as a result, boys outscored girls on it by a wide margin. This was OK; the right people got the item right.[24]

SOCIAL CLASS AFFECTS "STANDARDIZED" TEST SCORES

Most "standardized" tests, including the SAT, also correlate strongly with social class. Again, test bias is partly to blame, and again, looking at a prospective item illustrates the problem. Consider this analogy:

Spline is to miter as _____ is to _____[25]

In a heuristic exam I developed, the "Loewen Low-Aptitude Test," I provided these five alternatives:

a.   love . . . marriage
b.   straw . . . mud
c.   key . . . lock
d.   bond . . . bail
e.   bond . . . paper

Over the years, I have given this item to thousands of people. Among college undergraduates, no more than one person in a hundred gets it right and can explain why. It is a difficult item. First, it relies on terms that fair numbers of working-class Americans know but few members of the middle and upper classes recognize. "Spline" and "miter" are carpentry terms. A miter joint is a way to cut and glue two pieces of wood to form a joint often used in picture frames. Although attractive, because it conceals the end grain, this joint is weak. Weight placed on the top piece, for example, stresses the joint and causes the glue to let go. Hence such a joint is often used for a picture frame but rarely for a desk.

A spline is a piece of wood inserted into a miter joint to make it strong. A carpenter uses a table saw to cut matching notches—called "kerfs"—in the angled faces to be joined. Then s/he cuts or carves a small piece of wood—perhaps in a contrasting color like walnut—to fit the newly created space. When the three pieces are glued together, a downward force on the top piece no longer stresses the glue; the spline locks the joint in place.

Note that as with the dashiki item, knowing the vocabulary does not make this question trivially easy. Straw goes into mud to make bricks, to be sure, but doesn't love also go into marriage to make it stronger? The computerized grader replies, "Well, no. There is no evidence that love strengthens marriages. In most countries, including the United States, arranged marriages last longer, with fewer divorces, than love marriages."

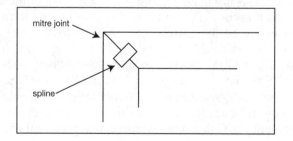

Besides, even if data showed that love *did* strengthen marriage, the analogy is not as close, not as physical. Bricks made with straw can literally support a weight placed on top of them, as can a miter joint made with a spline.

What about the alternatives? A key goes into a lock to lock it, "strengthening" in a sense, but it also goes in to *un*lock the lock, making it "weak." The other two choices make no sense whatsoever—although they draw votes from people who don't have a clue as to the vocabulary.

Thus, unlike the sake item, choosing among three of the alternatives on the spline analogy tests higher-level reasoning. Thus, among working-class students who know the vocabulary, it might correlate with and hence help predict college GPA.[26] Why then doesn't this question appear on an SAT? Why has no item using working-class vocabulary *ever* appeared on an SAT?

The obvious answer, after having viewed the graphs presented in this chapter, is that the wrong people—members of the working class—would get a working-class item correct. Working-class students are "wrong" in that on average they will score lower overall—partly because other items on the test rely on upper-middle-class culture. This obvious answer seems right but is too elegant. In fact, test-makers rarely even *propose* a working-class item, because they don't know working-class culture. Test-makers come from the same social class background as the students taking my test—the upper middle class. Like them, they have never heard of "kerf" or "spline" and just barely know "miter." They could never make up a question based on carpentry terms.

These problems of test bias afflict any test that uses point-biserial correlation coefficients, which includes most multiple-choice tests in U.S. history.[27]

INTERNALIZING EXPECTATIONS

Most students—for that matter, most adults—do not understand that "standardized" tests are biased and inadequate ways of measuring aptitude. We noted that the SAT is supposed to predict first-semester college grades. It does this badly: correlations between SAT scores and college GPA are often as low as .33. A better predictor of aptitude for most colleges is high school GPA. Indeed, for more than fifteen years, "SAT" has not stood for "Scholastic Aptitude Test." In June 1989, the U.S. Civil Rights Commission held a "consultation" in Washington, D.C., entitled The Validity of Testing in Education and Employment. I was the lead presenter, followed by Nancy S. Cole, then executive vice president of ETS (soon to be president), and several other testing experts. In the ensuing discussion, I stated,

> I don't think that the "A" in the SAT is merited. I don't think it should be called the "Scholastic Aptitude Test." I don't think SAT scores measure who will be an apt student next year in college precisely enough to label a student as "inept" or "apt."

Cole then said,

> The word "aptitude" in the Scholastic Aptitude Test has existed for a very long time. . . . The word "aptitude" has become associated with intelligence or an inherent characteristic in an individual. This is not the intended meaning of the word, but because those associations are made and wrong interpretations follow, I would also prefer that the Scholastic Aptitude Test didn't have the term "aptitude" in its name.

At that point Lloyd Bond, professor of education at the University of North Carolina, chimed in: "I agree."[28] Two years later, bowing to such arguments, ETS renamed the SAT the "Scholastic Assessment Test." After three more years, during which time it became painfully apparent that "Scholastic Assessment Test" was repetitive, said the same thing twice, and repeated itself, the ETS renamed the SAT once more—to *"SAT"*! "It does not stand for anything," as the College Board, ETS's governing body, put it in 1994.

Few people know this history. More than fifteen years after "aptitude" was dropped from the name, published test preparation books still call it the "Scholastic Aptitude Test," counselors call it the "Scholastic Aptitude Test," and students still think it is called the "Scholastic Aptitude Test." ETS knows this. Indeed, ETS makes use of it: when "Scholastic Aptitude Test" is typed into a search engine, the home page of the SAT comes up.[29] "Get ready to take the SAT!" it begins cheerfully. Yet "Scholastic Aptitude Test" does not appear on that page—the webmaster has made the text invisible, but it resides there nevertheless, rewarding the seeker who mistakenly enters it. Nowhere on the site does ETS let on that "Scholastic Aptitude Test" is a misnomer, indeed has been wrong since 1991. Nowhere on it does ETS provide any warning that the SAT does not measure aptitude.

As one result, some students who score poorly on "standardized" tests infer that they have low aptitude. One of the most brilliant undergraduates I have ever taught came to this conclusion. She was a psychology major at Tougaloo, but because psychology did not then offer a course on statistics and research methods, she took my course in sociology. It was tough, requiring thirteen different assignments during the semester. When I brought the course to the University of Vermont, I had to make it easier, because its demands were too far out of line with existing courses there.[30] My Tougaloo student not only mastered everything the course threw her way; she also learned the statistical technique called chi-square on her own. Yet she scored only about 370 on the Graduate Record Exam. Her school of choice, Vanderbilt, rejected her on that account, despite my glowing letter of reference. She internalized the rejection, concluding she probably could not have succeeded there anyway. I had graduated from a program at Harvard that put me in classes with many psychology graduate students and I knew she was as capable as most of them, but my protestations did not convince her. She believed what her test scores told her.

If the GRE could have such an impact on a brilliant college undergraduate, the SAT can have far worse effects on capable—but still developing—high school students. To be sure, some eighteen-year-olds have the audacity to say that the tests are wrong and the self-confidence to go on to do well enough to disprove them. Other low scorers preserve some self-esteem by saying, "I just don't test well," while still believing they are capable. Often, however, their self-assurance is part bravado; they are no longer sure they are good college material.

TEACHERS AND "STANDARDIZED" TESTS

The SAT and its competitor, the ACT, are the last "standardized" tests taken by most K–12 students. Even more damaging can be the "Iowas," the "Metropolitans," the "Californias," the "Stanfords," and of course, the grandfather of them all, the "IQ test," because children take these tests much earlier. Not only do they affect students' self-esteem, but also how students get treated. From kindergarten to 12th grade, most teachers subtly expect more from students who score higher. Sometimes these expectations are not subtle. Many school systems use scores on the exams mentioned above to group and track students, encouraging high scorers to take advanced placement courses and suggesting "general" classes for low scorers. Using these scores is only slightly better than setting different expectations based on first impression or even mere photographs. Indeed, although the correlations between test scores and ensuing performance are typically weak, what relationships we do see may derive from differential teacher expectations—high for students with high test scores—rather than from genuinely low aptitude.

Different expectations aren't all teachers' doing. Students participate. We all can remember that day or school subject that caught us unprepared.

How we hunkered down behind the student in front of us, avoiding eye contact with the teacher, hoping and praying not to be called upon! We were signalling our teacher that to expect much from us, at least that day or in that subject, would be a waste of time. Some students behave that way all the time, sending out vibrations to their teachers and fellow students that they are incapable. Others strain to get called upon, implying that they are capable. After only a short while, these behaviors become mutually agreed upon, creating a classroom hierarchy that seems "right" to teacher and students alike. Indeed, that may be why the Rosenthal and Jacobson study did not generate an expectancy effect in grades 3–6. After all, the researchers conveyed nothing directly to the students about their performance. Unless turned around by teacher expectations, students who had been selected randomly never knew they were supposed to excel. They probably continued to show the same behaviors they had used in the past to cue their teachers with regard to their performance level. After a few attempts at expecting more from them, based on the false information leaked by the researchers, teachers may have given up and let "nature" run its course.

At the beginning of this chapter, we noted that the performance gap between have and have-not students is larger in history/social studies than in any other subject. Now we have uncovered part of the reason why. In history and social studies classes, teacher expectations as well as student self-expectations play a particularly large and unfortunate role. More than chemistry or geometry, more even than English literature, history is tied to everyday experience and the potpourri of knowledge that children pick up more or less automatically from living in mainstream America. Unfortunately, the degree to which children live in mainstream America varies widely.

Journalist Susan Eaton showed that many black and Puerto Rican 3rd graders in Hartford, the capital of America's richest state, live so constricted by poverty and race that they have never seen the Connecticut River, which forms the eastern boundary of the city. On a field trip, seeing it for the first time from the windows of their school bus, the children give it a standing ovation! Although they live in New England, these children have never been sledding or even seen a sled up close. What chance do such children have to pick up, semiautomatically, useful facts about historic sites, the president, or anything else in mainstream culture? The "new math" is new to nearly everyone, which is one reason why the gap between have and have-not students is smallest in math. Students like those that Eaton observed signal to teachers that they don't know the basics in social studies, the things that teachers want to assume so they can go further.[31]

TEACHERS CAN CREATE THEIR OWN EXPECTATIONS

Such children are not stupid. They are merely ignorant—ignorant of many of the things needed to do well in school. What they have not learned, they do not know.[32] Teachers must not be swayed by what children like these do not know. They must see beyond their low scores on IQ tests and other "standardized" exams. Betty Hart and Todd Risley recorded the behavior of parents in different social classes as their children grew from age 6 months to age 3. Poor parents talked much less with their babies and used shorter sentences with fewer modifiers. Such patterns then made a huge difference to the children's vocabulary growth by age 3, their measured IQs, and their scores on the Test of Language Development at age 9.[33] Moreover, they do know lots of stuff. Many children of poverty are put into positions of major responsibility at young ages. They prepare supper, care for younger siblings, translate for mom at the doctor. It is not poor children's fault that they were talked with less. Teachers must expect them to be adequate first—and excellent later on—even though they seem to know so little of the knowledge they need to do well in school.[34]

Absent such intervention, differential expectations often get written in stone by the time students reach high school. Sections at Woodrow Wilson Jr. High School in Decatur, Illinois, were numbered 7.1, 7.2, and on down to 7.8, when I attended. Section 7.1 one was the "smartest," 7.8 the "dumbest." Two criteria mainly explained who got assigned to which section—ability, measured by teacher recommendations and "standardized" test scores, and the music group one was in. Being in the band played a key role, as did being in the best choral group. In 9th grade came another choice point: whether the student chose a foreign language—and which language—was key. Students in 9.1, by my memory, chose Latin; many were in the band. I remember pondering for a long time the choice between Latin and auto mechanics. Since then, owing to a fondness for old sports cars and pickup trucks, I have spent many roadside hours regretting my choice of Latin. It did get me into the college of my choice, though. Not the language itself, of course. Except for "habeas corpus, Corpus Christi," I've forgotten all that. High teacher expectations resulting from being in section 9.1, continuing into high school the next year, did the trick.

What happened to me was no isolated anecdote. The same thing happens all around the U.S. Sociologist James Rosenbaum showed the process in a wonderful book on a working-class city near Boston. Because this city was overwhelmingly white and working class, Rosenbaum did not have to deal with the claim that differences in race or socioeconomic status lay behind the school system's decision to track its students. He found that, like Decatur, the choice of foreign language in junior high school "determines both the group of students that a student is placed with for all his classes and the level of difficulty of all his classes." Rosenbaum describes how it worked:

> There are actually nine tracks in each of the junior high years. The choice of a foreign language leads to placement in one of the first five tracks (labeled A to E); any other elective leads to placement in the last four tracks (F to I). Tracks are ranked within these two groups according to teachers' assessments and IQ scores.
>
> Students in each track have all their classes together and even sit together at lunch and in assemblies. Furthermore, each class is paced by the ability level of the section. Thus the top language group has the most difficult history class, English class, and mathematics class. The second-highest language group has a slightly easier class in each of these subjects, and so on. Moreover, language tracks have more difficult classes than nonlanguage tracks.[35]

Admittedly, I attended junior high school in the 1950s and Rosenbaum studied his Massachusetts city in the 1970s. No longer are school systems so insensitive as to label the "smartest" section "7.1" or "7-A." No matter. My mother tutored math at Woodrow Wilson two decades later, after the system had progressed to numbering its still-tracked sections randomly. She was helping the "slowest" section in mid-September when a student complained about the workload. "You expect too much from us, Mrs. Loewen," said the boy. "You *know* we're the dumbest section in the school." "Oh, no, you aren't," she assured the lad. "Then name a dumber one!" he replied. Although his section was now arbitrarily designated 7.4 and school had been in session for less than a month, students already knew exactly how they and everyone else ranked.

Today, most school systems have done away with junior high schools. Many have formally abandoned tracking in middle school. Nevertheless, some schools that no longer overtly divide students into "ability-based" groups have let tracking sneak back in through the rear door. Strong performance in gateway courses like algebra are legitimately required for advanced math. First-year French is legitimately required for advanced French. By the time students reach 11th grade, sections of American history are inadvertently programmed by the scheduling computer into ability groups to accommodate students who must take advanced math and foreign language at certain hours. Other schools test in math and group students in math courses by achievement level. Either way, inexorable demands of the schedule mean that courses in history (and other areas) wind up also grouped. History teachers can unwittingly accept labels like "slow" or "smart" that students themselves apply to these sections, even though such labels may derive from proficiency in algebra long ago in 7th grade. Teachers must expect students to be excellent, even students in the "slow" section.

Many high schools offer IB (International Baccalaureate) or APUSH (Advanced Placement U.S. History) classes, "regular" U.S. history, and history for students in the "general" or vocational curricula. Doing so overtly divides students into three groups and inevitably expects more from the first. However, research shows that when students are lifted from "slow" classes to "average" classes and then to "high" classes, their performance often increases to match their new environment.[36] A given student might do B– work—just below average—in "slow," "regular," and AP classes. Of course, it would be better if these students performed at the A– rather than B– level. Nevertheless, they do much more work and do it much better when they earn a B– in APUSH compared to a B– in the slow track.

LouAnne Johnson (played by Michelle Pfeiffer in the movie *Dangerous Minds*) made this point anecdotally:

> Inside the classroom I learned that the more difficult the material I presented, the harder my students worked, especially students who had been labeled underachievers. They might moan about having to read the classics, but they didn't want to read "dumbed down" versions of the books. They wanted to suffer like the "smart" kids in regular classes.[37]

History courses taught in innovative ways can challenge students to do excellent work, some for the first time. All people have strengths and weaknesses. The excellent student, always prepared, a sponge for information, a whiz on multiple-choice tests, may be only ordinary when challenged to represent an event—for example, the Depression, and FDR's response to it—as a graphic poster. The slow reader who performs poorly on timed multiple-choice exams may come up with fine ideas for a group project outlining a museum exhibit about the women's movement of the 1970s with its successes and failures. A teacher can quietly point out to an underperforming student that this next task is different—"you are *good* at *this* skill"—whether it is art, music, talking, or even physical prowess. For perhaps the first time, that student may believe that s/he will excel, or at least do adequately. Then the teacher builds from there.

An increasing number of teachers, high schools, and entire school districts are making AP and honors courses open enrollment, available to all. Some teachers and districts have taken the next step and explicitly recruited students of diverse racial and class backgrounds to their fast-track courses. "Personally, I cast a wide net when it comes to letting kids take the course," wrote one teacher of the Advanced Placement history course in 2004. "I love the fact that I can get some kids with lower abilities into my class and watch their writing improve and contribute to their understanding of U.S. history." Another teacher agreed:

> I have an open enrollment position regarding students who want to take my APUSH class. . . . For whatever reason—students' parents take little interest, the students don't think it's a "cool" thing to do, they doubt themselves, nobody has ever suggested it to them—many students in my high school never even consider an AP class.

He went on:

> Many times students have never really thought that they could succeed in an AP class. Many times these students internalize the message that they will never succeed in a course filled with the "brains" from their class. Even worse, many of these students have been institutionalized into self-identifying mediocrity through the shortsightedness of counseling advice. But when I have been able to encourage these students to accept the challenge of AP, almost always they surprise themselves with how capable they really are.[38]

These teachers have recruited students with low self-expectations into their Advanced Placement classes. They then expected them to succeed, taught them effectively, and gave them bad grades if they did not perform well. From their own responses, doing so seems to have worked.[39]

Another way to handle the problem of tracking while making honors available to all students is by adding an optional honors component to regular courses. Having students do history, discussed in Chapter 4, is a good way to add such an element into U.S. history courses. Also, whenever a class does a good job, whether a "regular" or honors class, teachers can call them "scholars" or "intellectuals." Maybe no one has ever called them that before. Maybe it will even be believed.

Forming quick assessments of children's abilities or tracking them on the basis of test scores would be fine if the underlying theory were correct—if children really possessed markedly different aptitudes for school, probably genetically determined, and surely fixed by the time they enter school. Rosenthal and Jacobson show these assumptions to be false. If merely being observed by a team from Harvard can raise 1st graders' IQ scores by an average of 12 points (the Hawthorne effect), and if merely leaking the "fact" that students A, B, and C are likely to spurt can cause randomly selected 1st graders to raise their scores by another 16 points, then IQ can hardly be either innate or fixed.

Even within homogeneous white upper-middle-class classrooms, some students give off the aura that they don't like history and are not prepared in it. "I don't do well in history," they say, as if that explains anything. To this, teachers must reply, "Until now." Allowing students to admit they are bad at history gives them permission to be bad at history. Withhold that permission! The sentence "I never did well in history until now" sends quite a different message.

We must conclude from the research summarized in this chapter that teachers must not let pupils' appearance, their own self-expectations, or low "standardized" test scores influence what teachers expect from them. If a teacher cannot convince herself that a student has *any* ability, s/he (the teacher) can fake it. Besides, every student is good at *something*, or at least less bad at it. Build on students' strengths. Herein lies another benefit of the 30–50 topics regimen. Teaching topics in very different ways during the school year lets students excel in at least some of the activities that are assigned. A boy may shine in debate who had previously not finished his written assignments. A girl who had been quiet in class discussions and inattentive to lectures may conduct and write up a terrific history of her grandmother. A student who does little homework on his own may work well with others on a project. Experiment with different groups. A have-not student may hold her own when grouped with privileged students, working at their level, thus performing at a higher level than she had reached before. Or, grouping have-not students together may coax at least some of them to do good work, just so their group can complete the assigned task and report to the class. A student whose background is problematic—perhaps a recent immigrant, with inadequate command both of English and of general knowledge about the United States—can make use of precisely that background when asked to learn about and write up the history of his/her family.

If, well into the school year, some students have not responded to their teacher's expectations for them, the teacher might show the class the first half hour of the PBS video *A Class Divided*. This video reviews the now-famous "Iowa eye-color experiment" devised by Jane Elliott. She divided her all-white 3rd graders in Riceville, Iowa, on the basis of eye color. She then told them that blue-eyed children were smarter than brown-eyed ones; within minutes they believed her. More astonishingly, the next day she reversed the expectations, telling the children that she had lied to them; in fact, brown-eyed children were superior. Among other outcomes, on that 2nd day the brown-eyed students whipped through a flash-card exercise in 2.5 minutes that had taken them 5.5 minutes the day before, when Elliott had expected them to be slow. Before showing the video, ask students to watch for the effects of the teacher's expectations on the children. (In a sense the entire film is about her expectations and their impact.) After viewing, and after a discussion that notes the impact of expectations on flash cards performance, the teacher can turn the discussion to her own classroom. Do students see their teacher as having different expectations for different students? Do students have different expectations for themselves? By talking about the expectations elephant in the classroom, a teacher may be able to challenge those self-expectations—or perhaps learn something about how s/he helps maintain them.

"In every child who is born, under no matter what circumstances, and of no matter what parents," wrote James Agee, "the potentiality of the human race is born again."[40] A teacher's job is to help that child realize a portion of that potential today. The job includes that same task tomorrow. To keep expectations high, day after day—even when students do not respond—is truly a challenge. Some students *are* less able—partly because they believe they are. A teacher cannot reach everyone, but history teachers can come close. Owing to the multifaceted nature of its subject matter and the diverse ways it can be taught, history can bring out *some* worthwhile performance from almost every student. "You say you're 'just not good at history.' I don't know you very well yet, so I'm not going to challenge that statement. I just want you to change the verb tense, and just for the rest of the fall semester. Say 'Up until now, I just wasn't good at history.' OK?"

On that high note, the chapter should end. First, we must tie up two loose ends. Earlier, we saw that the performance gap between have and have-not students is larger in history than in any other subject. We also noted that differential teacher expectations—strong as they are—explain only part of that gap. Something else is also going on: a special alienation of have-not students. Much of American history is taught to justify, not merely analyze, our nation's past. The biased and inaccurate account of Reconstruction learned by my Tougaloo students, described in the introduction to this book, is merely a particularly flagrant example. So is the counterfactual "$24 myth" discussed in Chapter 7. Faced with material like this, students who do not hail from the establishment often develop a special alienation from history. For example, they may not be articulate enough to describe how the way in which their textbook presents the past implies that the nation is just, in turn implying that their family's lack of status must be its own fault. They only know they "don't like" history.

Don't let this happen in your class! History can be a tool of liberation or oppression. Surely, learning the truth about the past is a tool for liberation. Teachers need to look within and ensure that their course and their thinking about the U.S. does not gloss over our misdeeds or imply that Americans did them with good intentions. Western civilization will not come to an end if our students face the past without flinching. On the contrary, our nation can only benefit from its newly informed citizenry.

The second loose end concerns the rising number of "standardized" tests in history that students—and by implication their teachers—face. Under pressure from the federal No Child Left Behind Act (NCLB), some-times derided as "No Child Left Untested," many states now rely on multiple-choice exams to test students' knowledge and skills in history. There is nothing wrong with an increased emphasis on accountability. Teachers should be accountable. The problem lies in how we measure student progress.

Legislators and state administrators do not adopt multiple-choice tests out of a belief that such exams measure skills that children need. Everyone knows that after students leave school, most will *never* have to answer another multiple-choice item again. In the workplace, we may be asked to write, to speak, to read critically and summarize, to understand tables. In our job as citizens, we need to be able to do all those things and also listen critically, develop ideas, and persuade others of our point of view. In adult life, we are not asked to choose a letter:

The War of 1812 began in

    a.   1811
    b.   1812
    c.   1815
    d.   It never really began because Great Britain backed down
    e.   All of the above[41]

To state officials, multiple-choice tests come with a gloss of fairness. They seem defensible and uncontroversial because they look objective. They claim to test factual knowledge because they come with "right" or "wrong" answers.

This chapter has shown what is not fair—and *cannot* be fair—about "standardized" tests. The claim that multiple-choice items are defensible and uncontroversial unravels when we consider the "right" answer to this fill-in-the-blank item: "Columbus discovered America in ____." A further unraveling comes when we recall the problems with "twig tests" discussed in the previous chapter. Although multiple-choice items can be constructed that test subtle matters of understanding, such questions are rare. Most multiple-choice tests ask for mere recall. Teachers will teach to the tests. We even want them to. If the test is multiple choice, teachers will teach twigs, students will be bored, and we will return to square one, with U.S. history being the least-liked subject in the curriculum.

Meanwhile, students who have done powerful work in a course in U.S. history for the first time—partly because they were expected to, and partly because some of the varied teaching methods resonated with their strengths—are unlikely to do well on these statewide exams. Multiple-choice twig tests are precisely the barriers that have been defeating these students for years.

In the real world, twig tests get adopted because they are cheap. Indeed, developing and grading them can be cash cows for their manufacturers. Despite their economy, however, end-of-the-year exams should not be twig tests, state-mandated or not.

Mind you, simply doing away with the test in history offers no solution. The only thing worse than a statewide twig test in history is *no* statewide test in history at all—because then principals and superintendents will concentrate their resources on those subjects that *are* tested. So my final suggestion about "standardized" tests in history is this: Teachers can influence their state's test. They can be active. Teachers can persuade first their district and then their legislators that relying on multiple-choice items is false economy. Teachers can learn about states that refuse to trust such tests—Vermont and Rhode Island, for two.[42] Instead, states can ask students to prove in various ways that they possess the historical knowledge and skills that will allow them to be creative citizens. These are the same skills that equip them to be effective in the workplace, after all, and state legislators and administrators want to produce capable workers. Twig tests don't test useful skills. Who better to create a test that does than teachers who have given a lot of thought as to why and how U.S. history should be taught and learned? In short, who better than you?!

FOCUSED BIBLIOGRAPHY

Robert Rosenthal and Lenore Jacobson, "Teacher Expectations for the Disadvantaged," *Scientific American, 248* #4 (4/1968), 21–25. This article sparked the now-vast literature on teacher expectations, so it is hardly the last word on it, but it still reads well and raises the key concerns.

CHAPTER 3

Historiography

H ISTORIOGRAPHY IS ONE OF THE GREAT GIFTS that history teachers can bestow upon their students. Unfortunately, many college history departments reserve this blessing for their history majors in upper-level courses. Every college student needs to learn the term. For that matter, every high school graduate needs to know it. (Don't worry: I've taught the idea to children as young as 4th grade. If they can learn supercalifragilisticexpialidocious, they can handle "historiography.") The term and the underlying concept are one of our best tools for developing critical reading and analytic thinking.

Most concisely, historiography means "the study of history," but not just "studying history." Historiography asks us to scrutinize how a given piece of history came to be. Who wrote this book? Who put up this marker? Who *didn't* put it up? What points of view were omitted?

When I was in high school, I believed history was to be memorized, like the times tables. After all, Columbus did discover America in 1492, didn't he? Doesn't $8 \times 8 = 64$? Historians know better. History is not like arithmetic. To be sure, there is a bedrock of fact in history. What happened in 1492 happened. But that is not history. History is what we *say* happened. What we say about 1492 changes as we change. Historiography is the study of why and how history changes.

A TALE OF TWO ERAS

On the landscape, every historic site is a tale of two eras: what it's about and when it went up. The historical marker for the Almo massacre in southern Idaho offers an unusual exception to this rule. While researching *Lies Across America: What Our Historic Sites Get Wrong*, I read thousands of historical markers. Of them all, the one presented here is perhaps the most attractive—a piece of slate carved into the shape of the state of Idaho. It is also the most deceitful. It claims that on some day in 1861, Indians killed some 300 pioneers in their wagon train near present-

While this marker commemorates a massacre that never took place, it does reveal something about Idaho in 1938.

ALMO IDAHO
DEDICATED TO THE MEMORY
OF THOSE WHO LOST THEIR LIVES IN A MOST
HORRIBLE INDIAN MASSACRE 1861
THREE HUNDRED IMMIGRANTS WEST BOUND
ONLY FIVE ESCAPED
ERECTED BY S.& D. OF IDAHO PIONEERS
1938

day Almo. In reality, 300 immigrants did *not* perish. Thirty did not . . . three did not . . . *it never happened at all.*

It isn't easy to prove a negative. I can write about what didn't happen in Almo with such authority only because a fine Western historian, Brigham Madsen, spent much of four decades researching the topic. He makes a compelling case. First, he showed that the *earliest* mention of the massacre was in 1927—66 years after it allegedly took place! Other, much smaller incidents won extensive newspaper coverage at the time; but not Almo. Throughout the entire West between 1842 and 1859, of more than 400,000 pioneers crossing the Plains, fewer than 400, or less than 0.1%, were killed by American Indians.[1] Two years later, almost as many more allegedly perished in one incident, yet no one noticed? Next, he found no mention of the event in the records of the Indian Service, War Department, and state and territorial bureaucracies. "A massacre involving the deaths of 294 emigrants would have engendered a massive amount of material," he pointed out. "There is none." Finally, Madsen found inconsistencies, even impossibilities, in the tale as told in 1927. To cite just one: supposedly the men of the party, inside their circled wagons, dug wells during the three- or four-day siege, trying in vain to reach water. Afterward, these wells proved deep enough to accommodate all 294 corpses![2]

We must conclude that *this* historical marker is *not* a tale of two eras. It has nothing to tell us about what it's about, because in 1861 nothing much happened in southern Idaho.

What can it tell us about 1938, when it went up?

By the 1930s, the Almo anecdote resonated with the familiar American archetype of whooping Indians circling around the circled wagons. In reality, Indians rarely circled like that—doing so would merely have exposed them and their horses to danger. The tradition of circling Indians does not begin in the real West, but in 1883, in Buffalo Bill's Wild West Show. There Indians *had to* circle because they were in a circus ring! Buffalo Bill became the biggest show business act in the world; by 1893 fifty imitators were touring the United States. Hollywood picked up the tradition, and the real West became the reel West: one-third of all Hollywood movies made before 1970 were Westerns! Today, as Western novelist Larry McMurtry put it, "Thanks largely to the movies, the lies about the West are more potent than the truths."[3]

According to Hollywood myth, made visible on the landscape in Almo, Native Americans were the foremost obstacle that pioneers faced. Actually, although Natives did defend their homes and lands against intruders, on the whole they proved to be more help than hindrance to westering white pioneers.[4] All this was forgotten in the culture of white supremacy that arose during the first decades of the twentieth century. By 1938, the Sons and Daughters of Idaho Pioneers were happy to believe any story about savage Indians, with no basis beyond a writer's memory of something "an old trapper" told him around 1875. Thus, the Almo marker does deserve to be on display, perhaps in the Idaho State Historical Society Museum. There it could be accompanied by a label, "Artifact of 1938," that explains to visitors what the marker reveals about white culture in southern Idaho.

As soon as students understand historiography, they get twice as much stimulation from every historic site they visit. I have watched as students poke around at the rear of a war memorial until they find the date when it went up. Now they can put it in context: This is what South Carolina said about Gettysburg *in 1965*. Simply adding the last two words hangs a context around whatever the monument says. No longer is it written in stone; now it is written in 1965. Intrinsic to that context is the possibility of a different context—1865, perhaps, or 2015. Thinking critically about the message cannot lag far behind.

THE CIVIL RIGHTS MOVEMENT,
COGNITIVE DISSONANCE, AND HISTORIOGRAPHY

If every historic site is a tale of two eras, the same holds for every historic source. Different editions of the same textbook provide an inexpensive introduction to historiography. Treatments of John Brown offer a case in point. As white supremacy increasingly pervaded American culture during the Nadir of race relations in the early years of the twentieth century, textbook authors increasingly saw the abolitionist as insane. Indeed, they even lost sympathy for nonviolent abolitionists like William Lloyd Garrison, considering them somehow responsible for the Civil War. Not until the Civil Rights Movement of the 1960s was white America freed from enough of its racism to accept that a white person did not have to be crazy to die for black equality. In a sense, the murders of Michael Schwerner and Andrew Goodman in Mississippi, James Reeb and Viola Liuzzo in Alabama, and various other whites in various other southern states during the Civil Rights Movement enabled textbook writers to see sanity again in John Brown.

John Brown's sanity provides an inadvertent index of the level of white racism in our society, and students can trace Brown's sanity level in textbooks published from 1870 to the present. Different editions of the same book offer a particularly effective demonstration of the importance of historiography. *Rise of the American Nation*, probably the best-selling textbook of the 1960s and 1970s, labeled Brown's 1859 Harpers Ferry plan "a wild idea, certain to fail," in 1961. The same textbook in 1986, now retitled *Triumph of the American Nation*, called it "a bold idea, but almost certain to fail." How economical! The typesetter changed *wi* to *bo* and added "almost," and students can see Brown becoming more sane, right before their eyes.

I asked a class of 5th-graders what John Brown had done between 1961 and 1986 to cause this change in his treatment. "Nothin'," they chorused. "Well, he *moldered* a little more!" volunteered one. Then I asked the class, "What changes took place in American society between 1961 and 1986 to cause this change?" Immediately a student replied, "The Civil Rights Movement." Right before my eyes, they were doing historiography. They now understood that *when* one writes about John Brown helps to determine *what* one writes about him. When students return to their textbook, they realize they are reading what *this* book, published in its specific year, says.

Why did the Civil Rights Movement cause such change in how historians wrote? Cognitive dissonance, an important concept developed by the social psychologist Leon Festinger, can explain the transformation. Cognitive dissonance has such important implications for history that every high school graduate should understand it. Briefly, Festinger teaches that

Book Review

He Took Orders
Only From God

John Brown is Russell Banks's
hero in "Cloudsplitter," a novel not
about history but about living
and dealing with fanaticism.
Reviewed by Walter Kirn 9

Two portraits of John Brown show him edging back toward sanity as the twentieth century drew to a close. First is Brown as John Steuart Curry saw him in 1937. This gaunt man is obviously disturbed; in Curry's mural at the Kansas State Capitol, Brown's outstretched hands drip blood. Like the tornado behind him, he spins out of control.

Next is how the *New York Times Book Review* would have readers see Brown in 1998—as a religious fanatic. "He took orders only from God," headlined the *Times*. In reality, Brown never claimed God dictated his plans. "I see a book kissed here which I suppose to be the Bible, or at least the New Testament, which teaches me that all things whatsoever I would that men should do to me, I should do even so to them," said Brown in his last words to the court at his treason trial in 1859. "It teaches me, further, to remember them that are in bonds as bound with them. I endeavored to act up to that instruction." That teaching is Jesus's "Golden Rule." It can indeed be found in the New Testament and does imply that slavery is un-Christian. Rather than present Brown's religious motivation honestly, the *Times* parodies it. Even in 1998, more or less our time, neither its illustration nor its prose helps readers see Brown as he was.

when our ideas or ideals are out of harmony with our actions, there is a mental push to change our ideas. We cannot change what we have done, after all, and often we cannot easily change what we are doing.

Festinger devised ingenious experiments to demonstrate cognitive dissonance. For instance, he recruited undergraduates to participate in a boring task involving repetitive hand motions. After an hour, when time was up, he asked each to tell the next student that it was interesting. Some subjects he paid $20. Others got only $1. The $20 recipients did not know that others had got less; the $1 participants never knew that others had got more; hence no invidious distinctions could be drawn. Finally, he asked each student a series of questions about the hourlong session: Did they find it boring or interesting? Did they think it was useful to science or probably useless?[5] Take a moment and ask yourself: responding to the final questions, who were probably more positive about the experiment, the $20 recipients or those paid only $1?

The answer surprises most audience members: the $1 folks rated the task more interesting than those paid $20. Why? Put yourself in the shoes of a $20 recipient. You have wasted an hour of your life doing a dumb experiment. You even lied—well, maybe only fibbed—to a fellow student, about how it was actually interesting. But then, you did get $20 for it, not bad for an hour's work. Now empathize with a $1 recipient. You spent an hour doing a dumb experiment. You even told a fellow student that it was actually interesting. For this you got exactly $1. You are a jerk! A patsy!

Few of us like to say that about ourselves. We cannot go back and retrieve the hour we have wasted. We can modify our opinion about it. It wasn't *so* bad. It was kind of interesting. It probably benefitted science. So we become more positive about the experience than those paid $20. Nor are we lying now. Our more positive opinions are our real opinions, just as real as those held by the $20 recipients. We did not first hold negative views, then change them overtly when asked at the end. But we did alter our opinions to bring them into harmony with what we did. Modifying one's opinions to bring them into line with one's actions or planned actions is the most common resolution of cognitive dissonance.

Now consider the impact of the Civil Rights Movement. Imagine yourself the parent of a white 2nd grader, your daughter, as late as 1969. All your life you have been told by your state, Mississippi, and by the federal government as well,[6] that African Americans are inferior beings—so inferior that they must be kept away, in separate and unequal schools, lest they hold white children back. Local industries hire them only as janitors, not as line workers. Blacks cannot live on the white side of town, and the city has not even paved some of the streets on the black side. Indeed, African Americans are a pariah people who cannot even be allowed to eat in white restaurants or rest in white cemeteries. Exactly *what* menace they represent is left vague—crime, surely, and mental inferiority, maybe also a sexual threat. Your daughter has been in an all-white school for two years—well, not quite all-white; under your district's "freedom of choice" desegregation plan, two black children have enrolled in her otherwise white elementary school.

It is easy for such parents to believe that African Americans *are* inferior. They do make less money, after all, and live in worse homes. Besides, the

alternative would be to think of ourselves as bad people. For we all participate in a society that confines blacks to the worst jobs, the worst schools,
even the worst streets. To treat others so badly while considering them
reasonable human beings like ourselves creates a dissonance between
act and attitude that demands resolution. No one can erase what society
has done, and no single parent can have much influence on its current or
future actions. Even to try would not be in our best interest, lest we be
called "nigger lovers" and lose our position in the white community. To
change our attitude is far easier. So we agree with what authority figures
tell us. We conclude that African Americans *are* inferior, and that segregation is appropriate for such people. Would we let our daughter marry a
black person? Surely not! Indeed, only 4% of whites approved of interracial marriage before the Civil Rights Movement, and that was the national proportion, not just in the Deep South. Almost as few whites agreed,
"It is OK to have Negroes as foremen over whites."[7]

In the fall of 1969, in *Alexander v. Holmes*, the U.S. Supreme Court finally ruled "freedom of choice" desegregation plans unconstitutional.
Giving black children the right to attend white schools put all the burden of desegregating society on their heads. Besides, there should not *be*
white schools, or black schools—just schools. So on January 5, 1970, public
schools desegregated across Mississippi. Your daughter's white elementary school became the school for all 3rd and 4th graders in town; all 1st and
2nd graders had to attend the former black elementary school. Ninety-
three percent of white parents kept their children in the public schools.
Some hastily organized a private school in the Sunday School building of
the Baptist Church, but it hardly equalled public school facilities. Moreover, your daughter got to keep her former teacher at her new school. As
a white parent, you may have hoped that this day would never come, but
of course you were upbeat about it with your little girl.

Imagine now that a year has passed. Your daughter is now halfway
through 3rd grade. The sun still rises in the east and sets in the west. She
still comes home bubbling with enthusiasm about school and shows you
her art drawings. At this point, you have another cognitive dissonance
problem. You can continue saying to yourself, "African Americans are inferior. They are so inferior mentally that they must be kept in separate
schools, lest they hold white children back." But then you would have to
conclude, "I am sending my little daughter off to school with them. That
is bad parenting. I am a jerk!"

Again, Festinger would remind us, people don't want to say that
about themselves. To change behavior would be hard: scrimping to pay
tuition for what looks to be a second-rate private school anyway. So attitudes change. "They aren't so bad. My husband served under a black

sergeant in the Army, and he was all right." Within months of school desegregation, most white Southerners agreed with the statement, "It is OK to have Negroes as foremen over whites." By 2003, nationally, 66% of whites "would not object to a child or grandchild's marrying someone of another race."[8]

Although my imaginary parent was a Southerner, the impact of the Civil Rights Movement was national, like the Gallup poll referred to in the previous citation. Before 1954, every white American had been complicit to a degree in denying African Americans equal rights, because the federal government had played a role. Not only did it do little or nothing to enforce the Fourteenth Amendment, promising equal rights to all without regard to race. As well, the FDR administration built eight all-white "model towns," from Greenbelt, Maryland, to Richland, Washington, that flatly prohibited African Americans after dark. Throughout the United States, the Federal Housing Administration told banks not to make loans to African Americans trying to buy in white suburbs and suggested that realtors not show them properties in white neighborhoods. White registrars across much of the South absolutely denied African Americans the right to vote, yet the U.S. did not enforce the Fifteenth Amendment, which had promised all races the right to vote. In this setting, historians found it easy to assume the inferiority of African Americans and write bad history about abolitionists, including John Brown.

What happened during Reconstruction got especially distorted in the decades before the Civil Rights Movement. No wonder, since Reconstruction was the one period when African Americans were granted and exercised their rights as citizens. Looking at what textbooks written in different eras say about Reconstruction engages students. Quickly they see that the time period in which authors wrote—as well as their race and region—can influence their writing more than what actually took place. Within the South, after 1890, only white supremacists had the power to determine how Reconstruction would be remembered, having disfranchised African Americans outright and terrorized white Republicans into submission. In the North, too, from the start of the Nadir of race relations in 1890 and persisting through World War II and up to the civil rights struggle, most historians emphasized tales of corruption and bad behavior during Congressional Reconstruction, when blacks had some influence on state and local governments. Indeed, the entire enterprise of Congressional Reconstruction seemed corrupt to historians who "knew better" than to presume that blacks could or should enjoy equal rights. Once the Civil Rights Movement wrested our society onto a path toward racial justice, these distortions no longer seemed appropriate. Bernard Weisberger's article "The Dark and Bloody Ground of Reconstruction Historiography"

chronicled the changes in historians' views up to 1959; Eric Foner continued the chronicle to 1982 in his article "Reconstruction Revisited."[9] These
sources can underpin an assignment inviting students to assess old and
recent textbooks or secondary works on Reconstruction. Not everything
has been made right; to a degree even new textbooks still reflect the influence of the "Nadir" in their terminology and treatment of Reconstruction
(and other topics).

As the changes in attitudes toward African Americans reverberated
through our culture in the 1970s, not only the history of black-white race
relations improved. The introduction suggests that textbook portrayals of
the incarceration of Japanese Americans on the West Coast in concentration camps also got better. Students can research this topic as an example
of historiography. They might begin by reading newspaper accounts from
1942–45, now available on the Web. Then they can compare textbook treatments over time. I would suggest dividing the books into four periods:
"early" (1943–50), "pre-civil rights" (1950–70), "post-civil rights" (1970–
88), and "post-reparations" (1988–present). They may find that early accounts were cursory, sometimes omitting the matter entirely, and justified
the action. After the Civil Rights Movement, coverage in textbooks may
have increased and treatments may have become more critical. After the
United States apologized and paid reparations in 1988, coverage may have
grown still fuller. Such improvement cannot be credited to better sources,
because journalists covered the internment well at the time. Cognitive dissonance leads us to hypothesize a reciprocal relationship between truth
about the past and justice in the present. That is, after Japanese Americans
achieved some measure of justice after 1988, their incarceration became a
success story of sorts. The U.S. wronged them, yes, but then the nation did
something to make it right. So now authors can give it major coverage.[10]

STUDYING BAD HISTORY

Students find it intriguing to think about what topics textbooks handle
especially badly. This is the flip side of our earlier discussion of the incarceration of Japanese Americans. The following ten questions—or a
subset—can be applied to a feature film, field trip site, documentary,
novel, newspaper article, textbook, or other historic source.

1. When was it created? The theory of cognitive dissonance suggests that
    the actual social practices of the period when history is written largely
    determine that history's perspective on the past. How did that time differ
    from ours? From the time of the event or person described?

2. Who created it? Representing which participant group's point of view? What was their position in social structure?
3. Why? What were their ideological needs and social purposes? Their values?
4. Who was/is the intended audience? What does the work ask that audience to go and do?
5. Did the intended audience include powerful people and institutions? For example, is the source a textbook that is striving to win government adoption? Is it a book that needed to win an editor's approval? Did the process of getting approved by the powerful influence what it says?
6. Who is left out? What points of view go largely unheard? How would the story differ if a different group had told it? Another political party? Another race, sex, class, or religious group?
7. Are there problematic words or symbols that would not have been used today, or by an author from another social group?
8. How was it received? Is it largely forgotten? Remembered? Why?
9. A critical question to ask at any historic site is: What does it leave out about the people it treats as heroes?
10. Is the presentation accurate? What actually happened? What do other sources—primary as well as secondary—say?

What difference does each point make to what is said? Under #2, for example, how does the creator's point of view and position in social structure influence what s/he wrote? Does the source appear inadequate—or worse—in the light of these questions?[11] Of course, all ten questions should not be applied tediously to every text or picture. On the contrary, students can choose which question(s) are most important for a given source.

Armed with these questions, students can read between the lines of their textbooks, or whatever source they are studying. Then the book (or movie, etc.) can furnish insights not only about the era it describes, but also about the time in which it was created. Indeed, the worse it is, the more it reveals. I know at least two high school teachers of U.S. history who deliberately adopted the worst book they could find on their state's approved list. After all, even the worst book gets the basic chronology right—South Carolina did secede in 1860, and World War I did precede World War II. So a bad book won't interfere much with twig learning, while it might provoke critical reading and thinking.

Why are textbooks so bad? The example of the Nadir of race relations, treated in Chapter 10, provides a way in to thinking about this question. Not one high school textbook I have seen uses the term. Of the eighteen on which I based *Lies My Teacher Told Me*, only one treated it adequately (albeit without naming it), and it has been out of print for more than twenty years.[12] Why such inattention? Perhaps because various elements of the Nadir, such as sundown towns and suburbs, still plague our nation today. Therefore, we can hardly call the Nadir a success story.

A still more likely reason for the neglect of the Nadir has to do with the basic story line underlying American history textbooks: the archetype of progress. As a nation, we started out great, and we've been getting better ever since—pretty much automatically. This notion of perpetual progress legitimizes ignoring anything bad Americans ever did, because in the end it turned out all right; indeed, our history led to the most progressive nation in the history of the world. In this view, progress is what doomed the American Indian, for example, not bad things "we" (non-Indians) did. Progress as an ideology always supports the status quo: because things are getting better all the time anyway, all groups should support the system. Unfortunately, this line of thinking disempowers students (and everyone else), for it implies that simply by working and living in society, Americans contribute to a nation that is constantly improving and remains the hope of the world. The very notion of a Nadir—that things got worse, and for a long time—is contrary to the ideology of progress.

The most pervasive reason why textbooks supply bad history is that they simply don't want to offend. Speaking badly of the dead is unkind, after all. Take the case of Franklin W. Pierce, perhaps America's least popular president. Certainly his home state of New Hampshire came to detest him, for his administration committed two key blunders, both on behalf of Southern slaveowners: the Ostend Manifesto and policies that led to Bleeding Kansas. The 1854 Ostend Manifesto was a memo signed by three important Pierce appointees—his ambassadors to Spain, Great Britain, and France. It suggested the U.S. should force Spain to sell us Cuba as the first parcel of an expanding Southern slave empire. If Spain refused, we should simply take it. When the memo leaked, it ignited a firestorm, since it showed the Pierce administration aligned with pro-slavery expansionists. In Kansas, Pierce openly supported the pro-slavery territorial government that had been elected with the help of men from Missouri who crossed into Kansas and voted illegally. This disregard of democracy precipitated near-war between pro-slavery and pro-freedom settlers in Kansas, aware that the conflict would not be solved under the rule of law.

To this day, Pierce remains the only elected president ever denied re-nomination by his own party. He slouched back to New Hampshire in silence and then managed to alienate his few remaining supporters by growing even more pro-Southern as the Civil War approached. In 1860 he endorsed Jefferson Davis as the best presidential candidate. He called the Emancipation Proclamation "an attempt to butcher the white race for the sake of inflicting freedom on blacks." In a speech on July 4, 1863, the very day that U.S. forces took Vicksburg and won the battle of Gettysburg, Pierce attacked the idea of saving the Union. In 1869, he died of cirrhosis of the liver, the result of years of heavy drinking.

A case can be made for Pierce as the worst president in the history of the republic. Do textbooks make it? Here is the entire treatment of his presidency in *Holt American Nation*, published in 2003:

> Pierce won the election by a landslide.[13] In his inaugural address, he called for national harmony and proceeded to appoint a cabinet that included both southerners and northerners. Pierce proved to be a weak leader, however. He was unable to control his diverse cabinet or to convince northerners that he was not caving in to southern pressure. Abolitionists labeled him a "northern man with southern principles."[14]

While it does not try to make a positive case for Pierce, this paragraph excuses his failings as human weakness, implicitly blaming his cabinet for whatever went wrong. Also, he suffered from a public relations problem, according to these authors. In reality, Pierce's problem was not that he couldn't "convince northerners that he was not caving in to southern pressure." Even to write "he caved in to southern pressure" would be too kind, for no evidence supports the claim that he opposed slavery but caved in to pressure. Pierce favored the Confederacy during the Civil War and pursued overtly pro-Southern and pro-slavery policies before it. *Holt American Nation* is far from the worst. Another recent textbook, McDougall Littell's *The Americans*, supplies as its entire treatment of Pierce this phrase: "With the help of President Franklin Pierce, a Democrat elected in 1852," in a sentence that tells how Stephen A. Douglas got the Kansas-Nebraska Act through Congress.

Saying bad things about our fourteenth president, to be sure, might cost a few textbook adoptions in New Hampshire. In the twentieth century, New Hampshire residents developed amnesia about Pierce. They erected his statue at the State Capitol in 1914, called him an "effective political leader" on his historical marker, and named Franklin Pierce College, founded in 1962, after him. Pierce remains the only president to come from the Granite State. No need to say anything about him that might offend his home state, reasons the marketing department of the textbook publisher. Surely no school district will refuse to adopt our book because it is too *kind* to Pierce, while a district in New Hampshire might reject our book if it treated Pierce accurately. Of course, if textbooks cannot present Pierce in a way that might offend anyone in New Hampshire, surely they cannot treat the Alamo in a way that might offend someone in Texas, a much larger market. The upshot is: honest history might always offend *someone*. So instead, textbooks offer dishonest history.

Whatever the specific reasons that prompt textbooks to lie or omit, what is distorted or left out usually points to times and ways that the United States went astray as a nation. The reciprocal relationship between truth and justice suggests that such issues usually remain unresolved in our own time. For that reason, it may be more important to understand what textbooks get wrong than what they get right. Thus, Americans need history courses that make us thoughtful—that tell of our past honestly, warts and all.

Americans share a common history that unites us. But we also share some more difficult events—a common history that divides us. These things, too, we must remember, for only then can we understand our divisions and work to heal them. Questioning the myths told in our textbooks is a first step toward good citizenship. Whether maintaining the status quo is a good thing depends on what the society is doing today. Usually it's a mix of good and bad. Perhaps the United States has been both "the last great hope of mankind," in Lincoln's words, and an ethnocentric empire robbing some members of mankind, at home and abroad, of their chance for a decent life. So we have to be thoughtful citizens—neither cynics nor nationalists, but thoughtful citizens. Being critical readers and critical thinkers about the past is great preparation, and historiography helps.

Asking students to question their textbooks may not be a lightweight assignment. The task may require serious historical research. Chapter 1 told of a 6th-grade teacher in Illinois whose students critiqued their textbook for leaving out the fact that most early American presidents owned slaves. To show that they *did* own slaves was easy. To show how textbooks distort the Vietnam War would require much more work. Indeed, it almost demands that students create a superior account of the war. This they can do—but only as a group project, supplied with enough time, guest speakers, and other resources. "Critique your textbook" assignments must therefore be made thoughtfully, taking into account the size of the task and amount of research required to do a credible job.

OTHER WAYS TO TEACH HISTORIOGRAPHY

Content analysis provides another way students can see history changing right before their eyes. The key is to use a standard unit of analysis that makes sense, such as a column inch or paragraph. Or students might count the illustrations of a group over time. After the Civil Rights

Movement, coverage of Native American societies increased dramatically, for instance. In 1961, among 268 total pictures, *Rise of the American Nation* included 10 that contained Native people, alone or with whites. Twenty-five years later, the retitled *Triumph of the American Nation* had 15. By 2003, *Holt American Nation* had at least 53, although admittedly, the total number of illustrations had also soared.

Students can assess not only quantity but also quality. They might classify Native American images to see if they depict or caption Indians as one-dimensional primitives or as people who participated in struggles to keep their identities and their land. Native treatment in the main narrative also changed, becoming more critical of governmental actions after the Civil Rights Movement.[15] The 1966 edition of *The American Pageant* labeled the Dawes Act of 1887 a "legislative landmark" and said it was "designed to help the Indians." Forty years later, *Pageant* called the act "the misbegotten offspring of the movement to reform Indian policy." Its much longer discussion of Dawes went on to tell how it "struck directly at tribal organization" and "ignored the inherent reliance of traditional Indian culture on tribally held land." The tone with which authors described American Indians became more respectful, as well.

Throughout the school year, classes can keep handy an alternative text, to see if it treats each topic differently than does the main textbook. Several titles listed at the end of this chapter provide different viewpoints.

Considering issues in the recent past provides another way to get students to think about historiography. Drawing upon a distinction made in Kiswahili, I have found useful the terms "sasha history" and "zamani history." Events in the sasha remain in the memories of the living, who can call them to mind and bring them to life in anecdote. When the last person to recall an event dies, that event leaves the sasha for the zamani, the distant past. For myself, born in 1942, the period from about 1952 to now is the sasha. Before that, history is zamani for me.

This distinction has implications for the question of historical perspective. The passage of time, some people assume, somehow provides perspective. However, historical perspective does not automatically accrue from the passage from sasha to zamani. On the contrary, more accurate history—certainly more detailed history—can often be written while an event lies in the sasha. Then people on various sides have firsthand knowledge of the event. Primary sources, on which historians rely, come from the sasha. To assume that historians or sociologists make better sense of them later in the zamani is merely chronological ethnocentrism, a subject we shall revisit in Chapter 5. Moreover, writers working in the sasha know that they may be critiqued by others who lived through the events they are describing, so they may be more careful.

Whether on the women's movement of the 1970s, the Gulf War of the 1990s, or the ongoing issue of gay rights, with a teacher's guidance students can invite to class guest speakers and can find newspaper articles and other primary sources from various sides of the issue. Indeed, with the advent of websites like the American Memory project at the Library of Congress and the archived and indexed *New York Times*, students can be challenged to write the history of events in the zamani entirely from primary sources, making sure to include material from all acting groups. Then they can compare their result with their textbook's treatment. The next chapter tells more about how to get students actually doing history.

FOCUSED BIBLIOGRAPHY

Every middle school or high school U.S. history classroom needs at least one college-level textbook. Used bookstores sell older editions cheaply; they will do fine. I suggest Eric Foner, *Give Me Liberty* (NYC: Norton), or Mary Beth Norton, *A People and a Nation* (Boston: Houghton Mifflin).

Each room should also have two alternative textbooks: Howard Zinn, *A People's History of the United States* (NYC: Harper & Row), and Joy Hakim, *A History of US* (NYC: Oxford UP), because it reads so well. Any edition will do.

In addition, consider Paul Johnson, *A History of the American People* (NYC: Harper-Collins, 1999), a book avowedly both conservative and celebratory. John Hope Franklin and Alfred A. Moss, *From Slavery to Freedom* (NYC: McGraw-Hill, 2008), offers a distinctive emphasis on African American history. *Through Women's Eyes*, by Ellen DuBois and Lynn Dumenil (NYC: St. Martin's, 2005), does the same from a feminist viewpoint.

CHAPTER 4

Doing History

HISTORY COMES ALIVE WHEN STUDENTS *DO*, rather than merely read, history. Doing history, broadly defined, means identifying a problem or topic, finding information, deciding what sources are credible for what pieces of information, coming to conclusions about the topic, developing a storyline, and marshaling the information on behalf of that storyline, while giving attention to information that may seem to contradict the argument. That's a long sentence, and it's a big job, but most students—maybe all students—can do it. They can research something that happened, learn about it, write it up (perhaps using other media, such as photography, video, or a website), and thus create history.

DOING HISTORY TO CRITIQUE HISTORY

Recall the history teacher in Chapter 1 whose class challenged her claim that most American presidents before Lincoln owned slaves. Her students had to do history to investigate her claim. They had to find out about the family living conditions of George Washington, John Adams, and the others.[1] Critiquing offers an easy way in to doing history, because the storyline situation has already been structured by the work being examined. Several chapters suggest turning students loose to critique their textbook's treatment of an important topic, perhaps one the textbook handles particularly poorly.

Alternatively, after locating the historical markers and monuments in the area, students might critique a particularly bad one. Who put it up? Who wrote it? What point of view was left out? Students might write an alternative marker text, telling the history as seen from that (omitted) viewpoint. If the marker has the same text on both sides, students might collaborate to fit their alternative text onto one side, eliminating the duplication and improving the marker.[2] Perhaps other positions are still left out and a four-sided marker is in order.

As they do history, most students will surely use the web. Teachers use it; why shouldn't students? Of course, the web has problems. Several years ago, working on my book *Lies Across America*, I needed to know something about Franklin W. Pierce. Pierce is not a popular subject for biographers. Indeed, he is my candidate for the second worst president in U.S. history. He is so bad that the Library of Congress listed not a single biography of him. So I turned to the web, typed in "Franklin W. Pierce" and "biography," and up came a site called "Franklin W. Pierce: A Biography." It looked promising until I saw misspelled words; it turned out to be by a 7th-grade boy in Pierce's home town of Hillsborough, New Hampshire. So it was not the best source.

Some students have no working computer at home with internet access. Some schools don't have computers available for students' easy use. Given the low cost of used computers today, this is an outrage. It might make for a good student project itself—comparing computer availability across schools and school districts. Hopefully all students can get to a library, but since some have never been, starting a history project with a field trip to a nearby major library is useful. Teachers can arrange for a librarian to show students sources relevant to their topic and how to find them, in hard copy and online. Every student who does not have a library card gets one, of course.

Teachers can impose two requirements that help students do good history while using the internet. First, although students can (and should) use the web, they must not stop there. Books still exist in the library, after all. Local historical societies have archives and objects that reveal the past. People who lived through historic events remain to be interviewed. We still have the census, newspaper archives, and many other sources, many of which, unlike the web, have been vetted, making them arguably more credible.[3] Second, every source—from the web, the library, or their textbook—needs to be annotated. The annotation—as short as a sentence or even a phrase—tells why this source is credible. Credibility is not just a matter of credentials. The website of an Arkansas Ku Klux Klan leader is probably credible when addressing the question "What does today's Klan believe?" even if its author dropped out of high school. I learned something from the Hillsborough student's web page on Franklin Pierce, despite his lack of credentials, partly because he did include references.

Students can apply four tests to sources to assess their credibility. First, locate the speaker, audience, and era. (This is, of course, a large part of historiography.) Then look for internal contradictions, external contradictions, and problems with verstehende. Let me illustrate these tests—and explain the word "verstehende," new to many readers—using a source known to all of us and read (or seen) by all too many of us: the book and movie *Gone with the Wind*. The dominance of this book and movie is massive. It has sold more than twice as many copies in hardcover as any other novel. In constant dollars, *Gone with the Wind* is by far the most profitable and most widely seen movie ever made.[4] In 1988, the American Library Association asked patrons across the U.S. to name the "best book in the library." *Gone with the Wind* won. But that's not the full story. Consider that more than one billion different books have been published in the history of the world. More people chose *Gone with the Wind* than all the others combined.[5] Of course, *Gone with the Wind* is first and foremost a romance. However, set in Georgia between 1861 and 1871, it also purports to be a historical novel. Is it a trustworthy guide to the eras—slavery, the Civil War, and Reconstruction—that it treats?

Let us locate the speaker, audience, and era. Margaret Mitchell was a white Southerner. Her parents were upper middle class; they named her older brother for the vice president of the late Confederacy. She wrote during the Nadir of race relations era when, as Chapter 10 tells, racism rose to its highest level in U.S. history. Few white Northerners at that time believed in racial equality, and Mitchell lived in Atlanta. During her most important sojourn outside of the South, at Smith College in Massachusetts, she protested bitterly when she found a black student in a history class with her and demanded to be transferred to another class. After a year, she left Smith and returned to the South. To characterize her as limited by and to her race, social class, region, and era seems fair.[6]

Speaking in the role of author, telling readers what happened during Reconstruction, Mitchell uses these words:

> Aided by the unscrupulous adventurers who operated the Freedmen's Bureau . . . the former field hands found themselves suddenly elevated to the seats of the mighty. There they conducted themselves as creatures of small intelligence might naturally be expected to do. Like monkeys or small children turned loose among treasured objects whose value is beyond their comprehension, they ran wild—either from perverse pleasure in destruction or simply because of their ignorance.[7]

The flat racism in passages like that makes for chilling reading nowadays. Mitchell repeatedly uses animal imagery to describe African Americans—both en masse and as individual characters. In the 1930s, however, neither her overt racism nor her false analysis of Southern race relations were offputting to white Northerners, including Olivia de Havilland, who won an Academy Award for her portrayal of Melanie Wilkes in the movie. Instead, it won them over. "The whole cast, all of us, became Southerners," de Havilland said in 2004. "Our sympathies lay with the South, and to this day, I think they still do."[8] As the previous chapter on historiography explains, a historical source—novel, movie, newspaper story, even textbook—may reveal more about its own era than about the period it treats.

With a little guidance, students can do similar analyses of speaker, audience, and date for a newspaper article, historical marker, or history textbook. Doing so stimulates critical reading. Learning about the writer, audience, and era is only a step, however. Stopping there amounts to an ad hominem attack. After all, some writers, moviemakers, and other creators of culture have transcended all limitations of place, race, and age. Students of history must still consider the product.

Students can look first for internal contradictions, because that search requires no examination of anything beyond the source at hand. In the case of *Gone with the Wind*, internal contradictions suggest it is not trustworthy history. For example, Margaret Mitchell portrays the enslaved African Americans at Tara, the huge plantation where Scarlett grew up, as content with their lot, even happy. When war comes, however, all but three decamp as soon as they can. Mitchell seems not to notice the contradiction. Later in the novel, during Reconstruction, African Americans are voting, determining public policy, going to school, and in other ways acting as if they consider themselves equal to white people. Again, this behavior contradicts the alleged happiness they had with their assigned inferior position during slavery. Mitchell does notice this contradiction and blames their newfound audacity on outside agitators from the North, who are in it only for financial gain. This deus ex machina papers over the contradiction but does not really resolve it.

Other internal contradictions mar *Gone with the Wind*, but my task here is not to critique the novel to death. Contradictions and tensions often exist within a source. U.S. history textbooks are replete with contradictions, partly because different authors often wrote them, and in different decades. For example, a textbook tells that before 1492, most Native Americans farmed. Forty pages later, explaining U.S. Indian policy, the same book says, "They [government officials] tried to get Indians to settle down on farms and become 'good Americans.'"

By external contradictions, I mean what other sources say about this period or issue that may be different. An interesting source to compare to *Gone with the Wind* is Margaret Walker's *Jubilee*. Set in the same part of Georgia at the same time as *Gone with the Wind*, *Jubilee* is said to tell a similar story from a black point of view. Certainly, Margaret Walker was an African American poet and novelist. Students who compare excerpts from *Gone with the Wind* about Reconstruction, say, to the treatment in *Jubilee* face a dilemma: both books cannot be accurate. They are forced to locate additional sources to learn more. Eric Foner's *Reconstruction* and Lerone Bennett's *Black Power U.S.A.: The Human Side of Reconstruction* can help.[9]

Once students understand the term, they can find many problems with verstehende in *Gone with the Wind*. Sociologists have brought this German word into English. It means "empathetic understanding"—placing oneself in someone else's shoes and imagining how they see the world and what they would do. It's fun to teach students, en masse, how to pronounce this word (vehr-SHTAY-end-deh), and then invite them to dazzle their parents with it. A problem with verstehende underlies the internal contradiction described earlier. Mitchell does not take time to understand why slaves would vote, talk politics, and otherwise be "uppity" during Reconstruction. If she did, she would be able to explain why most slaves left Tara as soon as they could.

Gone with the Wind is riddled with these verstehende problems. Consider the most important black character in *Gone with the Wind*, Mammy. From the first pages of the book and the first minutes of the movie, Mammy is obsessed with raising Scarlett, with helping her make a good impression on others, even with making sure she eats before going to the barbecue because men are said to favor women with small appetites. No doubt such a character is possible, and Margaret Mitchell can make her characters have whatever motivations she wishes. But if students put themselves in Mammy's place, would they be concerned only with their white charge? What about her own children? Or, if childless, what about her parents, siblings, and fellow slaves? Throughout the book, almost never does an African American display a plausible emotion about or a connection to another African American.

WRITING A PAPER

When students use these four methods to critique a claim in their textbook, a historical marker in their town, or a passage from *Gone with the Wind*, they are doing history. They are seeking more information, assessing sources, developing an argument, and collecting evidence to persuade their reader. The next step is to invite students to write a paper entirely their own, not structured as a critique. An old-fashioned term paper can be the key method for teaching and learning one of the 30–50 topics in a U.S. history course.

Too many students leave high school never having been challenged to write one scholarly essay. This is terrible preparation for college.[10] It is also poor preparation for life. Many jobs require nonfiction writing—from a job description, to instructions on how to use a product, to arguments for a new organizational policy. Furthermore, writing a nonfiction paper helps students be more discriminating in what they read. Once they understand how to compose a storyline, create the trappings of scholarship, and distinguish good writing from bad, they can critique others' work with more authority.

Among my own list of 36 topics, "immigration and Americanization" seems particularly inviting as a term paper assignment. Each student can pick a different group. I would let two or even three students pick the same group if they wished. From some students I might require independent papers, while suggesting they talk with each other about what they are discovering. Others I might let work together, handing in a joint product with a specified division of labor so I knew who was doing what. Indeed, teachers may ask students to work in pairs or triads. They may group students who rarely speak in class or have been underachieving. Then at least one person in the group has to step up and perform, to avoid a fiasco. Alternatively, weaker students can be grouped with stronger ones. Then the former can see what excellent work looks like and experience success at least this once, while the latter can mentor the former. One way to ensure that every student works is to devise a different role for each member, such as hard copy researcher, web researcher, and writer, for a triad. Another is to share at the beginning a one-page form for students to evaluate their group's work, their own contribution, and that of the other members.[11]

Textbooks handle some topics so badly that they leave them wide open to student efforts. Among the subjects that most textbooks treat poorly are the arrival of the people who became Native Americans, various possible pre-Columbian explorers, diverse American Indian societies, the Nadir of race relations, and labor unions. For example, *A History of the United States*, by Daniel Boorstin and Brooks Kelley, supplies just four pages on Native American societies before European contact. This is about the same as what they grant to two explorers, Magellan and Cartier, who never even reached what is now the U.S.[12] Students might conclude that such skimpy coverage won't do. They could then jointly construct a chapter on American Indians to supplement their textbook. This might be done as a wiki, a dedicated website where all students (and the teacher) participate. Wikis allow students to collaborate to create a better treatment of the topic while maintaining a log so the teacher can keep track of who contributed what. Near the end of the school year, the teacher might print out the result as a resource for next year's students, especially for those who cannot access the web at home. The class might also send it to the publisher of their textbook, along with a letter explaining why they felt the need to construct it. Students might write coordinated local history papers that combine to show how a major topic played out at home. Each student might pick a labor union in the community, for example, learn about its history, and write it up, following a uniform structure. Bound together at a copy shop, the results form a "book" worth placing in the local history collection of the community library, as well as a resource for future students.

Many guides exist to help students write papers. These range from a one-page list of do's on the web ("How to Write a History Paper," history1900s.about.com/c/ht/00/07/How_Write_History_ Paper0962934264.htm, 2/2008) to entire (small) books, including one, Jules Benjamin's *A Student's Guide to History*, that is available for free in a shorter version on the web.[13] I won't duplicate them here, except to note that students must understand that their paper needs to have a storyline, sometimes called a thesis or argument.[14] The storyline is the paper's reason for being, the message the student wants the reader to remember, the case s/he is trying to make.

Students may be unfamiliar with the notion that a history article might be trying to convince the reader of something. In a sense, most textbooks do not, after all.[15] Thus, an immigration storyline like "Chinese people came to America; here is what you need to know about them" won't do. "Brainstorming" can help show students the need for a storyline. Ask the student to put "Chinese come to America" at the top of a blank page and then write every question that comes quickly to mind about that topic. "How many came? Why did they come? Where did they go? What religion were they? What jobs did they do when they arrived? How did they change after they lived here?" and so on. Then help him/her see that the answer to almost any one of these questions—such as the last one—is a declarative sentence that can form the storyline of a good paper.

Another way to get students to understand the need for a storyline is to ask all of them to propose a paper on the same immigrant group—again, say, Chinese Americans—as an in-class exercise. Each must come up with his/her own storyline. Each student can do a few minutes of research on the group overnight, using the web, a few resources available within the classroom, or some help from the school librarian. The next day, they will bring in many different storylines. In class discussion, students can help each other see how some of these storylines are more usable or plausible than others.

Eliciting good papers requires a multistep process. Some people call this scaffolding. Early while students are working on their papers, teachers should ask for an opening paragraph and outline, complete with preliminary bibliography. Teachers as well as librarians can give bibliographic advice. They need not be experts on every topic and need not limit their suggestions to books and websites. Often a person is the best resource— maybe a member of the ethnic group who lives in the community, or a professor at a nearby university or community college.

Requiring an introductory paragraph and outline early can head off papers with no storylines, wrong storylines, or storylines so broad that they cannot possibly be handled in a term paper. Teachers must be clear about how to use and footnote sources, so students don't veer toward plagiarism. They probably need to learn how to do footnotes. Teach them. Like any authors, most of the time students need to footnote the sources of the information that they are putting into their own words. Students need to realize that footnoting makes them look good, giving their work more authority.[16]

Students also need guidance on how and when to quote sources, how and when to summarize sources, and how and when to write with no sources at all. Most students quote far too much. Teachers may infer they are trying to avoid work, and some are. More often, students don't understand that it's OK to tell something in their own words. "What do *I* know about Chinese coming to America?" is their thinking, especially if they are not Chinese American. They need to understand that *they* are the creator of their storyline. The main reason to quote others is if they have said things so well that the student feels compelled to use their words. Also, they do not need to quote or footnote facts that are common knowledge, such as "Most Chinese entered the U.S. through Angel Island in San Francisco Bay." Being clear at the beginning ensures that students don't disappoint later on by amassing quotations by others (footnoted or not).

The National History Day competition demands that students understand the difference between primary and secondary material. So do some state history standards. Primary sources derive from the period under examination. They include not only private sources like diaries and letters, but also Supreme Court opinions, speeches, newspaper articles, census tables, photographs, illustrations done by someone who was there, and memoirs and oral history from participants. An example in this chapter is the quotation about *Gone with the Wind* by Olivia de Havilland. Secondary sources include standard histories like Eric Foner's *Reconstruction*, mentioned earlier; biographies like Darden Pyron's *Southern Daughter*, footnoted earlier; and illustrations like Theodore de Bry's famous engravings of Native Americans on Haiti. De Bry never left Europe. He based his engravings on the writings of Spanish historians and published them almost a century after the events they described, when no living witness remained alive who might validate or invalidate them. Secondary source material can play a critical role, especially for students, who usually do not know enough context to base their interpretations on primary sources alone.

The importance of primary materials can be overstated. Such sources are not intrinsically more reliable than secondary sources; indeed, often they are *less* reliable. After all, the actors in an event have vested interests to portray their own actions positively. Historians coming along ten or a hundred years later may be much less biased. Primary sources can also mystify students and put them off. Taking class time to figure out the references in a political cartoon or the abbreviations in a letter can make a primary source appear like an inviting puzzle rather than a baffling obstacle. Moreover, historical interpretations do build up, encrusted like barnacles upon a fragile bark of primary sources, so it's a good idea to revisit the sources themselves. Students are well situated to generate primary sources by interviewing older residents in their community.

Midway through, require a first draft. Before students hand in their drafts, they should pair up, perhaps randomly, and swap papers for peer editing and suggestions. Students can be terrible editors, especially if they are reluctant to criticize their friend's work and just say, "It's fine." What is needed is a "critiquing supportive environment." Criticism without support is often too harsh to be heard, but support without criticism is useless. Teachers can help students learn to peer-edit by asking one or two students to do so in front of the class.[17] After the editing suggestions, the class can critique the editing, adding further advice. After peer editing, some students may decide their draft needs more work before handing it in, even as a draft. With intermediate steps like these, the final deadline will not loom ominously, because students have been working with guidance, taking one step after another. Such a process also negates any chance of fraud, such as buying a paper off the web. The final deadline should come before the end of the school year, to allow time for revision by students who hand in inadequate work.

BRINGING FAMILIES IN

Teachers can invite parents of all social classes and ethnic groups into the process of doing history. All might be assets to their children. Ask them to come to a half-hour session in the evening, repeated on a weekend day, called "Parent Academy."[18] There they learn that their child is about to undertake a research project. That project might be critiquing their textbook's treatment of a topic, assessing a historical marker or a movie, a group project, interviewing a family member (with a focus), writing a paper, setting up a website—whatever. More than one research project may be assigned during the year. Provide a one-page handout describing the task, listing and explaining the interior deadlines, telling why and how to cite sources, giving clear rules for working together, and suggesting sources of help.[19]

The more parents know about how to go about doing a research paper, the better. Then they become a resource and an ally for their child.

Parents reinforce the idea that the task is important. Parents may appreciate knowing that during the days or weeks until this project is complete, their child *always* has homework in history. Parents can also help students understand the importance of the storyline, simply by asking their child, "What is your storyline?" This helps parents understand that history does not equal memorization, but involves organizing evidence, and so forth. Involving parents can also bring them on board in case their child's topic involves controversial content.

At the Parent Academy, teachers can demystify web research by asking for a question from parents, then quickly searching for it. There will be missteps, of course, but that's OK. Led along by the teacher, the group can then assess the websites found in this initial search. The point is not to do good research, but to introduce the research process and to show that it is doable. Although it is elementary and predates the web, the book *Helping Your Child Learn History* may be useful, especially for parents of younger students. It is in the public domain and is available online.[20]

Teachers can also set up a "research corner" available to parents or guardians as well as students. It might go in their classroom or in the library, shared with other teachers. In the research center, put:

- a schedule of the steps in the overall research project, along with the guidelines for each step
- a checklist complete with writing and organizational tips that students can apply to their semifinished drafts
- a one-page list of useful websites
- a list of places where students can go to learn more history. These include nearby historic sites, the community library, cooperating senior citizens centers, and the local college library if it will be receptive to pre-college students. If the school library can be open at least once a week after school hours, then every student has at least one option within reach
- examples of good work by prior classes
- materials students can use for displays, like foam board and construction paper

Teachers must not set up an assignment that depends upon family members, however, because some children simply cannot count on help from any relative. Making mentors available can help. Older students who did well in history the previous year can mentor. So can local college history majors, who might get internship credit for doing so. "Big brother" and "big sister" programs supply mentors. So do adult organizations; try Mentor, at mentoring.org/, a website that lists mentoring organizations within fifteen miles of one's zip code. Senior citizens can be tapped, if they can write. Mentors need to understand their role. They do not write a single word of the project, but they critique and support it with suggestions from start to finish. They can make use of Parent Academy and the research corner and might even help set them up.

Doing local history helps level the playing field. Suddenly the student from Central America finds her background a help, not a hindrance. She can interview family members in Spanish, transcribe the result, and translate it into English. Already she has a terrific appendix to the paper she will write, and her own family's experience helps provide a storyline.

LOCAL HISTORY

A great way to get students doing history is to get them doing local history. Historians often consider local history to be the backwater of their profession. That's due to interminable self-congratulatory coffee-table tomes that never say anything meaningful because they never say anything critical—like *One Hundred Years of Progress: The Centennial History of Anna, Illinois.*[21] But local history does not have to be like that. All history is local. It happened *here*—in this town. The woman's movement happened here. The Civil Rights Movement happened here—or if it did not, then the absence of African Americans or the absence of the movement is at least as important. People from this town supported (or perhaps opposed) the Korean War; people from this town went to Korea and may have been killed or wounded; today "the forgotten war," as it is called, is forgotten (and also remembered) in this town. These and other national and international issues affected every community, and in turn the community played a role in our national response to these issues. Viewed this way, local history is neither local nor trivial.

For the last fifteen years, I've been studying local history nationally. My 1999 book *Lies Across America* examined 100 historic sites, at least one in every state, that presented the past poorly. These places treat such national matters as relations between American Indians and non-Indians, slavery, Reconstruction, the place of women in our society, and even our war against the Philippines—all in the context of local history. My more recent book, *Sundown Towns*, treated the roughly 10,000 communities, most in the North, that for decades were all-white on purpose (some still are). This phenomenon must be researched locally but matters nationally.

Another sort of local history can be equally significant. Consider a natural disaster—a flood, for example. Some disasters are so enormous as to be national events—Hurricane Katrina in 2005, for example, or perhaps the Great Chicago Fire of 1871.[22] Smaller local disasters can be historically important, however, if the student historian makes them so by investigating important themes. A town's response to a flood, for example, can reveal schisms in the community. After the great flood of 1927 inundated much of the Mississippi Delta, the alluvial floodplain between Vicksburg and Memphis, white leaders called in the National Guard to keep African American sharecroppers from fleeing and to force them to do relief work. This laid bare the state of peonage that many African Americans endured on plantations in those years.[23] Alternatively, a community in disaster may pull together to mute and even moot its social divisions, at least temporarily. That, too, is interesting. An economic disaster, such as a plant closure, also provides a fine topic, because "micro" details like its impact on an individual family are as important as "macro" history like the globalization of the textile industry.

A field trip to the cemetery can provide an effective and structured way to begin doing local history. Jim Percoco, history teacher at West Springfield High School in Virginia, has his students visit Congressional Cemetery in Washington, D.C. Before they go, he supplies them with the names of famous people who are buried there, accompanied with an identifying phrase, such as "Pushmataha, Choctaw chief." Each student signs up to learn about and prepare a short biography of one person who is buried in the cemetery. When the class tours the cemetery and reaches Pushmataha's tombstone, the student who selected him makes him come alive for the class. Of course, Percoco has the advantage of living near our nation's capital. But many schools are within field trip range of the state capital, or a major city, and not just New York or San Francisco. I searched the web for "famous" and "buried in Omaha," for example, and came up with all kinds of interesting people in that Nebraska city. If the cemetery has no historical marker, students can propose one, complete with mention of a few of its most distinguished residents.

Going beyond the cemetery, students might select the most important people and ideas that have come from their area, or the most prominent graduates of their high school. In the process, they must ponder such matters as what is "important," whom history should remember, and why. They might then begin by interviewing the oldest teachers, including retired teachers, and the oldest members of the community. Old high school yearbooks can jog the memories of retired teachers and members of the community. Of course they will search the web, with phrases like "Plainville High School" and "famous" or "distinguished." They will browse online and printed compendiums of famous people, such as *Who's Who in America* and the various regional and occupational guides. In the 1880s, county histories became a profit-making rage among publishers. Typically, these contain boilerplate accounts of the state, several chapters about the county and its larger communities, and then at least a hundred pages of vignettes of community leaders, with marvelous illustrations of each—just what may be needed for a cemetery or "distinguished graduates" project.

In the process of doing history on their own family, school, or community, students will learn that their lives have larger meaning. The stories they uncover and construct will display themes that resonate across our society and over time—immigration, working-class families having a hard time at upward mobility, the costs of war being borne by a few families. Conversely, all major events in national and world history can be seen in their impact on the local community. Doing so brings them alive. Consider the women's movement of the 1970s (continuing to today, to some degree). It did not just take place in Washington, in the attempt to pass an Equal Rights Amendment for women, or in the sexual desegregation of the army. It is reflected everywhere—in the history of the local Presbyterian church, for instance. In 1950, that church was run by a Board of Elders, all men, and a Board of Deacons, usually all men. It employed a senior minister, always male; perhaps an assistant minister, also male; a minister of music, possibly male; a director of religious education (Sunday school), probably female; a secretary, female; and a janitor, male. By the late 1960s, women were on the Board of Deacons; a few might have been on the Board of Elders as well. By 1995, perhaps most members of both boards and maybe even the senior minister were women. Institutional records provide the number of women and their names. Many of them (and many men) are still alive to talk about the strains and benefits of this transition. A wonderful student paper beckons to be written.

The school and school system also provide likely subjects for good history. Many high schools resulted from the merger of two or more predecessors. In states that had de jure segregation—from Arizona through southern Illinois to Delaware and all points south—today's high school may result from combining former black and white schools. Students can interview adults who were students at that time. As suburbs or urban attendance zones change in their residential composition, school populations also change. Students might interview the first Asian Americans to attend their high school, the first Jewish students, or refugee students from Hungary (1956), Cuba (1980), or Sudan (2008). In rural areas, today's consolidated high schools may take in students and teachers from several communities that formerly had their own smaller schools.[24]

GETTING STARTED

A minimal local history project asks each student to interview one person and record the conversation as fully as possible. Students can take

notes and reconstruct the interview immediately afterward or can au-
diotape or videotape the interview and transcribe it. Most students have
never done an interview before, so every step must be discussed before-
hand. Ethical issues need to be discussed before "inflicting" students on
the community. Would-be subjects must be free to refuse. Students must
treat the record of the conversation with professional discretion. The
teacher must review the subject areas to be covered. Students should not
ask about personal matters that might hurt the interviewee or put him/
her at risk, like sexual orientation, possible illegal activities, and the like.
In conversation with the student, the teacher will influence whether the
interviewee's name should be kept out of the paper and off the interview
summary. In many cases, students should share the transcript or reconstruction of the interview with the subject, for approval. This can lead to
another interview that clarifies the first. Then the student writes a paper
based on the interview(s), with the interview summary or transcript as its
appendix. Like a term paper, this essay tells a story. Most essays will not
follow the chronology of the interview at all.

Students might coordinate their interviews. Each student could interview one family member and one "stranger" to learn if and how they were
affected by the Korean War—what they thought of it, whether they served
in the armed forces or knew people who did, and so on. The best resulting interviews become the appendix, introduced by an overall narrative
composed jointly by the class. Interviews of residents of the same nursing
home or users of the same senior citizens center can also focus on a common topic. What was everyday life like in a neighborhood that was later
altered by urban renewal? Where did people go to have fun? For a date?
How did World War II affect the neighborhood?[25]

I cannot provide a treatise on how to help students become good interviewers here, but the bibliography at the end of this chapter does suggest
sources that help. Having taught interviewing to hundreds of undergraduates, however, I can supply a few tips. Most students will choose to record
their interviews, but doing so can make the subject feel uncomfortable,
casting a chill on the proceedings. Students may decide to turn off the
recorder conspicuously at a sticky point in the conversation. They can still
take notes, but interviewees may talk more freely when they are not being
recorded word for word. Also, transcribing a one-hour interview takes
from two to ten hours, and interviews must be transcribed. To avoid fum-
bling and false starts, students should be completely familiar with their
equipment before their first interview. They need to show courtesy: take
off their hat or hood, don't yawn, and so forth. Taking notes while record-
ing expedites transcription, takes the subject's mind off the recorder, and
promotes a thoughtful atmosphere. The student should sit at an angle to

the subject, not directly opposite. Open-ended questions are important, and the student needs to pause and let the subject fill the silence. Of course, students need to bring a list of questions to the interview; these should be in the form of abbreviated handwritten notes on the otherwise blank pad of paper used for taking notes. All these things—and more—must be rehearsed in class as students interview one another for practice. Indeed, the teacher might select one student interviewer and adult interviewee who are brave enough to do the interview before the entire class. Afterward, students can critique what went well and not so well.

Besides oral history, many other sources can help students learn about their own community. Students will start with the web, of course. So did I, trying to learn who of historic importance lies buried in Omaha. But they must not stop there. I've yet to see a community library with no local history collection.[26] Some even boast a local history room. Every library also has its staff member who knows the most about local history, even if they only know a little more than the *other* librarian. The librarian can also point to the person in the community who is considered the local "expert." Most towns also have a local museum, even if it is only open one afternoon a week. Members of the local historical society are splendid resources, although sometimes they are overly protective of their community, and hence might not be forthcoming with information on controversial topics. Genealogical societies are usually more candid.

Weekly community newspapers may also self-censor, but students can skim them at a rate of about a year per hour. The daily newspaper in the nearest larger town may be more likely to print real news about the town. City and county records may prove useful, including plat books, city directories, and WPA files from the 1930s. Like the Presbyterian Church, many institutions keep files for years that are useful. School records may be sealed for recent years, but students may gain access to older records. They can then study, for example, the racial desegregation of the school district. Or, using information from the manuscript census (see below), students can compare the distribution by race, sex, parental occupation, and parental education of students in "college-track" courses to those in "general" courses.[27] Do teachers help girls more than boys? If so, does this favor girls in the long run? Does the school do things that prompt boys to drop out more than girls? I used school yearbooks to learn about the changing social position of Chinese American students in Mississippi. Many yearbooks list organizational memberships opposite each senior's picture. Over time yearbooks showed Chinese students moving into more important clubs and teams.

U.S. census tables for towns for all years are available online at census. gov/prod/www/abs/decennial/index.htm.[28] If information by county or state will do, much easier to use are the census tables at the University of Virginia, at fisher.lib.virginia.edu/census. The "manuscript census"—the raw data from which census tables derive—is on the web through 1930.[29] It consists of the actual names as written by enumerators, with age, sex, race, occupation, address, education and literacy, and some other information. With these data, students can do all sorts of things, from tracing the occupations and movements of a family to forming conclusions about an entire town and its changes over time. The website of the National Archives, archives.gov, is more oriented to researchers than teachers, but with encouragement many students can dig around and find documents useful to their topic.

FINAL PRODUCT

When students have finished their papers (or websites or whatever their products), celebrate them. The teacher can start a local history archive in the school library. Copy shops can bind every good local history paper to go into this archive. Then next year's students can refer to the archive to see what good work looks like. For really good papers— perhaps chosen with input from students themselves—an additional copy should go into the local history collection at the community library. Now the student has created "a book," complete with call number! Moreover, it may prove priceless to some future researcher. I know, because twice while doing research for *Sundown Towns*, I came upon local history papers that treated my topic, race relations. I was thrilled; my work benefitted immensely.

If student papers relate to a coordinated class project, they can be bound into one book with a table of contents—perhaps "Plainville Confronts the Korean War" or "Memories of a Lost Neighborhood." Again, bind an extra copy for the community library. Also, "publish" the collection on the school's website.

From the outset, students can plan to enter their projects in National History Day. Three of their competitions particularly foster historical research, critical reading, the development of a storyline, and a persuasive presentation. These are the exhibit, paper, and website competitions. All are described at NationalHistoryDay.org.[30] In many states, National History Day is not yet well known. There, teachers may have to organize a local competition from scratch, but the national headquarters will help. Of course, the point isn't whether students win and advance to the state or national level. The point is to have 2 or 20 or 100 students actually learn how to do history and and have a blast. Even teachers who choose not to participate in National History Day can enlist representatives from the local historical society or other appropriate outsiders to judge and comment on their students' papers or exhibits. The bibliography at the end of the chapter includes student projects that became published books, articles, websites, and videos.

Local history is hardly the only route to success in the National History Day competition. One year when I was judging the national competition, a black 10th grader mounted an exhibit on "Jackie Robinson as Turning Point." Perhaps to encourage students to have a point of view, every year National History Day assigns a theme like "turning point." It's never very restrictive; possibly 75% of all topics can be made to fit. In 1947 Jackie Robinson *was* a "turning point." This teen had read the standard juvenile biography of Jackie Robinson, of course. Then, from his home in South Carolina, he had pulled off telephone interviews with Robinson's widow, two former teammates, and at least one member of the Brooklyn Dodgers front office, and had transcribed them accurately. He had loaded his tape recorder with an interview making a particular point that tied in with his thesis. He knew about the Nadir of race relations (see Chapter 10), so he understood that Robinson was *not* the first black player in the major leagues, but rather the first in the twentieth century, after the Nadir had set in. He did not walk on water, but our team rated his project the best of the dozen we judged.[31]

USING THE PRODUCT

If students researched the most prominent graduates of their high school, then each student might create a plaque listing the accomplishments—positive and negative—of one graduate, with a short biography. These might then line a corridor (a "Wall of Fame") and comprise a website.

Research by students may unearth history that needs to be remembered more permanently. They might then suggest a new historical marker to remember something that happened or someone who lived in their community. Such a person or event might be uplifting, symbolizing the aspirations of the community at their highest. Some students might choose to bring back to memory a more tragic event, showing divisions that may still reverberate through the community. The challenge is to create a public history that functions for citizens as they go about their business as Americans.

In the fall of 1990, a 6th-grade teacher in Springfield, Illinois, challenged her students to enter a project in National History Day. Two white eleven-year-olds, Lindsay Harney and Amanda Staab, decided to work

together. Staab's great-great grandfather had been a reporter for a Springfield newspaper in 1908, when whites tried to drive the entire black population out of Springfield and turn it into a sundown town. He had left a
family memory of the race riot that had reached Amanda's ears, so the
girls decided to make that their topic. They found it quite researchable
and wrote a good paper on the riot, eventually winning an "excellent" and
advancing to the state meet.

After finishing their research, the girls realized that while Springfield
was festooned with historical markers about happier subjects like Abraham Lincoln, its landscape was silent about this seminal event. Most residents in 1990 had never heard of it. So the students got up a petition for
the city council, that read in part:

> No marker or memorial exists in Springfield to commemorate this historic
> event. Although the Springfield Race riots of August 1908 were a tragedy for
> the hometown of the "Great Emancipator," Abraham Lincoln, they focused
> national attention on the issue of civil rights and served as the catalyst for the
> formation of a biracial organization that works for political, social, educational,
> and economic equality. This organization is the NAACP. We, the undersigned,
> petition the Springfield City Council to commemorate the Springfield Race Ri-
> ots of 1908 with a marker or memorial so that we might learn from the past and
> strive for equality and harmony in our community.

They got 251 of their fellow students to sign and presented the petition to
the city council. The eventual result was not one but eight historical markers. It is a "Race Riot Walking Tour," an apology on the landscape, and a
statement of memory. Springfield will never forget this event again, and to
make doubly sure, the University of Illinois developed a half-hour documentary, "Springfield Had No Shame," that became part of the 6th-grade
curriculum of the Springfield Public Schools, honoring the age Harney
and Staab were when they first rekindled the memory.[32]

The class who wrote the publisher, which was mentioned in Chapter 1,
concerned that their textbook never alluded to slaveowning by U.S. presidents, was similarly trying to correct an omission. Student research can
also open a window on social processes that favor certain groups at the
expense of others. In 1995, two students at Cass Lake-Bena High School
in northern Minnesota began a movement that eventually convinced the
Minnesota Legislature to strike the word "squaw" from geographic and
place names in the state. Other students have acted to make sure that communities that kept out African Americans (or others) admit doing so in the
histories included in their entries on Wikipedia. Acknowledging the past
is a first step toward apologizing for such practices and declaring a town
now open to all.

When students use their research to try to right wrongs, either individually or collectively, they learn that doing so is fun. As Theodore Roosevelt put it, "Far and away the best prize that life offers is the opportunity to work hard at work worth doing." Doing so is citizenship in action. After all, we—those of us alive now—get the duty of changing the world. No other job is more exhilarating or important.

Earlier, I suggested that one challenge Americans face is to create a public history that functions for our citizens as they go about their business as Americans. What is their business—our business—*as Americans*? Surely it is to bring into being the America of the future. What should race relations be like in that America? How should that America handle gays in the military? What about gay marriage? How should that America deal with whatever domestic or foreign policy issues arise next year?

Preparing students to live in that America, making them ready for that important task, is why we teach U.S. history in the first place. Having students *do* history—not just read it—is the best way to equip them for that crucial responsibility.

FOCUSED BIBLIOGRAPHY

Here are seven examples of local history mostly done by middle and high school students:

In Relentless Pursuit of an Education (Lexington Park, MD: Unified Committee for Afro-American Contributions, 2006). The catalog of a museum exhibit done by adults and students about the black schools that predated desegregation in St. Mary's County, Maryland. A similar volume should be completed in every locale that had segregated schools, from California to Delaware.

Bernadette Anand et al., *Keeping the Struggle Alive: Studying Desegregation in Our Town* (NYC: Teachers College P, 2002), tells how teachers got students to research race relations in their New Jersey home town.

Anderson Valley High School, Boonville, C0A, *Voices of the Valley* (website, ncrcn.org/vov/, video, books). These students interviewed nonagenarians and used their results to make a video, books, and website.

Khmer Legacies, at KhmerLegacies.org. Cambodian American students interview their parents about life in Cambodia, escaping, and life in the U.S.

R.O.C.C., *Minds Stayed on Freedom* (Boulder: Westview, 1991). Written by students in a Mississippi high school, this book tells of the Civil Rights Movement 25 years earlier in their county, researched through interviews. I wish the students had integrated the accounts into an overall narrative, but for a collection of separate interviews, it is still uncommonly interesting.

Robert A. Scappini, "Teaching High School History in the Context of Performance-Based Standards," *The History Teacher, 37* #2 (2/2004), 183–91, tells how his inner-city students have researched poverty, local inventors, and deaths in the 1918 flu epidemic.

Peter Wallenstein, "The First Black Students at Virginia Tech," *VPI&SU Diversity News 4* #1 (Fall 1997), 3–4, at spec.lib.vt.edu/archives/black-history/timeline/blackstu.htm. Not by a student, but a good example of research students could do among the alumni of their high school.

The following three items help teachers to help students do local history:

David E. Kyvig and Myron A. Marty, *Nearby History: Exploring the Past Around You*, (Walnut Creek, CA: AltaMira, 2000). A bit dull and plodding, putting off students, but contains many possible topics that can be researched locally, along with pointers toward sources of information.

Robert K. Lamb, "Suggestions for the Study of Your Home Town," *Human Organization, 11* (1952), 29–32, though old, offers a compact introduction to the use of plat books, city directories, and other local records.

Glenn Whitman, *Dialogue with the Past* (Lanham, MD: AltaMira, 2004). Whitman has his high school students do oral history with everyone from their grandmothers to high officials in the federal government. He reports improved work by students at all ranges of past performance and tells how to avoid pitfalls.

CHAPTER 5

How and When
Did People Get Here?

W E NOW TURN TO THE FIRST OF SIX SPECIFIC content areas that prove problematic in U.S. history courses. The earliest of the 30–50 topics in such courses turns out to be a hot issue: how and when people first reached the Americas. Teachers must not present any one date—such as 13,000 BP[1]—as "the answer," because the field of archaeology is riddled with debate. Nor should teachers present the Bering land passage as fact. The second edition of *Lies My Teacher Told Me* and its footnotes provide a brief introduction to these controversies,[2] but any published summary rapidly goes out of date.

Luckily, U.S. history courses reach this issue at the beginning of the school year. I say luckily, because the controversy provides a teachable moment to caution students about the voice in which textbooks are written. It is a monotone of certainty, providing answers for them to "learn," as in rote memorization, and it simply won't do. Since no sure answer yet exists, teachers must instead teach the conflict. Better yet, let students choose a position themselves and support their choice with evidence. It's wonderful to get this lesson across so early in the school year.

How can teachers get students thinking about these matters? One way is to ask on the first day of class, "When did people first reach the land that we now call the United States?" Each student jots down a number. Then ask, "How?" and ask them to jot down a phrase. After everyone has written something, I launch the discussion by calling on someone and asking for their date. In the style of an auctioneer, "Do I hear older?" I ask, if the date proffered is within the last 12,000 years. "Do I hear more recent?" I ask, if the date proffered is farther back than 50,000 years. Eventually a range of dates comes forth. Don't flinch at offbeat answers like "1620," "millions of years ago," or "We have always been here." If students have access to computers—in class, in the library, or at home—turn them loose to find information to refine, change, or back up their answers.

Another good way to get students thinking about how and when people got here is by listing the disciplines that help answer the question.

These include:

- cultural anthropology, the study of human cultures. Cultural anthropology can help determine whether similar cultural elements—pots, words, architecture—show a common origin or independent invention.
- glottochronology, the study of language similarity and decay. Glottochronology can help tell if various languages have a common origin and, if so, when they split from each other.
- physical anthropology, the study of anatomical differences among groups. Physical anthropology can help show how similar and different various peoples are, helping to infer when they split from each other.
- human genetics, our increasing knowledge of the human genome. This fast-moving field now contributes much of the new information about the ancestors of American Indians, with implications for when they arrived and from where.
- epidemiology, the study of diseases. Since different diseases arose at different times and in different places, the susceptibility of today's populations to them gives clues to their history.
- botany, the study of plants. Did such plants as cotton require human help to cross the Atlantic? Did sweet potatoes require help to cross the Pacific?
- zoology, the study of animals. Animal remains in garbage dumps and human feces can tell what Native Americans were eating, when.
- archaeology, the study of artifacts and remains and their dates
- history, including oral history of descendants, sometimes called ethnohistory

A class can distribute itself (or be distributed) across these areas of study. Each team of two or three students has the job of finding out what their field says about how and when people got here, in the process assessing its strengths and weaknesses. Then the class combines the information from the assorted disciplines, seeing what alternative dates and routes emerge and which seem more likely.

Because no consensus exists, and because new information keeps coming forth, the web is a good resource for investigating this issue. Of course, all websites are not equal. This is a good point to introduce the values of vetting, credentials, and peer review. Journalists don't have credentials in archaeology, but they do have professional standards about accuracy. Editors vet articles in major newspapers and newsmagazines. Journals like *Science* and *American Antiquity* have the additional advantage of peer review, meaning that professionals who know the research literature have to approve an article before it can appear in print or on the organization's website.[3] On their own websites, individuals can put up anything they want with no review by anyone. Of course, any website might be right. Students can apply the same four tests used to assess the credibility of sources in the previous chapter: locate the speaker, audience, and era; look for internal contradictions; seek confirmation in outside sources; and check for problems with verstehende. Teachers can kindle this process by suggesting two or three sites—including one that is not very reputable—for students to critique.

A CRASH COURSE ON ARCHAEOLOGICAL ISSUES

Until recent decades, archaeologists of the Western Hemisphere agreed on the answers to the main questions in the field. How had people come to the Americas? They had walked. From where? Siberia, of course. When? During the last Ice Age, around 13,000 BP, when much of the Earth's water was stored in massive ice formations on Antarctica and the Earth's northernmost land masses. At that time, ocean levels were so low that the Bering Strait was dry land that we now call Beringia. Yet an ice-free corridor beckoned southeastward through Canada.

Today, this consensus is in disarray. Students will quickly discover at least five controversies that now enliven archaeology:

- people may have come by boat rather than on foot
- people from many places may have washed up in the Americas
- clovis points (explained below) haven't been found in Siberia
- a comet may have hit North America around 13,000 BP, causing a firestorm and transforming human life
- humans may have spread throughout the hemisphere before 13,000 BP, including throughout Amazonia

Teachers need not be experts on these possibilities. They can let students do the work of convincing each other which positions are based on sound evidence. The more teachers know, however, the better they can guide their charges.

There turns out to be almost no evidence that the ancestors of today's Native Americans walked across Beringia. They might have. But the archaeological record does not disclose older and older sites of human habitation as we move from British Columbia to Yukon, Alaska, and finally Siberia. To be sure, absence of evidence is not evidence of absence. Archaeologists have not done enough excavation in northwestern North America. In addition, most sites may now be underwater, since the ocean

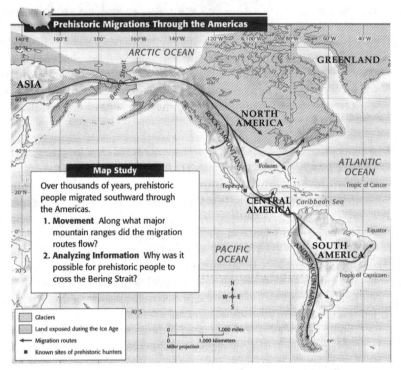

Prehistoric Migrations Through the Americas

Map Study

Over thousands of years, prehistoric people migrated southward through the Americas.

1. **Movement** Along what major mountain ranges did the migration routes flow?
2. **Analyzing Information** Why was it possible for prehistoric people to cross the Bering Strait?

Glaciers
Land exposed during the Ice Age
Migration routes
Known sites of prehistoric hunters

Five of six current U.S. history textbooks in my collection include maps like this, showing the "correct" route the first settlers of the Americas took to get here. (The only exception has no map but says the same thing in words.) I would suggest these answers to the questions this map asks: 1. None. No evidence suggests that migration routes "flowed" along any mountain ranges. More likely, migration flowed along the seacoast, by canoe and small boat, but since the seacoast then may have been miles to the west compared to the seacoast now, no archaeological evidence supports boat travel, either. 2. They had boats, and even today, it's only 55 miles across.

level has risen dramatically since the alleged crossing. Nevertheless, the Bering crossing remains only hypothesis, not fact.

Besides, it's a hypothesis that disrespects Indians. Implicitly it assumes that, so long ago, people *could not* have come by boat because they were too "primitive."[4] Yet people reached Australia more than 40,000 years ago, and humans could never have walked from Asia to Australia, no matter what the ice was doing.[5] Before about a thousand years ago, few artifacts survive except those made from stone, and no people ever made stone boats. Hence, archeologists have no evidence of boats from this ancient period. Again, absence of evidence is not evidence of absence.

Evidence for a land crossing consists mainly of one fact: there are cultural and genetic similarities between Native Americans and Siberians, and perhaps also Ainus, the early settlers of Japan. Evidence for a boat crossing consists mainly of two facts: first, boat passage is easier than walking.[6] Second, most Native Americans show unusual genetic uniformity, such as we would expect from a handful of settlers—a few boats full, perhaps.[7] There's not much hard evidence on either side! So we must leave open the question of how people got here.

Until recently, the consensus that ruled archaeology resolutely denied diffusion—the possibility that elements of Native cultures might have come from beyond the Americas. Archaeologists still call pre-1492 cultures "pre-contact." Good reasons underlay this bias against diffusion. The amateurs who had dominated archaeology before it became a science were a gullible lot who seemed to see diffusion everywhere. When they found pyramids in Central America, that proved to them that Egyptians had been there. When they found scratchings on rocks in central Canada, they "translated" them as words the prehistoric Irish had written in Celtic Ogham script. When they found long straight lines and landscape figures in Peru that could only be fully appreciated from above, they concluded that visitors from other planets had drawn them.[8] Minimizing diffusion also meant that archaeologists did not have to become experts on ancient non-American societies and cultures like Egypt, China, or the Celts.[9]

Diffusionists now get more attention within the field of archaeology. Most scholars now realize that allowing for the possibility of diffusion need not imply that Native Americans were stupid or primitive. To be sure, little evidence suggests that any crossing of the Atlantic or Pacific resulted in transoceanic trade. The Atlantic Current is fine for crossing from Africa but a barrier for returning. To get back to Europe or Africa from America by sea, one must make use of the Gulf Stream or its southern branches. One would land in the Atlantic islands or Iberia, not in West Africa. In *Black Africans and Native Americans*, Jack Forbes cites interesting examples of what seem to be Native American navigators washing up in Iberia, but none of Africans doing so.[10] It is unlikely that any round-trip voyages were ever made from Africa before the Europeans did it. Round trips from China or Japan are equally unlikely.[11] Still, ruling out the possibility that people—shipwrecked stragglers at the least—might have found their way to the Americas from Africa, China, and Europe before 1492 seems baseless. After all, people in tiny boats have crossed the oceans repeatedly in both directions—on purpose and by accident—in the last few centuries.

Moreover, stragglers may have influenced Native culture while not influencing Native genetics. For decades, archaeologists used Clovis points—the well-made spearheads and arrowheads first found in Clovis, New Mexico—to label what they thought was the earliest important culture in North America. However, "not a single Clovis point has turned up in Siberia," according to *Newsweek* reporter Andrew Murr, summarizing research by Smithsonian archaeologist Dennis Stanford. Stanford suggested that "Clovis people"—who made the points—came by boat from Spain, 15,000 years before Columbus. "They were from Iberia, not Siberia," he quipped.[12] Of course, the *idea* of Clovis points may hail from Spain, rather than the people. Put another way, just one person could have crossed the Atlantic around 15,500 BP, joined Native Americans, and made beautiful spear points in a style that Natives then adopted. In any event, it used to be rare for a major archaeologist to suggest a problem with the Clovis hypothesis, but now it is happening.

Further complicating the record is increasing recent evidence that a comet probably exploded in the atmosphere above North America about 13,000 BP. It split up as it crashed, perhaps setting much of North America on fire. This firestorm, not Native Americans, may have killed most of the large mammals—mammoths, mastodons, giant sloths—that formerly inhabited the Americas. It may also have decimated Native Americans, perhaps killing everyone who did not happen to be in a cave or within seconds of a body of water. Surviving mammals and people then faced a difficult time, because the climate change resulting from soot in the atmosphere killed many plants on which they relied, further reducing the population. Such a reduction in numbers may complicate our present efforts to learn about the first settlers. For instance, this event, rather than a boat crossing, may explain why surviving American Indians are so closely genetically related to one another.[13]

Finally, parts of the Americas now viewed as wilderness may have been thickly settled long ago. This includes even the Amazon basin, now a sparsely settled forest. As summarized by journalist Charles Mann,

> [A] growing number of researchers have come to believe that Indian societies had an enormous environmental impact on the jungle. Indeed, some anthropologists have called the Amazon forest itself a cultural artifact—that is, an artificial object.

Anthropologist Clark Erickson suggests that the regular mounds and straight berms crisscrossing northern Bolivia were built by South American Natives as part of an elaborate agricultural and fish-catching system. Then the residents were decimated by the new diseases brought after 1492, as well as by the warfare and deculturation caused by European conquerors.[14]

Again, the issue is not whether this claim is correct. Rather, teachers must help students grasp the fact that our knowledge of the history of the Americas before 1492 is tentative. These are exciting times for archaeology. Major new theories arise every few months. But most textbook authors have no particular insight into archaeology. They have no credentials to warrant the certainty that they adopt in their first chapters about pre-1492 America. They are consumers of archaeology, just like K–12 teachers and students. There is no reason to limit what students learn about the millennia of human activity in the Americas to the conclusions that textbook authors have selected for them. Teachers must let students in on the excitement.

PRESENTISM

Historians sometimes accuse each other of "presentism"—applying concerns of today to the past so as to distort our understanding of what happened. Presentism is a useful word, worth teaching to students, because it names a bias. Therefore, it helps students understand that biases exist and helps them become more critical readers.

Presentism can wreak havoc upon our understanding of the ancient past, probably more so than with any other era. This is ironic, considering that the ancient past is so distant from the present. The reason is simple: knowing about the distant past is so hard. Some archaeologists think that the petroglyphs dotted across Western rock formations are omens to ensure a successful hunt. Others think they were done by shamans while they were high on hallucinogenic drugs. Yet another serious hypothesis holds that they are mostly female genitalia. An onlooker might conclude, "Archaeologists don't really have a clue." Their confusion is perfectly reasonable, because they don't have much data. They try to infer an entire culture and social structure based on a few rock tools and what's left of a garbage midden after ten thousand years of erosion. With so little to go on, notions from the present about the past can sneak in without scholars realizing it.

Absent solid evidence whether people and ideas from China or Egypt reached the Americas before 1492, for instance, ideas from their own times have unduly influenced archaeologists' conclusions. The belief that pyramids had to have come from Egypt, for example, fit with the Nadir of race relations, that terrible period from 1890 to 1940 when the United States grew more and more racist. The possibility that Native Americans might have built the pyramids all by themselves seemed unlikely to archaeologists at that time; they assumed that such an "advanced civilization" required "white" intelligence.[15]

As the Nadir waned, archaeologists and anthropologists came to feel that minimizing diffusion gave Native Americans full credit. Doing so also helped the new generation of social scientists look more professional, since they sought more rigorous proof than their amateur predecessors had required. Laudable as these motivations were, presentist bias is still bias. They tended to go to the opposite extreme. For example, during and after the Civil Rights Movement, archaeologists were even skeptical that the Norse had reached Canada, for example, despite detailed evidence from Icelandic sagas. Applying harsher standards for claims of cultural diffusion than for claims of independent American development is not defensible, even when done for the finest reasons.

TODAY'S RELIGIONS AND YESTERDAY'S HISTORY

One particular form of presentism—projecting ideas from present-day religions onto the distant past—can make it particularly hard for teachers to connect with some students and their parents. Consider how the questions posed in the title of this chapter get answered in Utah. In my many workshops in Utah, I have encountered *seven* commonly held local answers to the question of how Native America came to the Americas. They are:

1. the common textbook answer, stemming from the old archaeological consensus: people walked across the Bering Strait from Siberia about 13,000 years ago
2. newer answers from archaeology, DNA research, and other sciences: by boat or perhaps on foot much earlier, around 35,000 or even 70,000 years ago
3. one Mormon answer: ancient seafaring Israelites, the so-called lost tribes of Israel, came about 2,600 years ago. (Most Mormons still believe this. DNA research has convinced many Mormon leaders, however, that most people came to the Americas from Siberia; the Israelites were only a small later addition.)[16]
4. a Navajo answer: Long ago, after being rejected by three former worlds owing to quarreling, the first people came up into this world but found Pueblo people already here
5. the most common Fundamentalist Christian answer: from Adam and Eve, who were formed about 4004 BC. Fundamentalists are not sure just how Native Americans arrived, but it had to be no more than 6,000 years ago
6. a Shoshoni answer: Long ago, from a water jug carried by a mythical being (Coyote)
7. a Ute answer: we have always been here

How is a teacher to cope with that panoply of preexisting views?

Teachers should not shy away from discussing religion at any point in U.S. history, including here at the beginning. Avoiding a topic only disempowers teachers. But teachers should not impose their religious preference or point of view in the classroom. Indeed, it's usually a poor idea even to share one's religious beliefs with students. I learned this early in my career when, in response to a student's question, I replied honestly that I (then) was an atheist.[17] A curtain descended in front of his eyes, and I was unable to reach him for the rest of the semester.

The way out is to teach students the word "compartmentalize" and what it means. Compartmentalizing is not mere hypocrisy, or, if it is, everyone does it at times. I know I do. Years ago I contemplated the northern lights, for example, in northern Wisconsin. As a college student, I worked summers at a canoe base for Explorer Scouts just east of Boulder Junction. For three straight nights one summer in the early 1960s, the northern lights covered almost the whole sky, to within 30° of the southern horizon. This display went far beyond the usual pale yellow-green bands. We saw curtains of red, of white, of yellow-green with vertical folds, and other formations as well. They swayed and soared. Sometimes the whole sky throbbed. For two nights, the camp staff stayed out in a field in our sleeping bags, eyes on the sky, speaking in whispers, not sleeping until well past midnight, marveling at what we were witnessing. Astronomy had been a major interest of mine in high school, so I understood the scientific explanation. I knew that prior sunspot activity threw off electrons and protons. Some got captured by the magnetic attraction of Earth, which drew them toward the north and south magnetic poles. They then collided with molecules in the upper atmosphere, causing them to glow. At the time, I think I even knew how that glow was created, though I don't now. Nor do I understand what caused the folded drapery effect, the rapid movements, or the throbbing.

They were so astounding that they communicated a spiritual energy as well. Even decades later, typing these words, I get stirred again, recalling the power that they had over all of us. Did this display prove the existence of a higher power? Well, no, it did not prove it. It did show that science does not offer the only way to fathom the northern lights.

Not only the magnificent sights of nature inspire awe. Walt Whitman instructs us that nature's mundane aspects are equally miraculous:

I believe a leaf of grass is no less than the journey work of the stars. . . .
And a mouse is miracle enough to stagger sextillions of infidels.[18]

When a person dies, one perfectly reasonable response is, "God have mercy on her soul." Another is, "What did she die of?"

Likewise, there is more than one way to understand the distant past. To let a student claim that God formed the world a few thousand years ago, and formed today's animals fully modern within six days, will not do, however.[19] About the question posed in this chapter, teachers want students to know and understand the first and second commonly held answers in Utah, listed above. Teachers need not argue with answers three through six, which are in essence religious. They can say frankly that those answers are appropriate in some circumstances, but not in school. After all, professors of epidemiology at Wake Forest Medical School, affiliated with North Carolina Baptist Hospital, believe in evolution, at least while teaching epidemiology or treating tuberculosis. Evolution is not compatible with the notion that God formed people whole a mere 6,000 years ago. What these professors believe in church on Sunday morning is another matter. Answers one and two to the question, how and when did people first reach the Americas, do not fit in some religious settings, just as the scientific explanation for the northern lights did not seem appropriate to me lying on a Wisconsin meadow at night.

No longer do Americans pay any attention to former religious views of the solar system from the Middle Ages, owing to advances in the science of astronomy. No longer do people pay much attention to religious views of the human body, owing to the science of anatomy/physiology. Religious views about our earliest history still have some influence, precisely because knowing the ancient past is so hard. Nevertheless, they need to be labeled religious presentism and kept separate from the historical and scientific approach.

CONCLUSIONS ABOUT PRESENTISM

Presentism is evident in archaeology about the distant past, especially in earlier archaeology that is now regarded as manifestly preposterous. That's why it's good to bring it up in the first unit of a U.S. history course. Presentism is a complicated charge, however, not to be tossed around lightly. Therefore, teachers need to complexify the discussion before moving on. After all, we always look at the past from where we stand. We have no alternative. Students especially have little interest in learning about the past for its own sake. Teachers always need to "make it relevant" to the present. Moreover, simply lobbing the charge of "presentism" does not prove that the history being challenged is biased. Evidence is still required.

Presentism has often been invoked inappropriately about moral issues. For example, some people charge that criticizing Columbus for enslaving American Indians is presentist, because people did not consider slavery wrong in 1493. This charge is unconvincing. First, it implies a thorough-going moral relativism: if a culture deems a practice OK, who are we to say otherwise? But there are moral absolutes. The "golden rule," found in many religious and philosophical systems, is one. As we (or Columbus, for that matter) would not want to be chained and confined to a ship's hold and forced across an ocean to work for others for nothing, neither is it right to so chain and confine others.

As well, in 1493 many people opposed Columbus's plan to enslave Ar-awaks and send them across the Atlantic to Spain and the Canaries. Most of these opponents were Arawaks, to be sure. To leave them out of the moral calculus, notwithstanding, condemns us to write white history, not history. Furthermore, when historians look closely, they usually find that even among the oppressors, some at the time stood for justice and told the truth about what was going on. Among the Spaniards, these included Antonio de Montesinos, the Dominican priest who in 1511 denounced the Europeans on Haiti for their treatment of American Indians, and Barto-lomé de las Casas, the first great historian of the Americas.[20]

Related to moral presentism is the error historians call "Whig history." Herbert Butterfield coined the term in his 1931 book, *The Whig Interpretation of History*. He used it to criticize historians associated with the Whig Party in Britain around the middle of the 1800s, like Thomas Macaulay. They wrote about the past in a way that made Britain's dominion over other countries and the Whig Party's dominion over Britain seem altogether right and natural.

"Whig history" has come to mean any portrayal of the past that makes the present seem foreordained and natural. Because the term derives from specific circumstances in Great Britain, rather than teach "Whig history" to students, I prefer a more general sociological term, chronological ethnocentrism.

CHRONOLOGICAL ETHNOCENTRISM

Chronological ethnocentrism makes explicit the assumption that was implicit in Whig history: that our society and culture are better than past ones. That's why we developed whatever institution we are now trying to explain, and that's why we don't have to try very hard to explain it. It's just "natural" that people would do things better, as time passed and they and society evolved. A corollary of chronological ethnocentrism is that we are smarter and more knowledgeable than past peoples.[21]

In the nineteenth century, chronological ethnocentrism provided a splendid rationale for imperialism. Whites, allegedly more advanced, saw

themselves as necessary to perform the service of exploiting natural resources, which natives were too backward to do. It was Manifest Destiny,
Americans said, for the U.S. to expand to the Pacific, maybe to Panama
and Cuba as well. At its worst, this kind of thinking repeatedly led to
genocides. Spaniards wiped out most Canary Islanders in the fifteenth
century, Anglo Americans killed or dispersed into the West Indies most
Pequot Indians in 1637, the French shipped virtually the entire Natchez
nation in chains to the West Indies in 1731, British policies and diseases
ended Tasmanian culture between 1803 and 1833, Germans slaughtered
the Hereros in Namibia in 1904, and the list goes on and on. It didn't
seem to matter, because history had already consigned these peoples to its
backwaters. Their annihilations, while tragic, amounted to mere potholes
on our otherwise smooth highway to the present, in this view. After all,
things have gotten better since. Thus, despite such horrors, chronological
ethnocentrism lets textbooks present our American journey—and Western
civilization in general—as a morality play, but without suspense, for all
along students know that good triumphs in the end.

Chronological ethnocentrism is a distinctive form of presentism, with
distinctive and deleterious effects. For one, it can keep students from
grasping that individuals—sometimes just a handful—caused things to
turn out as they did. The godlike monotone used by textbook authors also
has this effect—one reason why textbooks are so dull. By removing contingency, chronological ethnocentrism removes tension from the narrative.
Things were bound to turn out as they did. Things were bound to turn out
well. Why, then, should students concern themselves?

PRIMITIVE TO CIVILIZED

We have seen how chronological ethnocentrism prompts archaeologists
and textbook writers to give inadequate attention to the possibility that
the earliest settlers came to the Americas by boat. Those "primitives" must
have walked. The same thinking imposes the idea of automatic progress
as the underlying storyline of U.S. history textbooks from start to finish.
Asking how people first got to the Americas provides a splendid moment
to point out the inadequacies in this storyline.

As historians project today's social relations onto the distant past, they
know without even thinking about it that human societies have much
more capability now than they did way back then. Consider medicine.
In earlier times, societies blamed various factors when a person became
ill. She ate too much "hot food" (not always referring to temperature),
someone "sang her" (put a hex on her), she did something bad, and so on.

People were ignorant of the germ theory of disease. Ignorant of anatomy and physiology too, many societies did not understand how problems with organs like the heart, kidneys, and even gums could cause symptoms elsewhere in the body. Since we moderns know more, we assume we must be smarter.

Of course, if we thought about the matter directly, we might realize that people probably aren't getting smarter. On the contrary, we may be growing stupider. I know a man whose job for years was to drill seven holes in a road grader frame as it passed him on an assembly line. I know a woman whose job—also for years—was refolding and stacking clothing after shoppers had unfolded it at K-mart. For them and many others, our modern division of labor does not provide experience in solving varied problems, and hence may not build mental capacity. Place an eighteen-year-old in the "wilderness," as we civilized folk have learned to call it, and watch (or imagine) what happens. Most likely, he does not know how to find food, shelter, or even north. He cannot tell a poisonous from an edible fungus, snare a rabbit, or start a fire without a match, and maybe not even with one. Not to put down our eighteen-year-old—he can identify thumbnail photos of Paris Hilton and Britney Spears at a glance, from the back. He can take a photo with his cell phone, add commentary, upload it, and post the result on a website. Perhaps the soundest conclusion is that the knowledge and intelligence of modern people may be different—neither more nor less—from that of our primitive counterparts.

At this point, students need to become sophisticated in their use of two terms: "primitive" and "civilized." "Civilized" is a problematic word, because it has at least two very different meanings. Anthropologists use it in contrast to "primitive" to denote societies with a complex division of labor. All societies show some division of labor, to be sure. Women do somewhat different tasks from men, and children engage in different activities from adults. In primitive societies, however, the division of labor does not go much further than that. The principal chief of a village does not "chief" for a living—he hunts, fishes, perhaps farms, just like other men. The same holds for the shaman or religious leader. Traditionally, every Inuit woman knew how to soften seal skin and combine it with caribou fur to make boots. Every man knew how to harpoon a seal.

In our society, few mayors know how to hunt and fish.[22] Few women can make footwear. Our jobs have become so specific that the Los Angeles metropolitan area boasts more than 100 businesses whose work is poodle clipping. Such specialization makes our society very capable—not only at clipping poodles well, but also at open-heart surgery, computer design, and a million other tasks. That capability is what distinguishes civilized from primitive societies.

Unfortunately, "civilized" has quite a different meaning in common discourse: polite, refined, even humane. Students can see the disjoint by considering this question: Did Nazi Germany show a high degree of civilization? An anthropologist would reply, "Of course," compared to such primitive societies as Shoshoni Indians in Utah, pre-1492. Which society was more civilized in the sense of polite and humane? The Shoshonis, of course.

Our society labels some ancient cultures—Iraq, Egypt, China, Rome—"higher civilizations," in contrast to "more primitive" peoples like Shoshonis or Australian Aborigines. These very terms—"higher," "primitive," "civilized"—are suffused by the notion of progress. Many societies apply the same labels to religions, viewing the "animist" or "pagan" beliefs of American Indians as less advanced than "religions of the book" like Judaism, Christianity, and Islam. Earlier, mankind believed in many gods, goes this line of thought; then in fewer and more abstract deities, like the Trinity; and finally, in just one god.

Anthropologists are uncomfortable ranking anything other than science and technology higher or lower. Most elements of culture—religion, family structure, language, law, and the like—cannot be graded higher or lower but only different. When we look carefully at schemes that purport to rank religions rationally, for example, we find weaknesses. In a sense, like Christians, Native Americans believed in one god, a "Great Spirit" that infused itself into sacred places like a meadow, beautiful lake, islet, and so on. In a sense Christians believe in several gods—Father, Son, and Holy Ghost for starters, and perhaps Satan, the Virgin Mary, and a whole realm of saints and angels.

U.S. history textbooks do recognize that some Native American cultures—usually the Incas, Mayas, and Aztecs—were civilized. But not cultures in the United States. "Throughout the continent to the north and east of the . . . Pueblos," says *The American Pageant*, "social life was less elaborately developed—indeed, 'societies' in the modern sense of the word scarcely existed." Such "analysis" exemplifies ethnocentrism. The authors of *Pageant* admire hierarchical Indian societies—more like our society today—and think little of those American Indian societies whose citizens were more equal. They are still in thrall to the outmoded primitive-to-civilized continuum.

COSTS OF CHRONOLOGICAL ETHNOCENTRISM

Chronological ethnocentrism deadens social studies/history classes. Because it excuses and minimizes past wrongdoing, it leads to genial shallow treatments even of gripping problematic topics. Because our present forms are better, everything seems to have led to our present situation naturally, so there's no real suspense. Because outcomes that were struggled over now seem appropriate, ordained, even commendable, textbooks are bland. They convert things that are worth thinking about into things that are taken for granted. Boring textbooks have payoffs for publishers. Their books will not offend, so they will not lose sales. Meanwhile, students fall asleep reading them.

Chronological ethnocentrism results in bad history, especially about the distant past. It distorts even the terms that we use. Europeans "explored," while earlier peoples "wandered." Europeans "settled," while the first settlers "roamed." Essays on Oregon, Kansas, Ohio, and Rhode Island in my *Lies Across America* attack these and other chronologically ethnocentric terms.[23] Students might critique their own textbook by comparing the frequency of these verbs when paired with Native American actors and European American actors. Or they might compare illustrations. Chapter 7 shows how our culture uses nearly naked images of American Indians to connote that nonwhites are "primitive." Conversely, the first Europeans appear triumphal, such as Hernando de Soto "discovering" the Mississippi River while wearing armor and carrying flags. Any competent historian knows de Soto did not approach the river in triumph. By the time he reached it, his forces had lost 40 men and most of their equipment to a Choctaw attack in Alabama, his men and women were near revolt, and he had to post guards at night to keep his followers from defecting to the Indians. Not one textbook shows the Spaniards in their makeshift boats, looking far more bedraggled than the Natchez Indians who chased them down the Mississippi in their canoes. Such a portrayal would not fit with chronological ethnocentrism.

The problem goes beyond twisted terms and triumphal images. Just as ethnocentrism makes it hard to learn from other cultures, chronological ethnocentrism takes away the ability to learn from other eras. We wind up profoundly ignorant about primitive societies, past or present. For example, Americans believe without thinking that modern times give us unparalleled life expectancies—perhaps twice as long as those of people thousands of years ago. We do now live much longer than people did a century ago. In the U.S., the average life expectancy in 1900 was 47 years. Five centuries earlier, however, life expectancy in North America was not very different from now. Childbirth was riskier, but once people reached 1 year old, they typically lived to be 70. Not just Native Americans, either. Psalm 90 in the *Bible* tells us: "The years of our lives are three score years and ten. Yet if by reason of strength they be four score, yet is their strength labor and sorrow . . ." So people routinely lived to be 70 and even 80 in Old Testament times.

Agriculture, especially when it included livestock, decreased life expectancy. This seems counterintuitive. Didn't agriculture assure a steadier food supply? Rarely did gathering and hunting peoples live on the edge of starvation, however. Many people mistakenly think they did, partly because today people gather and hunt only in the most difficult places on Earth, like the Arctic and the Kalahari Desert, where more modern peoples find it too difficult to live at all. Even there, starvation is rare, because gathering and hunting peoples rely on a variety of food sources. Famines are recent developments, resulting when people rely too much on one crop, and it fails. Even without famines, agricultural societies, far denser, are more vulnerable to disease, including pandemic outbreaks. Nor did gatherers and hunters spend all their time desperately seeking food, clothing, and shelter. Anthropologists have shown that they met these basic needs in as little as two hours per day, less than many people spend now.[24]

In 1651 in *The Leviathan*, social philosopher Thomas Hobbes famously wrote about the state of mankind, absent government and law:

> In such condition there is no place for industry, because the fruit thereof is uncertain: and consequently no culture of the earth; no navigation, nor use of the commodities that may be imported by sea; no commodious building; no instruments of moving and removing such things as require much force; no knowledge of the face of the earth; no account of time; no arts; no letters; no society; and which is worst of all, continual fear, and danger of violent death; and the life of man, solitary, poor, nasty, brutish, and short.[25]

Hobbes and his readers projected that condition backward onto the distant past. Primitive life was not like that. We should view his sentence not as a summary of our rise from savagery to civilization, but as an instructive example of chronological ethnocentrism.

Here at the start, treating the primitive societies that first came to the Americas, teachers can get students thinking complexly about this complex topic of progress.[26] In what ways might their societies have been more fun than ours? More interesting? Healthier? Better—leading to a discussion of the meaning of "better"? Do textbook authors recognize such possibilities? Or do they treat these societies as "other," not really to be empathized with—"wanderers," for example, rather than "explorers"?

A major goal of anthropology is to present primitive cultures as reasonable and understandable societies. A way to get this across to students is to compare our maternity wards to how Mbuti people in central Africa (whom Americans know as Pygmies) give birth. Anthropologist Colin Turnbull notes that expectant Mbuti mothers do not take leave from their jobs or lie in bed for weeks or even days before giving birth.

A few days before her time is due, the mother may restrict her activities and perhaps refrain from going off on the hunt each morning, though it is common enough for a girl to give birth while actually on the hunt, merely staying back either by herself or with a friend and rejoining the hunt an hour or two later.

When she goes into labor, she does not lie on her back in bed, legs elevated for the benefit of the obstetrician. Instead, she typically puts a specially chosen vine around a tree at whose base is a soft bed of moss. She then squats, facing the tree, holding onto the vine, in the same position as if having a bowel movement. A friend familiar with childbirth attends her.

The infant emerges easily . . . and is immediately placed to the mother's breast as she lies down. The umbilical cord is cut in anything from a few minutes to as much as an hour or more later. At that time or soon after, the father and close friends may be invited to see the child, who by then is happily suckling.[27]

Students might contrast this with our "scientific" birthing system, which is modeled on having an abdominal tumor removed. Even in a "normal" birth, Western doctors remove the baby uphill, against gravity, sometimes with forceps. Although no one is ill, this operation takes place in a hospital, a place for the very sick, rife with infectious diseases. Often the "patient" is sedated, at least from her waist down. Almost one-fourth of all births in the U.S. are genuinely surgical: Caesarean sections. Increasingly, these operations are done at the behest of the mother or for the convenience of the physician.[28] Whether Caesarean or "normal" delivery, the baby must be brought to consciousness, having been sedated along with the mother. Often the father does not snuggle his baby but only gets to look at it through a window.[29]

To be sure, modern medicine has cut infant and maternal mortality, even though Turnbull states that Mbuti birthing rarely results in death. Nevertheless, we may have things to learn from "less advanced" societies, and not just about childbirth. Our ways of rearing children, for example, may not promote happy, well-adjusted, effective members of our society as well as the Mbutis'. Certainly our children mostly play indoors and have become estranged from nature, which may have bad long-term consequences both for them and nature.[30]

Even our technology, though assuredly more powerful, may not be better in that it may not meet our needs over the long term—not if, for instance, it leads to global warming, ozone depletion, or other planetary changes that prove catastrophic for our descendants. Chapter 1 pointed to the need for every topic in U.S. history to relate to the present. This very first topic—most distant from the present in time—turns out to be intensely relevant. Not only is prehistory fiercely debated today, but how students think about primitive cultures may have ramifications for our society's future. Two anthropologists who specialize in studying gathering and hunting peoples, Richard Lee and Irven DeVore, put the question baldly: "It is still an open question whether man will be able to survive the exceedingly complex and unstable ecological conditions he has created."[31] We cannot go on forever increasing our use of Earth. Yet we still do not act urgently about environmental concerns. Possibly we must move quickly to a steady-state use of energy worldwide. Certainly we must change those behaviors that otherwise portend no long-run future.

Surely our educational system should help students address Lee and DeVore's "open question." Indeed, this is the most important question students could possibly consider. To take it seriously—to ponder thoughtfully the likelihood of global warming, other forms of pollution, and the accidental or even purposeful annihilation of human life on Earth—Americans need to rid our thinking of chronological ethnocentrism. Unfortunately, whether discussing forms of government, medical practice, or our technological future, our history textbooks are useless, because they are infected by the uncritical belief in progress that results from chronological ethnocentrism. As chronological ethnocentrism distorts our understanding of the primitive past, it blinds us about the future and makes it hard to face the possibility of ecocide objectively. So we hurtle ahead, secure that our past has led us to this point, basking in chronological ethnocentrism. Students who learn the term here at the start of their U.S. history course can apply it appropriately to later passages in their textbook.

We are also moving toward a one-culture world, because our ethnocentrism has convinced not only us but also many less advanced societies that our culture is the best. Native American writer Russell Means warns, however, that a one-culture world is a likely route to species suicide. If everyone does everything the same way, then we have no alternative models if that way fails. Again, planting a seed here at the start makes it easier for students to see that chronological ethnocentrism is problematic, that other cultures should survive, and that even we Americans may need some of their ideas.[32]

Perhaps the worst effect of chronological ethnocentrism is that it discourages student involvement in civic life. Not only does presenting our world as if it was bound to come out as it did leave little room for individuals to make a difference. Also, instead of explaining the present, chronological ethnocentrism absolves and celebrates the present. If things are fine, and getting better by themselves to boot, what's the point? That makes chronological ethnocentrism a particularly enervating form of presentism. When students realize that things don't get better automatically (which most already question in some rhetorical contexts), then they can take steps as individuals or within their history or social studies class to make something get better. So, from the start of the course, civic activism can be a component.

In another way, chronological ethnocentrism interferes with civic life. It promotes a general deadening of our moral sense. All Americans want to be good people. Progress provides today's secular equivalent of salvation. Belief that our nation leads the world can invest citizens' mundane roles with a moral purpose, even though they may be doing nothing worthwhile. Then they can imagine that doing their job well, whatever that job is, has meaning. Somehow it advances society. The man who drills seven holes in a road grader frame is not just drilling holes. He is building the American future. Viewed that way, almost every job conveys this extra legitimacy. It gives our lives meaning.

Nothing is wrong with drilling holes in road grader frames. Until people developed robot drill presses, someone had to do it. When people rely on chronological ethnocentrism to legitimize their jobs and their lives, however, they are unlikely to question societal policies. Not every job contributes to society. The idea of progress should not be a matter of belief, but of inquiry. To live a morally satisfying life, people need to assess the effects of the society within which they live upon the world, as well as the effect upon others of the jobs they do and the lives they lead. As the great American architect Louis H. Sullivan put it almost a century ago, "In a democracy, there can be but one fundamental test of citizenship, namely: Are you using such gifts as you possess . . . for or against the people?"[33] Chronological ethnocentrism makes it harder to answer this question honestly.

This first topic in a U.S. history course can set the tone for an important, rich, and deep experience. Students who come to their own conclusion—based on evidence—about how and when people first got to the Americas will likely remember that conclusion—and the evidence and competing views—for years. Some will acquire a lifelong interest to keep up with the discoveries that continue to pour forth from the many disciplines that study prehistory. Students will also realize that textbooks are imperfect and can be challenged. They will grasp that we comprehend the past with difficulty, sometimes based on scant evidence. Then they can appreciate how pressures from the present intrude upon that evidence and distort what we might learn from it. Now they are doing historiography. Finally, students who understand chronological ethnocentrism have gained a concept that can help them think through the thoughtless assumptions that historians, politicians, and the public make every day.

FOCUSED BIBLIOGRAPHY

Vine Deloria, *Red Earth, White Lies* (Golden, CO: Fulcrum, 1997). Pages 45–80 query the Beringia hypothesis, raising questions that are all the more interesting coming from a Native American.

Boris Weintraub, "A Seagoing Human Ancestor?" *National Geographic*, 11/98, unpaginated. This short article throws into question the received dogma from earlier archaeology about Beringia.

CHAPTER 6

Why Did Europe Win?

IT IS NOT ETHNOCENTRISM—chronological or any other kind—to teach that European societies (and their extensions, like the United States and Australia) became powerful and effective. If one looks over the Earth in, say, 1892, every country except perhaps three was dominated by the West.[1] Surely the most significant development in world history during the last millennium is Europe's dominance over the planet.

THE IMPORTANT QUESTIONS

Why did Europe win? This is perhaps the most important question a world history course might address. Yet it usually goes unanswered, because it goes unasked. In a U.S. history course, the related question is, Why did the United States become the dominant country on Earth? It, too, usually goes unasked.

Perhaps history teachers and textbook authors don't ask these questions because they don't see them as problems. They take the importance of the West for granted, and the rightness and growth of Christianity, and within that dominion, the supremacy of the United States. In particular, teachers may feel reluctant to discuss why Christianity spread so widely, because the answers they might give would be secular.[2] Giving secular answers to what some will view as a religious question may strike some parents as irreligious. Teachers know this and don't want to get into an argument about religion.[3] Whatever the reason, since they were never asked these questions, teachers can think it odd—almost a violation of some unspoken norm—to bring them up at all.

Teachers must ask them, however. Otherwise, their courses are not competent. Not asking these questions makes the present dominance of the West seem foreordained and natural. That is a classic case of Whig history, as defined in the last chapter. Not asking these questions leaves a vacuum at the center of the story. Like nature, minds abhor a vacuum. Racism sneaks in to fill it. The unspoken answers that emerge in response to these unasked questions are: Europe won "because whites are better." Christianity is winning "because it is right." The United States is dominant "because we're the best." If teachers ignore these questions, then these answers go unchallenged, even though wrong, with harmful consequences for society.[4]

Students can address these questions historically. Doing so becomes a way to decrease ethnocentrism, which, as pointed out in the introduction to this book, is higher in the U.S. than anywhere else.

LOOKING AROUND THE WORLD

One way to get students to ask the question themselves is to invite them to participate in a mental experiment. Imagine they are visiting Earth from a distant planet in 2000 BC. Obviously, having developed space travel, they come from a society with advanced technology. Like space travelers of yore, they want to land and say, "Take me to your leaders." Where should they land?

Looking around the world in 2000 BC, our visitors would probably choose Egypt. At that time, Egypt had agriculture, writing, a large population, and a unified government. Even more obvious were its immense public structures, including the pyramids. Mesopotamia—modern Iraq—also had agriculture, writing, and a fairly large population. A bit later, Hammurabi would have his famous system of laws chiseled in stone. In the Indus River Valley in Pakistan and western India, people had built cities, some laid out in rectangular grids. They had also developed writing, agriculture, and mathematics, complete with a zero. All three of these civilizations had mastered the art of making objects from bronze. All had trading networks stretching for hundreds and even thousands of miles. Nothing in Europe compared. As historian R. R. Palmer summarizes,

> Europeans were by no means the pioneers of human civilization. Half of man's recorded history had passed before anyone in Europe could read or write. The priests of Egypt began to keep written records between 4000 and 3000 BC, but more than 2000 years later the poems of Homer were still being circulated in the Greek city-states by word of mouth.[5]

Now imagine a landing in 1000 BC. Egypt was still paramount. India was in decline. Various kingdoms vied for power in Mesopotamia. Again, nothing in Europe compared.

If the space travelers returned in 1 BC, they would find the Roman Empire dominant over Egypt. The civilizations of Persia and Greece had already risen to impressive heights and then descended, though they were still important culturally. Clearly the spacecraft would want to touch down in Rome, the center of the Mediterranean, or perhaps in China, now unified under the Han dynasty.

Half a millennium later, around 500 AD, a new claimant had arisen, the Mayas. They mastered agriculture and probably aquaculture, lived in cities, and built pyramids larger in volume than those in Egypt, though not as high. The Eastern Roman Empire, its capital at the city now known as Istanbul, was the largest nation in Europe and western Asia. Another civilization had arisen in India, this time in the east, but was already in decline, about to be sacked by the Mongols.

By 1000 AD, the Holy Roman Empire, amounting mainly to modern-day Germany, eastern France, and northern Italy, might have received a visit from our space aliens, even though Voltaire famously derided it as "neither Holy, nor Roman, nor an Empire." More likely, they would have landed in China, now divided into two competing kingdoms that got along without much conflict. Probably, however, our visitors would have chosen Mecca. As British historian Felipe Fernandez-Armesto put it, in 1000 AD,

> A continuous band of territory under Muslim rule stretched from the Duero [a river in Spain] and the Atlantic, across North Africa and the western Mediterranean, to the Indus, the Jaxartes [Syr Darya River, in Kazakhstan], and the Arabian Sea.[6]

Not only was this "the biggest . . . civilization the world had ever seen," it was still expanding in 1000. Meanwhile, the inhabitants of Britain were about to be conquered by Normandy.

In 1500 AD, the world was in rapid flux. Several empires had arisen and already declined or were about to decline: the Aztecs and Incas in the Western Hemisphere, Ghana and Mali in West Africa, and Great Zimbabwe. The Ottoman Empire in Turkey and Mogul empire in India had just got under way. "In 1500 Europe . . . was still but one civilization among many," writes British historian Hugh Trevor-Roper, who mentions the Ottomans, the Moguls, and the Chinese.[7] If our space visitors had any inkling of what was to come, however, they would have landed in Spain. For Europe—first Italy, then Iberia, and later, as new crops from the Americas altered population patterns, northern nations like Britain, France, Germany, and Russia—would dominate the next 500 years.

The purpose of this exercise is not to summarize the history of the world. Rather, this thought experiment can teach humility: even the longest-lived civilizations are transitory. Ours has been going on for a far shorter period of time than ancient Egypt, but Egyptian dominance is long over. Ours, too, will end. Realizing this may prove useful, delaying our fall and humanizing our dominance.

The exercise also seeks to get students asking why these societies were so successful, if only for a while. None of these civilizations was inevitable, least of all ours. What does explain them? As soon as students ask this question seriously, any genetic explanation fails. Civilization can hardly relate to some innate capacity for progress that some people have while others don't, because very different people inhabited the various landing sites listed above. Some of Egypt's founding ideas—as well as some of its pharaohs—came downstream from the black societies living along the Upper Nile. Mayans are neither genetically nor geographically related to Arab Muslims. Nor are Chinese close to Romans.

Thinking across time shows even more dramatically than thinking across space the absurdity of the notion that differences among people might cause differences among societies and cultures. The western and northern Europeans who now dominate the world were mostly not part of any of the civilizations mentioned above, before 1500 AD. Quite the contrary: Romans considered them barbarians. Lingering in our speech today is the fear civilized people felt of such groups as Vandals, Goths, and Huns. Writing about the peoples and nations that surrounded the Roman Empire, Palmer notes:

> Throughout its long life the Empire had been surrounded on almost all sides by barbarians, wild Celts in Wales and Scotland, Germans in the heart of Europe, Persians or Parthians in the East. . . . These barbarians, always with the exception of Persia, had never been brought within the pale of ancient civilization. They remained illiterate, unsettled, townless, more or less nomadic, and frequently bellicose.[8]

If Celts or Britons were backward in 2000 BC for "innate" reasons, how could they have subdued much of the world by 1892? Obviously, genetics had nothing to do with it. Evolutionary theory does not hold that innate human intellectual ability can change rapidly within what is, in evolutionary terms, the twinkling of an eye. Nor does evidence suggest a drastic winnowing of barbarian babies to produce some marvelous eugenics transformation. On the contrary, the causes of the hegemony of northern and western Europe are historical, not psychological or biological.

EXPLAINING CIVILIZATION

At this point, it may be useful to help students uncover why civilization—defined as a complex division of labor—arose in the first place. Absent an answer to this question, it is easy to slip into the inference that civilized people were (and are) smarter. Jared Diamond opens his bestseller *Guns, Germs, and Steel* with exactly this issue. Diamond was a biologist, studying bird evolution in New Guinea. A Papuan asked him, "Why is it that you white people developed so much cargo [modern technology], . . . but we black people had little cargo of our own?" Diamond noted, "He and I both knew perfectly well that New Guineans are on the average at least as smart as Europeans." Indeed, Diamond presents reasons for concluding that Papuans may be smarter. Yet we—and they—consider their culture to be backward.[9] So Diamond started thinking about why civilization arose in some places and not in others. Eventually he identified several critical factors, including domesticatable plants for crops, domesticatable animals for livestock, nearby societies to borrow ideas from, and the absence of certain debilitating diseases. Most important is not his specific list, but his approach. He correctly notes that a complex division of labor requires some antecedent conditions. They, and not some innate characteristics of the people, are crucial.

Sociologists, anthropologists, and historians have devoted much thought and research time to explaining the rise of civilization. The change from food gathering to rudimentary horticulture seems easy to explain. Someone notices that a given plant that is good to eat likes a certain kind of habitat. So the person helps enlarge this habitat, to get more of the plant. It works. Maybe a blackberry vine likes the edge between underbrush and meadow to the south. Our "primitive" person girdles a tree to the southwest, thus extending the meadow. Voila!—more blackberries. Now people are not just living off the world but are manipulating it to get it to produce more. It's only a small additional step to dig up a blackberry vine and plant it on the north edge of a meadow closer to one's village.

Other steps are not so obvious. Did cities come after the full-fledged invention of agriculture? Perhaps, but some anthropologists think sizable numbers of people may have lived together first. Does irrigation play a role? Sociologists have theorized that the benefits of irrigation would have been obvious alongside rivers in dry lands like Egypt and Iraq. In turn, irrigation, at least large-scale irrigation, requires coordination. People have to keep doing their share of maintenance. People have to take their share of the water, but not more than that. There has to be a system for dealing with disputes. So irrigation may have led to the invention of some kind of government, which in turn helped lead to a complex division of labor. Perhaps, but evidence suggests that government may have preceded irrigation.

A U.S. history course is not the place to discuss the likely causes of civilization at length. The point is that civilization is caused. Therefore, students should not infer that civilization shows anything about a people, other than that various causes came together. To label some *people* as less civilized or more primitive won't do.

MAKING THE EARTH ROUND

The four voyages of Christopher Columbus are both a result and a cause of Europe's growing dominance over the rest of the world. Hence, their discussions of Columbus provide textbook authors with a natural place to address the why question. Instead of helping students think about the sweeping changes that Columbus's journeys caused in our world, however, most courses in U.S. history squander the opportunity. Textbooks focus on minutiae, like the name of the sailor who cried, "Land, ho!" When not flatly wrong, most of what Americans conventionally learn about Columbus is a diversion from the important questions that his voyages ought to raise.

Many textbooks used to tell this whopper about Christopher Columbus: that one of his key contributions was that he proved Earth was round. Some teachers still say this. Columbus did no such thing, and no competent historian who ever wrote about him ever claimed he did. Nevertheless, students learn it. Consider this item from the first edition of the new writing portion of the SAT in 2005:

> We must seriously question the idea of majority rule. The majority grinned and jeered when Columbus said the world was round. The majority threw him into a dungeon for his discoveries. Where is the logic in the notion that the opinion held by a majority of people should have the power to influence our decisions?[10]

The lackeys who formulate items at Educational Testing Service used this quote, from a 1926 speech by U.S. Senator James A. Reed, "Majority Rule," without correction. Their purpose was to trigger a student essay about majority rule. In fact, neither of the two sentences that treat Columbus contains a shred of truth. "The majority" already *knew* the world was round and did not jail him "for his discoveries." Queen Isabella jailed Columbus for his inhumane and incompetent administration of Hispaniola, including enslaving 1,500 Arawak Indians. Unfortunately, about 300,000 high school juniors read the paragraph and wrote essays in response. Thus, the flat Earth myth got passed to the next generation.

The world became "flat" around 1830, not 1491, when Washington Irving, the novelist who invented Rip Van Winkle, included the flat Earth fable in a biography of Christopher Columbus. It went on to become the most popular biography of the entire nineteenth century and stayed in print throughout the century.[11] As the controversy over how people first got here provides a hook to get students to challenge textbook certainty, so the flat Earth myth provides a way to help them see how popular culture

The flat Earth myth has become part of our shared understanding of the world, which writers then use as a basis for everything from Mother's Day cards to comic strips. This everyday usage further embeds it in Americans' minds. Notions that we take for granted can be the last to change, precisely because we take them for granted.

can intrude on what should be a scholarly topic. In short, students need accurate history to rid themselves of the wrong information that is presented to them all the time in our culture.

A good way to start is by having each student list Columbus's accomplishments and then amassing a class inventory. Usually some students include "proved Earth round." If no one does, teachers can elicit it from the class in discussion. "Before 1492, almost everyone but Columbus thought the world was ____." If they have not heard the legend, salute them for their ignorance, which puts them ahead of most Americans, who believe this groundless story.

Students can find many examples of the flat Earth myth in our culture, like the Mother's Day card presented on the previous page.[12] Students can also interview their parents to see if they have heard the flat Earth myth. Except for recent immigrants, most have. (Again, students whose parents are ignorant can feel proud of their ignorance.) Students can also ask their parents if they believe it, and if they do, they can then disabuse their parents of the myth. To do so, they need to know some information.

Students who live near an ocean or Great Lake can watch a ship disappear over the horizon: hull first, then sails or superstructure, and finally the little flag on top, as the roundness of the Earth gets in the way. If they live in the Midwest or Great Plains, they can see the same thing as an eighteen-wheeler disappears: wheels first, then body, and finally the little flapper on top of the diesel exhaust. If the Earth were flat, a boat or truck would simply get smaller and smaller, become a dot, and then disappear. Everyone understood that, especially sailors. Earth casts a round shadow on the moon during each lunar eclipse, and everyone understood that as well.[13] The Catholic Church, at the time the most important institution in Europe, said the world was round. So did philosophers at least as far back as the Greeks. My poster book, *Lies My Teacher Told Me About Christopher Columbus*, includes a photo of a globe of the Earth made in Europe in 1492. Columbus did not get back until March 1493.[14]

Once students understand that people already knew that the world was round, they can be nudged to think about why so many people believe the flat Earth myth today. It's a profound question: since no evidence exists for the claim that Columbus proved Earth to be round, why do teachers still teach and students still learn this curious story? As students address this question, they will uncover some of the influences on our thinking that do *not* derive from evidence.

One important part of the answer is because our culture takes it for granted. Consider this example. In *Star Trek V: The Final Frontier*, Captain Kirk and his crew discuss their travel backward in time to our era (which occurred in the previous movie, *Star Trek IV: The Voyage Home*). Explaining this feat to the captain, Sybok, a Vulcan, refers to Columbus, who he says added another dimension to travel when he proved the world was not flat. In 1989, when this movie was made, its director, William Shatner, either believed the myth himself or thought most Americans would not question it. Columbus's alleged feat is not important to the plot; it's just a throwaway line used to help explain time travel, which *is* important to the plot.

Another reason why the flat Earth myth gets passed on is sheer educational inertia. Many teachers learned the tale in their youth, and their later schooling never challenged it. To break this dreary cycle, middle-school teachers need to challenge the flat Earth story that their pupils may have learned in elementary grades, and high school teachers must remove any residue that is still stuck in students' synapses. Students enjoy taking on this responsibility for their younger brothers and sisters.

Perhaps many teachers never questioned the flat Earth myth because it's such a good story. This raises the question, good for what? Tied to the flat Earth myth is the tale of the near-mutiny that Columbus's crew mounted, fearful of sailing off its edge. This story fits in with emphasizing how great Columbus was, triumphing over every adversary, even his own sorry crew. It makes him smarter and more courageous than those under him. So the world is as it should be: those on top of our enterprises deserve to be there, because they're smarter than the rest of us.

The flat Earth myth is only one of the legends that cling like barnacles to the history of the admiral. Now students can return to their inventory of Columbus's accomplishments and question other items that may also be problematic.[15]

WHY DID COLUMBUS WIN?

Columbus's voyages showed the growing power of Europe compared to the rest of the world. The second chapter of *Lies My Teacher Told Me* is entitled "1493: The True Importance of Christopher Columbus." It points out that Columbus was hardly the first non-Native to get to the Western Hemisphere. People from other continents had reached the Americas many times. Columbus's voyage was epoch-making precisely because Europe was now poised to react differently. Thus, Columbus's importance owes to changes in Europe, not to his getting to a "new" continent. Other Europeans would have reached the Americas soon after 1492 if Columbus had not.

Moreover, in 1492 Columbus did little that the Vikings had not accomplished around 1000 AD. The next year, however, owing to developments in Europe, Spain found it possible to equip Columbus with 1,200 to 1,500 men, 17 ships, cannons, crossbows, guns, horses, and attack dogs. Now Columbus proceeded to make history. He and the Spanish took over the island of Haiti, an ocean away from Spain, renamed it Hispaniola ("little Spain"), and threw its inhabitants into serfdom and slavery. This was new.[16] It was followed by even more stupendous feats: Spaniards subduing Peru and Mexico, Portugal taking Brazil, and eventually Britain taking the Atlantic coast of what is now the United States and Canada.

What had happened to give European nations this capability?

Coming near the beginning of a course in U.S. history, this question provides an ideal hook to get students thinking deeply about some of the most important issues they will face in their high school careers. Five crucial factors explain Europe's growing dominance: arms, social technology, greed, religion, and practice in colonizing islands.[17] A critical element of social technology was the nation-state. Societies organized on the village or even the tribal level could not protect themselves against nation-states. A biological factor—resistance to diseases—also helped make possible the conquest of the Americas, Australia, and the islands of the Pacific.

Underlying the development of most of these factors is Europe's borrowing of ideas from other cultures. This is hardly surprising: cultural diffusion and syncretism underlie the flowering of most civilizations. Syncretism means combining elements from two different cultures to form something new. A good example is Christmas, which joins elements from the Jewish religion, such as monotheism and the idea of a Messiah, and Northern European "pagan" observances, like the winter solstice date and the emphasis on lights and plants that are green in winter.

Syncretism is critical to understanding the triumph of Western and Northern Europe. For example, superior military technology was the most important single reason why Europe won. But Europeans did not concoct this new technology from scratch. Cannons and gunpowder came from China. Ships with lateen sails that could sail against the wind probably reached Europe from the Arabs. Other military ideas came from the massed cavalry forces from the east that repeatedly threatened European farmers and cities. European nations refined these concepts further, added their own advances in archery, drill, and siege warfare, came up with grapeshot and eventually rifling, and cast bigger cannons and learned to mount them on ships. Eventually they became world-class military powers.

Unfortunately, U.S. history textbooks do not talk about syncretism. Nor do they credit the Muslims for preserving Greek wisdom, adding ideas from China, India, and Africa, and then teaching the resulting knowledge to Europe via Spain. Instead, they show Prince Henry of Portugal inventing navigation more or less from scratch. So students can critique their textbooks for overlooking obvious syncretism.

The same processes of borrowing and syncretism gave Europe advantages in social technology that proved at least as important as its military superiority. "Arabic" numerals came into Europe from the Arabs, who called them "Indian numerals," because they came from India. Zero and the decimal system also developed in India, as well as China, Peru, and probably elsewhere. These advances made mathematics available to everyone. Italians then invented double-entry bookkeeping. Bureaucracy has a bad name today, but actually it, too, is a powerful social invention. If one person supervises ten subordinates, each of whom supervises ten subordinates, with just a few levels one individual can supervise millions. Add in a few rules, measures of performance, and the idea that information flows up while decisions flow down. Now rulers and merchants can manage far-flung enterprises efficiently. The printing press and the widespread literacy it facilitated also played a key role.

The foregoing paragraphs hardly suffice to explain the triumph of the West.[18] Teachers need not become expert on why Europe won, however. They can set their students forth on a quest. The class might brainstorm the question. Each student might then pick one factor, research its impact, and present to the class its role. Merely getting the class to brainstorm the question for a few minutes may be all that a teacher has time to do, especially in a U.S. history course, but even that simple activity prods students to realize that here is a historical question that has historical answers.

In the Americas, three cultures—Western Europe, West Africa, and Native America—increasingly interacted after 1492. More syncretism resulted from these encounters. Textbooks present the "frontier" as a border between civilization and the wilderness. In reality, it was a wide band. Within this band, interculturation was the rule. From medical remedies to trails to canoes to crops to style of warfare to relations between the sexes, European and African Americans learned from Native Americans.

However, Native cultures changed even more. The transformation of the Plains cultures was only the tip of a cultural change iceberg. Natives traded for many elements of European technology, supplying slaves, deerskins, and beaver pelts in exchange. In the long run, they lost important elements of their own cultures. American Indians and non-Indians began to conclude that Native cultures were inferior.

THE COLUMBIAN EXCHANGE

The first edition of *Lies My Teacher Told Me* attacked textbooks for leaving out the Columbian exchange. After 1492, crops, animals, gold and silver, diseases, and ideas began to cross the oceans regularly. One result was

syncretism everywhere—in what people ate, for example. Imagine Szech-
uan cuisine without its "heat"—chile peppers. Or spaghetti and pizza
with no tomato sauce. Or Irish meals with no potatoes. Contact with the
Americas made all this possible.

The introduction of diseases new to the Western Hemisphere also
helps explain why Europe was able not only to subdue Native Americans, but also largely to displace them. Although he only started the process, the Columbian exchange is the key reason why Columbus was so
important—why, in fact, archaeologists and historians of the Americas
consider BC ("Before Columbus," usually written "pre-Columbian") as a
milepost for dividing time almost as useful as BC ("Before Christ").

Astonishingly, most textbooks published before 2000 did not treat the
Columbian exchange. Now most do. This improvement, long overdue,
means that teachers must retool to keep up. Again, teachers can set their
class loose on the point. Each student can choose a topic from this list:

cows	racially based slavery
pigs	capitalism
sheep	democracy
horses	hierarchy
chickens	corn
goats, other animals	potato
gold	cotton
silver	rice
syphilis	beans
the poxes	tomato
bubonic plague	chiles, other spices
anthrax, tuberculosis, cholera	wheat
guns	"wilderness" as a concept
the Bible, Christianity	steel tools

Then the student learns where the item probably came from, how it affected trade, and its impact on the hemisphere to which it was new.[19]

Some of the items that went each way were ideas. Our textbooks, improved as they are, still omit ideas from their treatments of the Columbian
exchange, especially ideas that flowed from Native to European cultures.
Perhaps some lingering white supremacy makes it hard for authors to
credit American Indians with much influence on our civilization. Nevertheless, impact they did have. The relative lack of hierarchy in many
American Indian societies shook European philosophers and helped
lead to democracy, for example. Students can find short quotes from
Locke, Montesquieu, Rousseau, and other philosophers about the liberty

American Indians enjoyed, how they governed themselves, and how the philosophers were affected by seeing American Indians in Europe.

The conquest of the Americas in turn helps explain why Europe beat the Muslims and Chinese and achieved world dominance. Again, the Columbus chapter in *Lies My Teacher Told Me* explains these matters. Gold and silver from the Americas helped European nations to outdo Islamic countries economically. Crops from the Americas prompted a population explosion, helping northern European nations to outdo the southern nations that had been dominant. More important yet were the changes in how Europeans thought about the world that stemmed from their encounters with Americans.

Syncretism is a crucial concept for Native Americans. Workshops with American Indian groups have convinced me that most Natives don't know the word or the idea (which they might understand without knowing the term itself). Therefore, many Native Americans mistakenly conclude that their main alternatives today are acculturation to the dominant (non-Indian) culture or reversion to Native American culture as it was before cultural imperialism damaged it. They know the latter is impossible: We cannot turn the clock back to 1890, let alone 1491. Therefore, many American Indians have a sense of futility, which contributes to problems of alcoholism, drug abuse, and suicide among the young.

Young Native Americans need not choose "Indian" culture or "non-Indian" culture. Instead, they can—and should—choose syncretism. All cultures—Native American cultures, too—move forward (or die). Abenaki students in Vermont, for example, may not speak Abenaki, but other aspects of Abenaki culture are still available to them, including values and aesthetic ideas. For that matter, several American Indian tribes in the U.S. and Canada are now making heroic efforts to preserve and revive their languages. Ireland, Israel, and other places show that even "dead" languages can be revived.[20] Abenakis can select which ideas from "non-Indian" culture to adopt and adapt, and which elements from Abenaki culture to retain and adapt. They can then develop new ideas and forms. Native Americans need to realize that the dominant culture is syncretic as well, not completely non-Indian. From place names to foodstuffs to basic values, American culture differs from European cultures partly owing to its incorporation of ideas from American Indian cultures.[21]

Native Americans cannot easily convince themselves that they still have important roles to play in American culture if non-Natives poohpooh the idea. When students understand the important influences that Native American cultures have had in the past, they can more readily believe that Natives still have important contributions to make to the larger society. For that reason, and because it's accurate history as well, all students need to understand the role of syncretism in U.S. history. Students can end their study of Native American history by finding ways that Native Americans are making syncretic contributions to our society today. Each student can identify and learn about one living distinguished Native person—in the arts, education, sciences, whatever. Most non-Natives have never heard music by Indigenous or Robert Tree Cody, seen sculptures by Alan Houser or Nalenik Temela, or watched a movie by Sherman Alexie. When they do, some become fans.

October and November are the two worst months to be Native American in our schools, thanks to Columbus Day and Thanksgiving. Teachers can transform these holidays into opportunities to learn new perspectives about Native American history. On Columbus Day 2003, a 7th grader in Connecticut, having read the Columbus chapter in *Lies My Teacher Told Me*, was moved to gather several of his friends and get them to try to break into their middle school and hold class! Teachers who are unwilling to incite such lawlessness can plant a seed by pondering, on the day before Columbus Day weekend, "Why hasn't the United States renamed Columbus Day 'Native American Day,' as South Dakota has done?" This question can lead students to a passionate debate, prompting them to study how Columbus Day got to be a holiday, the pros and cons of Columbus's voyages, and the various ways Native Americans have affected American society. The day after Columbus Day would then be a fine occasion to host a Native American as guest speaker.

IDEOLOGICAL RESULTS OF EUROPE'S VICTORY

Europe's unprecedented power—and the global dominance to which it led—had to be rationalized, or else cognitive dissonance would have set in. Columbus provides the first example. Initially he is full of praise for the Arawaks—"well built" and "of quick intelligence."

> They have very good customs, and the king maintains a very marvelous state, of a style so orderly that it is a pleasure to see it, and they have good memories and they wish to see everything and ask what it is and for what it is used.

Later, when Columbus was justifying his enslavement of them, the Indians were "cruel" and "stupid," "a people warlike and numerous, whose customs and religion are very different from ours."

Europeans did the same thing in their assessment of African cultures. At one point, they had known that Timbuktu was a center of learning, with a university and a library. Later, as European nations proceeded to take over all of Africa except Ethiopia, Europeans (and Americans) perceived Africa as backward. Timbuktu lay forgotten. Ethnocentrism had set in.

Eurocentrism is a special case of ethnocentrism. Indeed, imagining Europe as a continent itself exemplifies Eurocentrism. A continent is a "large land mass, mostly surrounded by water." By any consistent definition, Asia is the continent, of which Europe is only a peninsula, or perhaps a series of peninsulas (Scandinavia, Iberia, Italy, the Balkans). Europe has no justifiable eastern boundary; the Urals are a modest mountain range that does not come within 2,000 miles of the southern edge of Asia. Yet Europe not only is "a continent," to many Americans, it is "*the* continent," as in "continental cuisine."

Europe became the point of reference for our terms for much of the rest of the world. Americans usually write "Near East" for Iraq, Jordan, Israel, and so on, and "Far East" for China and Japan. This makes sense to an Italian, for Baghdad lies fewer than 2,000 miles from Rome, while Beijing is more than 5,000 miles away. From San Francisco, however, Baghdad is 7,500 miles, and that's only by flying over the North Pole; no commercial airplane flies this route. Reaching Baghdad by normal means requires a journey of almost 9,000 miles. Beijing, on the other hand, is less than 6,000 miles. Why should China and Japan be known by how far they are from Europe? Why not call them "East Asia"? Iraq, Israel, and their vicinity might be called "Southwest Asia." Europe itself might better be known as "Far West Asia."

"New World" is another Eurocentric term, of course—new to Europe, not to American Indians. Other Eurocentric terms include "discover," "savages," and "settlers."

CULTURAL DIFFUSION AND SYNCRETISM CONTINUE

It is vital for today's students to learn the terms "ethnocentrism" and "Eurocentrism" and reduce their own levels of these maladies. Air travel, radio and television, and now the web have multiplied the rate of borrowing that cultures do from one another. Any society that fails to learn from its planetary neighbors is destined to become a cultural backwater. The United States needs to reduce ethnocentrism so our society can continue to adopt and adapt ideas from other cultures. Yet in the introduction to this chapter, I pointed out that the U.S. is more ethnocentric than other nations.

A good way to combat ethnocentrism is to learn a lot about one other society. In a world history course or in middle-school social studies, teachers can invite each student to choose a favorite country they might fantasize about visiting. Where would they go? Why? What is most interesting about the country? Then, when the next issue arises—health care, women's rights, pollution—students can find out how their country handles it. What does their country think about our policies in the Middle East? (Oops! I should have written "Southwest Asia!") About our young people?

Another interesting exercise is to use the term "American exceptionalism," discussed in the introduction, in its unbiased form. Each student can find two ways that the U.S. is exceptional—one positive, one negative. Positive and negative as categories are a bit too simple, but putting the assignment that way helps students grasp that "exceptional" need not always be good. These examples might be characterized as "negative," though that might also be too simple:

> The U.S. wound up with the smallest proportion of Native people in the Americas (except possibly Uruguay).
> The U.S. is the only nation to have fought a Civil War over slavery.[22]
> The U.S. remains the only nation ever to have used nuclear weapons on another nation.
> The U.S. spends about as much for military expenses as all other nations combined.[23]

As that last item implies, some exceptional characteristics can be statistical. Another way to combat ethnocentrism is to ask students to locate current figures on such measures of social progress as life expectancy, infant mortality, "most livable countries,"[24] and proportion of the national legislature that is female. In many cases, the United States is no longer first and is falling in the ratings.

For example, the U.S. ranks 139th out of 172 nations in the proportion of its voting-age population who actually vote—not dead last, but probably lowest among industrialized nations.[25] How do other nations do so much better? Maybe tactics as simple as moving election dates to weekends or opening polling places near work places would help. If we look at other countries with eyes that are not clouded by ethnocentrism, we can emulate their effective practices.[26]

Students will also find that Americans use more energy per capita than residents of any other nation. We also consume more calories per capita. As a result of this combination, we lead the world in obesity.[27] Maybe we have things to learn about diet and exercise from Taiwanese, Dutch, Kenyans, or others. The U.S. also has the highest murder rate of any Western industrialized nation. Meanwhile, Americans incarcerate more of our citizens, proportionately, than any other country except North Korea.[28] Maybe we can learn from other nations that either have far lower rates of criminal behavior or incarcerate wrongdoers for much shorter periods.

The U.S. spends more money per capita on health care than any other country. More than 15% of our gross domestic product goes to health care. Yet according to David Wallechinsky, journalist and coauthor of *The Book of Lists,*

> 43 countries have more doctors per capita, including France, Switzerland, Mongolia, and Lebanon. 49 have more hospital beds per capita than the U.S.—the United Kingdom, Italy, and Ireland, for example. 33 nations, including Cuba, have a lower infant death rate than the U.S., and 28 have a lower maternal death rate. We rank 30th in life expectancy for women and 28th for men.[29]

Health care surely offers an area where Americans might glean ideas from other societies.

When students understand the historical reasons why nations won, they become less likely to fall for half-baked psychological reasons. At the other end of the academic year, students can usefully be asked, "Based on your knowledge of the U.S. and other nations over time, how long will Western dominance endure?" This question reminds them that Egypt, the Mayans, and Rome, the Indus River Valley civilization—all the earlier civilizations that dominated the globe—no longer do so. Their declines, like their ascensions, were historically caused. Students who have thought about such matters become more thoughtful citizens—not only of their own country but of the world.

FOCUSED BIBLIOGRAPHY

Jared Diamond, *Guns, Germs, and Steel* (NYC: Norton, 1997), has been annotated in the text above. If Diamond "hooks" you, read the chapter on him in James Blaut, *Eight Eurocentric Historians* (NYC: Guilford, 2000), for a critique.

John M. Hobson, *The Eastern Origins of Western Civilisation* (Cambridge, UK: Cambridge UP, 2004). Hobson tells how Europe combined ideas from India, China, and North Africa to construct its "Age of Exploration."

William H. McNeill, *The Age of Gunpowder Empires, 1450–1800* (DC: AHA, 1989). This pamphlet tells how Europe's development of cannons and other weapons gave Western nations hegemony. More for world history than U.S. history.

Lynn Townsend White Jr. (1960), "Tibet, India, and Malaya as Sources of Western Medieval Technology," *American Historical Review* 65 #3, 515–26 [517]. White shows that Europe adopted inventions not only from China, but from other Asian countries as well, then modified them, sometimes changing them into new forms.

CHAPTER 7

The $24 Myth

HISTORY AND SOCIAL STUDIES TEACHERS in middle and high school face a challenge that most math and English teachers do not: they must undo the damage done to their discipline (and to their students) in elementary school. Instead of teaching what happened, elementary teachers sometimes present anecdotes that did not and could not have happened. These myths rarely get put right in high school, so students go out into the world having learned things that are flatly wrong. We shall look at one example, the imaginary purchase of Manhattan by the Dutch from the Indians in 1626.

I have asked audiences across the United States, "What was the most important purchase in the history of the U.S. ever made for the exact sum of $24, in fact for $24 worth of beads?" Across the U.S., they chorus, "Manhattan." Acquaintance with this fable is hardly limited to the East Coast. Asked, "Did you learn this 'fact' in college? In graduate school?" they chorus, "No." Most think they were first exposed to this information in elementary school.

Only once did an audience let me down. I was speaking at Laredo Community College in Laredo, Texas. Both the school and the town are about 95% Mexican and Mexican American.[1] When I asked for the most important purchase made for $24 worth of beads, dead silence was the response. I saluted my audience for their ignorance for, as with the flat Earth tale, knowing nothing put them well ahead of most of their contemporaries. As Native novelist Michael Dorris put it, when learning about Native Americans "one does not start from point zero, but from minus ten."[2] Then I changed the subject.

DECONSTRUCTING THE $24 MYTH

In retrospect, I erred. Because so many Americans know the $24 myth, students need to know it, too, if only to inoculate themselves against encountering and believing it later on. It also provides a fine opportunity to show a class how our educational system teaches students material that is not even plausible. This happens particularly when our popular culture and public history convey the same inventions.

In Battery Park at the southern tip of Manhattan, at the exact spot where this deal never took place, stands the monument presented here. It incorporates a huge flagpole, and on its base is a bas-relief showing the transaction. It states in part, "The purchase of the Island of Manhattan was accomplished in 1626. Thus was laid the foundation of the City of New York." The monument was given to the city "by the Dutch people" in 1926, exactly three centuries after the transaction never happened.

The sculptor himself made two errors. Analyzing them can lead students into critiquing the whole story. Show students the picture and ask them what's wrong. If they don't respond, invite them to think about it overnight.

The alleged purchase of Manhattan for $24 worth of beads. It's hard to believe that one scene can get so many things wrong.

Usually, the first mistake students find has to do with the headdress. Around the world, the prototypical Native American is a Plains Indian warrior on horseback, complete with eagle feather headdress. Plains Indian culture was indeed a dramatic and colorful syncretic development. So this statue offers another opportunity to teach syncretism. Apaches, Crows, Comanches, and other Natives combined elements of their own cultures with ideas about horsemanship from the Spanish—including horses themselves—to form something new.

Plains Indian culture began in the Southwest, when Pueblo Indians learned about horses and horsemanship from the Spanish who temporarily conquered them. After the Pueblo revolt of 1680, Pueblo Indians traded horses to Dineh people (Apaches and Navajos), who in turn traded with Comanches and Utes. Slowly horses and ideas about horsemanship moved up the Plains and the eastern slope of the Rockies toward Canada. Some bands of Sioux (Dakotas), the prototypical Plains Indians, did not get horses until about 1770.

From Apaches and Comanches north to Sioux and Nez Perce, Native Americans adapted the horse to their hunting and gathering lifestyles. Horses allowed the development of tepees, much larger than the previous structures that dogs and women had carried or pulled. Indeed, horses made hunting and gathering so much easier that sedentary groups like the eastern Sioux abandoned agriculture for the new Plains culture and moved west from Wisconsin and Minnesota onto the Plains. Consider this description of the flowering that followed, from a diary entry on May 24, 1855, by Lt. Lawrence Kip of the U.S. Army, describing the entrance of a long file of Nez Perce into Fort Walla Walla, Washington:

> They were almost entirely naked, gaudily painted and decorated with their wild trappings. Their plumes fluttered about them, while below, skins and trinkets of all kinds of fantastic embellishments flaunted in the sunshine. Trained from early childhood almost to live upon horseback, they sat upon their fine animals as if they were centaurs. Their horses, too, were arrayed in the most glaring finery. They were painted with such colors as formed the greatest contrast; the white being smeared with crimson in fantastic figures, and the dark colors streaked with white clay. Beads and fringes of gaudy colors were hanging from the bridles, while the plumes of eagle feathers interwoven with the mane and tail fluttered as the breeze swept over them.[3]

Minus the horse, this is the image our Manhattan statue presents.

An eagle feather headdress works fine on a horse on the dry plains of eastern Washington. Walking about in the woods of Manhattan, a tree branch would have knocked it off within seconds. Not only is this statue off by at least 2,000 miles, it is also anachronistic. The year it celebrates, 1626, predates the heyday of Plains Indian culture by almost a century. The rise and fall of the Plains culture took less than 150 years, showing how fast cultures can develop when syncretism takes place.

Depicting a Plains Indian in New York is certainly wrong, but students have to know something to notice the error. At the least, they need to know that New York was (and but for interference by people still is) forested. It also helps if they understand that the prototypical American Indian is a Plains Indian. Teachers can supply hints and leading questions to help students catch this mistake.

The other problem with the statue requires no special knowledge. Nevertheless, it is often invisible to modern American eyes. If no one notices it, I say, "You know, I've been in New York City in August, and if this purchase that never took place took place in August, that is one hot Dutchman." Audiences snicker. If no one volunteers what is wrong, I continue, "I've also been in New York City in January, and if this purchase that never took place took place in January, that is one cold Indian." Again, I challenge them: "What am I driving at?" Someone will volunteer that the dress is inappropriate. They're right: no two people ever dressed like that at one point on the Earth's surface on the same day. So ask students why the artist did it. Hopefully they will realize that the sculptor never tried to depict the scene as it actually might have taken place. Instead, he presented a "primitive Indian" and "civilized Dutchman." Clothing helps to convey "civilized." Nearly naked connotes "primitive."

Not just sculptors but textbook authors, too, equate mostly naked with primitive. One textbook describes Columbus's 1492 arrival this way: "Who were these people who greeted them on the shore? They were practically naked. They were not dressed in fancy silk robes and jewelry. . . ." The book is right that the Indians were practically naked. Today many Europeans in Haiti are practically naked Club Med vacationers. It's a warm country. Being naked doesn't mean one lacks sophistication or culture.

Without hints, most students do not immediately see the absurdity of the paired costumes. It is worth taking time to discuss why not. Maybe it is because we've grown so used to the convention. Hollywood repeatedly used the same conceit, especially in older Westerns. In the more recent IMAX documentary, *Grand Canyon: The Hidden Secrets*, a Spaniard "discovers" the canyon in 1540. He is dressed much like the Dutchman, but wearing a suit of armor besides. A nearly naked Native American leads him to it. As it happens, I have been in the canyon in January and July. I can attest that if the moviemakers shot that scene in January, they had to treat the actor playing the Indian for frostbite as soon as they finished, while if they filmed in July, they had to cool down the man playing the Spaniard to avoid heatstroke.

What else is wrong with this little fable? Let's start with the price. So far as I know, the only evidence for the purchase of Manhattan written at the time is one sentence in a letter by Peter Schagen, 11/5/1626: "They have purchased the Island Manhattes from the Indians for the value of 60 guilders." Russell Shorto notes that a Dutch soldier was paid 100 guilders annually at the time. In 2008 a soldier in the U.S. Army got about $8,500 per year. So 60 guilders would be about $5,000 in 2008.[4]

The $24 figure turns out to be arbitrary and bogus. Schoolchildren have learned it for decades anyway. My father learned the $24 story in school—in 3rd grade, he guessed. That would be 1911. I learned it in 2nd grade, I think, which would be 1949. Last October, elementary schoolchildren learned it anew. Even if $24 equaled 60 guilders in 1626, it did not equal $24 in 1911, 1949, or today. Abraham Lincoln bought his home in Springfield, Illinois, in 1844, for $1,200. He did add a second story to it, but the original home would probably sell today for about $100,000— 83 times as much.[5] If $24 was the price of Manhattan in 1844 dollars, it would have been maybe $2,000 today. This $24 for Manhattan is the only figure in the Western world that has never been touched by inflation! Just like the clothing, this makes no sense, as soon as one thinks about it. A few well-placed questions can set students researching how prices have changed, so they can achieve this "aha moment" themselves.

Then there's the beads. So far as historians can tell—the documentary evidence is almost nonexistent—beads and trinkets were not involved. What the Native Americans wanted and could not make themselves were principally five items: steel axes; steel knives; metal kettles, which they used as kettles but also made things from; guns; and brightly colored woolen blankets. For perhaps $2,400 worth of such trade goods, the Dutch bought the rights to Manhattan, probably from the Canarsies.

A MORE ACCURATE STORY

Students can go to New York City today and take the subway to Canarsie. They can do so in cyberspace at urbanrail.net/am/nyrk/nyc-map.htm. When they come out, they are in Brooklyn. Indeed, they are in east Brooklyn, at the end of the line. That's where the Canarsies lived. Why wouldn't they sell Manhattan? No doubt the Canarsies were as pleased with the deal as the legendary New Yorker who sold the Brooklyn Bridge to some later hapless tourist, for they got paid for something that wasn't theirs in the first place.

The Dutch didn't really care. They used the transaction to legitimize their presence to the next English ship that came by. The deal also made allies of the Canarsies, who otherwise might have joined with the British or with other nearby American Indian tribes. The Weckquaesgeeks, who actually lived on Manhattan and owned much of it, were not so pleased.[6] They warred sporadically with the Dutch for years, until finally, around 1644, in Kieft's War, perhaps with help from the Canarsies, the Dutch exterminated the Weckquaesgeeks as a tribe. Survivors fled to what is now Westchester County.[7]

At this point, students confront two very different accounts. The first tells how a tribe chose to sell their village or villages to some newcomers for $24 worth of beads—symbolized in the strands between the two figures on the monument. Second is the Canarsie/Weckquaesgeek story. As students weigh the likelihood of each story, two primary sources—images from the time—can help. On the web, they can find a John White watercolor of a Native village in northeastern coastal North Carolina, painted between 1585 and 1590.[8] White's are the best portraits we have of how eastern American Indians lived before much European contact. Being farther north, the Indians on Manhattan may have been somewhat less agricultural but probably lived in villages much like those portrayed by White.

Then students can apply *verstehende* to the founding of New York City. The first story asks us to believe that Native Americans would give up their villages, gardens, fields, burial ground, and gathering and hunting rights throughout Manhattan, in exchange for some strings of beads. Would they (students)? Invite students to imagine they were the Native depicted on the bas-relief. After they put on warmer clothing (assuming the Dutchman is not crazy and it's not summertime), what would they do on the day after they made their bargain for the beads? Pack and move, of course, but to where? New Jersey? People already live there, so they'll have to fight or negotiate with them before moving in. When they do, what next? They'll face at least a year of hard work—clearing new fields, building new houses, planting new gardens. All for a few beads?

Of course, students today did not grow up on Manhattan around 1600, so they cannot know for sure how Native Americans of that era would have thought or acted. Notwithstanding that problem, as a first approximation it seems reasonable to project ourselves back into their moccasins. Certainly it's reasonable to assume that people everywhere want a good life for themselves and their children.

The second image is a map of New Amsterdam, made in 1660 or earlier.[9] Many students won't even need this image, because they already have a bit of information that can help them judge these two accounts. Surely the most famous street in the U.S. is Wall Street, laid out in an east-west arc across Manhattan at the northern edge of New Amsterdam. Just north of it ran the wall the Dutch built to keep out attacks by the Weckquaesgeeks. If Natives had honestly sold their land—whatever the price—why would the Dutch need to build a wall across the whole island? In the back of our minds, Americans have always known what that wall was for, hence that the taking of Manhattan wasn't just this happy little fable.

Indeed, asking students which account is more credible insults their intelligence. As soon as they subject it to scrutiny, the bead story falls apart. Its obvious falsity raises another question: Why, then, do teachers persist in teaching it?

FUNCTIONS OF THE FABLE

One way to approach this question is to think about what the story accomplishes. Sometimes the way in which a cultural element functions is more important than whether it is true or false. Moreover, the $24 story mythologizes much more than the taking of one small island. Excepting specialists, most Americans have no idea how "we" got our other islands, such as Martha's Vineyard, Nantucket, the islands in the Great Lakes, or Long Island and Staten Island, for that matter. The $24 myth is supposed to symbolize the taking of much of a continent. Indeed, just like the Dutch, European Americans repeatedly paid the wrong tribe or paid off a small faction within a much larger nation. Often, like the Dutch, they didn't really care. Such fraudulent transactions might even work better than legitimate purchases, for they set one tribe or faction against another while providing the newcomers with the semblance of legality to stifle criticism.

The biggest single purchase from the wrong tribe took place in 1803, when Jefferson "doubled the size of the United States by buying Louisiana from France," as all the textbooks put it. With just a little guidance, students can critique the map of the Louisiana Purchase in their own textbook. These maps invariably also show the route taken by Lewis and Clark in their famous expedition to the Pacific Northwest. This makes sense: the one followed the other, and the geography is the same. Unfortunately, these maps all portray "Spanish land," "French land," "British land," and sometimes "Russian land"—never "American Indian land." William Clark's own map of the trip is quite different. He reveals the people who lived there, whose land it was.[10] Well he should, after all, because the Lewis and Clark expedition relied on contact, guidance, and help from each Native group in turn, from the Mandans in what is now North

"If you think buying Manhattan for $24 was a bargain... take a look at what I bought!"

"How! I'll tell you How. Frank called me, he works for a company that barters television time for merchandise. He bought 180,000 pair of leather slippers from the most famous maker of cold weather slippers and was having a hard time finding a buyer. They usually barter with the major television users for food or hardgoods like televisions or lawnmowers...he didn't understand sizes and colors and he didn't know what they were worth...but I did. I offered him a price that I thought would be a starting point in the negotiations and he took it! What a deal for me and for you."
                                    - Judy Campion, Shoe Buyer

WHEN WE BUY BETTER...YOU BUY BETTER!

Students can collect references to the $24 story in our culture, such as this ad for shoes in a 1998 North Carolina newspaper. On the web, many sites refer to this conceit. Finding them will convince students that this is a cliché that cartoonists and marketers take for granted—part of our culture's common "knowledge." So is the joke about selling the Brooklyn Bridge, and students can find many references to this joke as well, including cartoons. The butt of the bridge joke is always the naïve tourist, who does not know that the seller has no rights to what he sells. Here, that would be the Dutchman. The Dutchman is not the butt of the $24 story, however. That would be the naïve resident, the Native American, who does not know that he is being swindled. What gets defined as funny and whose behavior gets defined as hapless depends on who holds the power today.

Dakota to the Clatsops on the Pacific coast. Students then may choose to ask the publisher why their textbook left Native Americans off the map of the Louisiana Purchase and Lewis and Clark Expedition.

Not one textbook points out that this vast expanse was not France's to sell—it was Indian land. Indeed, France did *not* sell Louisiana Territory for $15 million. France sold the land it did control—most of the present state of Louisiana—and its claim to the watershed of the rivers that flow into that land. In short, France sold the European *claims* to Louisiana Territory. To treat France as the real seller, as all our textbooks do, is Eurocentric. Students can prove this themselves. They can catalog the many Indian wars the United States fought in Louisiana Territory from 1819 to 1890 to take it from its real owners, the Native Americans. They can also compile a list of our treaties with and payments to Native American tribes to buy the territory. These total far more than what the U.S. paid France for the European rights.[11]

Sometimes how a cultural element works is more important than whether it is true or false. The $24 myth has at least two important effects. Students readily come up with both. First, it makes Native Americans look stupid. Twenty-four dollars won't buy a postage-stamp-sized plot of land in Manhattan today. Those idiotic Indians! They didn't know what they were doing! Second, it legitimizes the taking. We can infer that we didn't really take the land or invade the continent. We bought it, fair and square (it didn't cost much, either). Thus, the $24 myth sets us up to accept the idea that acquiring Native lands was never very problematic. In reality, how European Americans got the country remains very problematic. The U.S. and its predecessor colonies took other people's lands, uprooted their cultures, and moved them hundreds of miles in some cases, in the process killing and enslaving some tribes. Then it kept them from acculturating and succeeding in our society. It's hard to face these facts. We find the $24 tale much more comforting.

Surely these functions and the sense of entitlement and moral and intellectual superiority they engender help explain why the story still gets passed on, even though it's so obviously absurd. At this point, however, it's important to consider who is "we" in the previous paragraph. Literally, it is everyone *but* Native Americans. They cannot possibly embrace this anecdote. An experience resulting from the very first classroom use of *Lies My Teacher Told Me* shows their response to this kind of history. In the fall of 1991, while working on that book, I taught a special topics course at the University of Vermont titled "The Sociology of Social Studies: Lies My Teacher Told Me." Doing so allowed me to get undergraduate and graduate student feedback on chapters of my book, which I handed out in draft form. Unbeknownst to me, one student—we'll call him Bill—who planned to be an elementary school teacher, used one chapter as the basis for his practice teaching that semester. He was observing a class of 3rd graders taught by a master teacher in Swanton, in the northwest corner of the state. Later in the semester, under her supervision, he was to teach the class himself for a week. Intrigued by the chapter in the book titled "The Truth About the First Thanksgiving," and knowing it would be late November when he took over the class, Bill decided to make that chapter the basis for his practice teaching unit.

He ran the idea past his coordinating professor at the university. Shamefully, that person advised against it: "Too likely to draw parental complaints." Then Bill brought the idea to the teacher he was working under in Swanton. She saw no problem, so he went ahead and planned his unit. November came. Bill took over the class. As soon as he announced the topic of his unit, one pupil, seated toward the back of the room, put his head down on his desk and clamped hands over both ears. Bill walked over, seeking to learn the source of the boy's manifest alienation, only to elicit the following sentence: "My father told me the real truth about that day and not to listen to any white man scum like you!" The boy looked white but was not—he was a member of the Abenaki nation. Luckily, Bill was not teaching the usual Thanksgiving claptrap and could explain this to the pupil and bring him back into participation with the class. But that episode shows how the usual tripe that we teach about Native Americans, such as the $24 myth, offends them. Indeed, I think stories like these put off everyone who is not in the in-group. The alienation of non-Indians is more subtle, to be sure, but real enough. It helps explain why nonwhites and nonaffluent white students perform so much worse in history than in other subjects.

OVERT RACISM?

At this point, it's useful to peel one more layer off the onion. The $24 story is obviously false—a polite way of saying "a lie." Students can think about whether telling it makes teachers liars, and if so, are they lying on purpose? As I recall, Miss Elliot, my 2nd-grade teacher, taught me the story. Why did she do so? Because it is true? No, the story cannot withstand a moment of thoughtful scrutiny, so that cannot be the reason.[12] Did she teach it to convince her pupils—25 white children in central Illinois—that they were smarter than Native Americans? Did she wake up one October morning and ask herself, "How can I make them more white supremacist today? I know! I'll teach them that $24 myth!" My audiences don't think she had any such motive, at least consciously. Asked this way, students readily suggest that Miss Elliot—and their own 2nd-grade teachers—were just thoughtlessly passing on something they had learned.

After the Civil Rights Movement of the 1960s, followed by the American Indian Movement in the 1970s, overt white supremacy has gone out of style, in education as elsewhere in society. Many textbook authors used to imply that Native Americans were less intelligent than Europeans. Only a handful still do. Now they tell of a tragic misunderstanding. Native Americans no more imagined that people could buy or sell land than that they could buy or sell air. Air is for us all, of course. Our in-taken breath is our own, of course, but only while we are using it; then we expel it and it is everyone's again. So it is with land.

This claim turns out to be bogus as well. Native Americans held roughly similar views about land ownership as European Americans. They thought they could keep all their land, keep part of it, or sell part or all of it. They did not think members of their tribe could do this individually, but a village or tribe could do as it wished. Natives also thought they could retain certain privileges when they sold land, such as the right of free passage. So did European Americans. Until very recent years, for that matter, access to undeveloped land was usually considered public, within limits of good conduct. Even today, the public still can walk, hunt, and fish on undeveloped land, unless clearly posted otherwise. Moreover, tribal negotiators often made sure that deeds and treaties explicitly reserved hunting, fishing, gathering, and traveling rights to Native Americans.[13] There was no tragic misunderstanding.

Before we completely absolve Miss Elliot and textbook authors from the charge of racism, we do need to define the term. Racism means treating people unfavorably because of their racial or cultural group membership. The dialect that Margaret Mitchell uses for black characters throughout *Gone with the Wind* provides a classic example. We all speak in dialect. Most of us use the term "Iminna," for example. You might say to a friend, "After I finish this chapter, Iminna have a beer." We never write English like that, however, not even when writing dialogue. In an essay, novel, or memoir, we would probably write, "After I finish this chapter, I am going to have a beer," even though no one has ever pronounced that sentence so well. To connote informality, we might write, "After I finish this chapter, I'm going to have a beer." Not Mitchell—not when she is dispensing black speech. Here is Mammy, berating Scarlett:

> "Is de gempmum gone? Huccome you din' ast dem ter stay fer supper, Miss Scarlett? Ah done tole Poke ter lay two extry plates fer dem. Whar's yo' manners?"[14]

This is almost unreadable. But is it racist?

The answer is, yes. Years of residence in Dixie taught me—indeed, just a few days sufficed—that people from a given area usually talk a lot like others from that area. Most Southerners, both black and white, do say "tar" when they mean "tire," for instance. But Mitchell subjects only black speakers to the indignity of dialect. Southern *whites* seem to talk just fine. Mitchell even goes so far as to have her black characters say "wuz" for "was"—"I wuz awful tard," for example, instead of "I was awfully tired." Not only would a white Southerner also say "tard," *all* Americans say "wuz" for "was." "Was" is correctly pronounced "wuz." To write it that way for blacks, but not for whites, is a perfect example of treating people unfavorably because of their racial or cultural group membership.

Sociologists identify three types of racism: individual, institutional, and cultural. Most Americans are familiar with the notion of individual racism. For example, as Chapter 4 told, while enrolled at Smith College, an infuriated Margaret Mitchell got herself transferred to another history class because her first class included a black student.[15] Individual racism does not require such an element of racial animus, however. William Levitt's firm, Levitt & Sons, was by far the largest homebuilder in America after World War II, building perhaps 8% of all postwar suburban housing. Levitt flatly refused to show or sell to African Americans. Huge suburbs like Levittown on Long Island wound up all-white as a result. Yet Levitt claimed he was not racist. He only maintained his all-white policy to avoid offending white buyers; it was all strictly business. He even kept Jews out of some of his developments—and he was Jewish![16]

Institutional racism—unfavorable treatment by a social institution of a group of people, based on group membership—often not only has no racist animus behind it but sometimes has no element of intent at all. That would be true for the SAT, which discards items that are favorable to African Americans by a statistical process, as Chapter 2 showed.

Perhaps most deep-seated of all, deeper even than the psychic racism of a KKK leader like David Duke, is cultural racism. This is the ideology that one race is superior to others, expressed in etiquette, religion, law, in terms built into the language, and in countless other elements of our culture. The $24 story is an example. Soft-pedaling the invasion intrinsically entails making fools of Native Americans today. At the very least, how could Natives lose their continent to such nice folks? Specifically, how could they be so stupid as to haplessly welcome the Pilgrims? Or throw away Manhattan for $24 worth of beads?

Retelling the $24 myth to children today exemplifies cultural racism. Note that I do not use the "r word" to smear Miss Elliot. Any of us could be Miss Elliot. Rather, students need to come to three realizations: first, our culture contains elements of ongoing white supremacy. Second, these elements typically (always?) involve bad scholarship. And third, learning more accurate history gives students tools with which they can change our culture to make it more just and more factual.

Happily, most U.S. history courses are scheduled so that students can confront the $24 myth and other misinformation about Native Americans early in the school year. Students should leave the $24 myth aware that it stands for a larger class of misinformation. Until recently, for example, textbooks provided unreasonably low estimates of Native populations before Columbus arrived. "It was a virgin continent," went their phrase. As with the $24 tale, low estimates make for a more genial account of how "we" won the continent. Spending time deconstructing the $24 myth can help students see through all the rosy accounts our textbooks provide. Thus, it pays dividends throughout the year.

ADDITIONAL CONSIDERATIONS

Coupled with the problems discussed in the two prior chapters, students can now appreciate that all history education—not just that about Native Americans—is drenched in inertia. The $24 myth exemplifies a class of tales that teachers and textbooks usually pass on without checking their truthfulness or understanding their hidden agendas. If teachers are comfortable with them and do not question them, they are likely to pass on stories with no basis in fact. This is especially likely if the material is in line with our national ethos. Thus, the next generation may grow up racist and ethnocentric even while trying not to.

Sociologists teach us that education is largely socialization, especially in the early grades. Socialization is the process of passing on the culture so children can take part in society. It is so basic as to include toilet training—a requirement in any society—as well as "The Star-Spangled Banner." There is nothing wrong with socialization. On the contrary, the well-being of society and the individual depends upon it. Some conflict persists between the goals of socialization and education, however, at least as the latter is usually defined. *Random House Webster's Unabridged Dictionary*, for example, defines education as the "process of imparting or acquiring general knowledge, developing the powers of reasoning and judgment, and generally of preparing oneself or others intellectually for mature life." Teaching and learning the $24 story fits uneasily under such a heading, especially since it is not true.

Perhaps "mature life" offers a useful way out. Students relish being treated as mature. When informed that in their earlier schooling they have been told fantasies and partial truths, but now they are old enough to find out the true story for themselves, they jump at the chance. In a meta-conversation about the learning of history, students rarely say that if they learn about bad past acts of the U.S., they will become disloyal citizens. On the contrary, they aver that such learning motivates them to make the U.S. better. The $24 story can trigger that meta-conversation. Students may also find useful the distinction between patriotism and nationalism that was drawn in the first chapter. A true patriot rebukes rather than excuses a nation for its sins. A nationalist rebukes anyone who points out the nation's sins. Learning the $24 story may help create blind nationalists but cannot produce thoughtful patriots.

Regarding Native Americans, the antiracist idealism that can result from deconstructing the $24 myth will wither away if the only outlet students can see for it is to give Manhattan back to the Weckquaesgeeks. That's not going to happen. As poet Maya Angelou put it, "History, despite its wrenching pain, cannot be unlived."[17] History is not a movie that we can reel backward. Redress must come in the present, from this point forward. Much of what we teach and learn in elementary school social studies every October (around Columbus Day) and November (Thanksgiving) amounts to a continuing canard against Native Americans. Stopping that deceit is an important first step toward redress. At the very least, students will want to let their younger siblings in on the new information they're learning about Native Americans, Columbus, and so forth. They may want to challenge their elementary school teachers or a textbook that they now find inadequate.

Other acts students can take include questioning nearby high school or professional sports teams for their use of Indian names and symbols as mascots and logos. Students can also work to change names on our landscape that disrespect Native peoples, like Squaw Mountain or Heathen Meadows.[18] If a nearby historical marker presents bad history about Native people, perhaps because of its ethnocentric use of terms like "discover," "settler," "massacre," or "half-breed," students can agitate for a corrective.[19] Students can also examine library books on Native Americans intended for younger readers, suggest better books for librarians to buy, and insert in existing books critiques of them by Beverly Slapin, Doris Seale, or others.

When they take steps like these, students are using what they learn in their history course to engage in civic patriotism. No longer will they assert for a moment that history is irrelevant, a waste of time, or boring.

FOCUSED BIBLIOGRAPHY

In *Through Indian Eyes* (Berkeley, CA: Oyate, 2006, www.oyate.org), Beverly Slapin and Doris Seale review children's books and find many that display inhumane and incorrect portraits of American Indians.

CHAPTER 8

Teaching Slavery

ONE OF THE 30–50 TOPICS IN A COURSE IN U.S. history must be slavery. However, giving workshops at several plantation sites convinced me that many Americans of all races are uneasy teaching about slavery. Especially in middle school, teachers can find it hard to bring up. They don't want to embarrass their black students; they don't want to make white students feel guilty; so they just mention it in passing.

Unfortunately, minimizing slavery is treating slavery, and treating it incompetently. It implies that slavery is unimportant and can be underplayed without damaging our understanding of our nation's past. That is not true. Worse yet, we have seen how sugar-coating the European invasion of America amounts to ongoing racism against Native Americans. Similarly, downplaying slavery amounts to racism against African Americans and helps maintain white supremacy today. To avoid that, teachers have to teach slavery, regardless of their own racial background or that of their class.

RELEVANCE TO THE PRESENT

Every topic in a history course needs to be relevant to the present. Slavery certainly is. The cover of *U.S. News and World Report* for November 9, 1998, furnishes students with a nice way for them to see the relevance of slavery today. (True, 1998 is in a different millennium, but few students will claim that it is really a different era from the present.) Whether our third president and his attractive house slave did or did not have sex and produce children provided the lead story of a national newsmagazine two centuries later. That fact itself shows that slavery is relevant today.[1]

The cover also may point toward a deeper significance of slavery today. Asked "Is there anything wrong with this cover?" students usually stare silently for a while. Someone may suggest, "It has his picture but not hers." I reply, "Well, maybe that's defensible. After all, he was the third president of the United States. She wasn't. Besides, no image of her survives."

What's wrong
with this cover?

Sooner or later, someone notes the use of his last name and her first name. "Exactly," I reply. "Why doesn't it say 'Tommy and Sally'?" Students titter. "'Tommy' is disrespectful to the third president of the United States," I continue. "But if it's disrespectful to him, why isn't it disrespectful to her? To put this another way, Sally Hemings is one of the few African Americans of the eighteenth century whose last names we know. So why didn't the editors of *U.S. News and World Report* have the cover say 'Jefferson and Hemings'?"

Discussion follows. "The public would recognize 'Sally' faster than 'Hemings.'" "That's a good point," I reply. "Editors do want to sell magazines. They have but a moment to convince the public in an airport to buy their magazine, rather than a competitor's. But in turn, that just drives the question back one step: Why does the public recognize 'Jefferson and Sally'?" If there is a pause, I interject this comment:

Let's suppose someone in this class gets sick tonight after supper. Has to go to the emergency room. In the emergency room work two health care professionals —a doctor and a nurse. One of them keeps getting referred to by her first name. Who gets called by her first name—the doctor or the nurse?

Students chorus "the nurse," of course. Then they can give other examples of this phenomenon: a partner in a law firm and his secretary. The CFO of a corporation and the cleaning person who comes in to empty his waste-basket. Soon they generalize: the use of first versus last names encodes social status. Throughout this discussion, I deliberately use male pronouns for the higher positions. At some point, I ask who has noticed anything about my pronoun choice. I count out loud the number of students with hands up. It's worth noting how many people didn't notice, perhaps because we're still used to the doctor or executive being a male.

It's important to get students to volunteer the three dimensions on which Jefferson outranked Hemings. These are race, of course; sex or gender; and social class. To be blunt, Jefferson was in the highest status occupation of his day, large-scale plantation owner. As the Illinois 6th-grade teacher noted in Chapter 1, most presidents before Lincoln were of this occupation. Hemings, on the other hand, was in the lowest status position, slave, although the case could be made that as a house servant, she was higher than a field hand.

To this day, most Americans are far more likely to use first names for women and for African Americans than for men or for other racial groups. Compare "Oprah" and "Seinfeld," for example. It's not a hard-and-fast rule, and many women and African Americans play along—Winfrey certainly does. More importantly, to this day, as a result of slavery, most Americans still find it appropriate for white men to be on top of our institutions, while people of color are at the bottom. Like "Jefferson and Sally," this pattern just seems "natural." (That is why Obama's election is so important.) By "natural" we mean we're so accustomed to it that it's not something we think about. The faculty at Catholic University, for example, where I have a courtesy appointment, is profoundly white. Except one Chinese American sociologist, now deceased, I have yet to meet a single professor who is not white. I have also yet to meet a janitor or groundskeeper at the university who is not black or Latino. I have never heard anyone remark upon these starkly different ratios, however. They're just taken for granted.

If not for slavery, race would not make such a difference today. More professors would be nonwhite; more janitors would be white. The distance in social status and pay between professor and janitor might also be a bit narrower. If not for slavery, Americans would never take such different racial ratios for granted, either.

The foregoing example is anecdotal, of course. Stark, but anecdotal. The 2000 census showed that African American families made about two-thirds the median income of white families: $30,439, compared to $44,226. This alarming difference—not anecdotal in the least—summarizes the anecdotal realities of thousands of employers like Catholic University across the United States. Even worse is the wealth gap. While the income ratio is about two to three, the wealth ratio is far more severe, about one to eleven. That is, the median white family has 11 times as much wealth as the median black family. To some degree, this enormous wealth gap derives from the smaller income gap. A family making $30,000 can find it hard to save a dime. Meanwhile, a family making $44,000 can save $10,000 and still live better than the median black family.

According to sociologist Dalton Conley, however, "The wealth gap cannot be explained by income differences alone." Within any given income category, white families own much more than black families. For example, at the bottom of the spectrum (incomes less than $15,000 a year), the median African American family has a net worth of zero, while the median white family has $10,000 worth of equity. Intergenerational transfers provide the reason, Conley points out: "50% to 80% of lifetime wealth accumulation results from gifts from past generations of relatives: a down payment on a first home, a free college education, a bequest from a parent." In turn, by far the biggest single component of net worth for all families below the upper class is the equity they have built up in their homes over time.[2]

What role does slavery play in the wealth gap today? As Chapter 10 tells, between 1890 and 1940 racism increased in the United States. In the South, neo-Confederates were now securely back in the saddle, and they reimposed a racial hierarchy that was almost as rigid as slavery. If not for slavery, whites never would have done this. In the North, white Americans had acquiesced in the Southern removal of African Americans from citizenship, notwithstanding the 13th, 14th, and 15th amendments. Partly to rationalize this complicity, they, too, explicitly embraced white supremacy and defined African Americans as a pariah people to be avoided when possible. By 1940, even federal policy held that the races should be residentially separate.

Overlapping this era, beginning around 1900 and continuing to the present, suburbs grew. Keeping African Americans (and sometimes Jews and other groups) out of suburbs became the rule, not the exception. In such metropolitan areas as Los Angeles, Chicago, and Detroit, most suburbs did not allow black residents, except perhaps as live-in servants in white-owned homes. Even today, many whites think it "natural" for

African Americans to live in the inner city, whites in the outer suburbs. The whiteness of our suburbs is neither natural nor due to social class.[3] Only in the 1990s did many suburbs, such as Hemet, California; Cicero, Illinois; and Livonia, Michigan, begin to allow black residents. Excluded from suburbs of all social classes throughout most of the twentieth century and from the programs that financed home ownership in them, black families paid rent in the city. Meanwhile, white families paid off mortgages in the suburbs. Between 1949 and 1969, according to research by John Kain, suburban homes saw huge appreciation, providing the source of much of the wealth that many white families still have today. Since 1969, houses have continued to appreciate much faster than the consumer price index. Shut out not only from home ownership but also from the equity resulting from this appreciation, black families have had less to pass on to their children. In turn, this makes it harder for them to amass down payments. Today, 70% of nonblack families own their own homes, compared to just 47% among black families. Exclusion from suburbs in the past keeps African Americans from purchasing houses in the present. Indeed, today's residential segregation will still be affecting us in 2050, even if we end all exclusion tomorrow.[4] Again, if not for slavery, race would not make such a difference today.

For that matter, if not for slavery, people from Africa would not have been identified as a race in the first place. Nor would they have been stigmatized as an inferior race. Race as a social concept, along with the claim that the white race is superior to other groups, came about as a rationale for slavery. (Chapter 10 treats race as a social construct.) As Supreme Court Justice William O. Douglas famously put it in 1968, racism is a vestige of "slavery unwilling to die."[5]

Slavery's twin legacies for the present are the social and economic inferiority it conferred upon blacks and the cultural racism it spread throughout our culture. Slavery ended in 1863–65, depending upon where one lived. Unfortunately, racism, slavery's handmaiden, did not. It lives on, afflicting all of us today.

HOLD A META-CONVERSATION

Showing its relevance to the present is the first step in introducing a unit on slavery. The second step might be to hold a meta-conversation on the subject—a conversation about the conversations that the unit will generate. Such a meta-conversation is especially useful for teachers who have not given slavery much attention before. They can begin with an admission:

Until this year, my U.S. history classes did not give slavery enough attention. To some extent, this was not my fault. The textbook doesn't give slavery enough attention either, especially as a continuing problem in American life. Yet we have just seen that its effects are still a continuing problem in American life.

Or, without the admission:

My research in U.S. history—as well as things like this magazine cover (the *U.S. News and World Report* cover)—convince me that we have to cover slavery and its impact better than the textbook does.

Either way, students can be challenged to go beyond the textbook and learn more about slavery—and the racism that derived from it—on their own. "You will have to join me in going beyond the book to learn more about slavery. It's important. It might be interesting. Can you do that?"

One reason teachers give for avoiding much focus on slavery is concern about how their students will handle the subject. It is not a "feel-good" subject. Teachers of majority black classes may worry that all they will accomplish is making their students mad. Teachers of classes with only a handful of African Americans do not want these students to feel singled out. Teachers of all-white classes don't want parental complaints from students who think they are supposed to feel guilty.

Again, a meta-conversation can help. "Some people tell me that an all-black class cannot handle the subject of slavery because it will get too angry to do good history." After a pause, the teacher continues, "Is that accurate?" In the ensuing discussion, few students will agree. In the process of disagreeing with the premise, they are signing on to be other than angry, to study slavery and its impact seriously. Teachers can also ask, if anger *is* a reasonable response to learning the truth about slavery, what action should that anger lead to in the present? Surely the answer is, Students can identify and then counter vestiges of slavery that still linger in our society.

If the class is majority black while the teacher is not, that difference has to be acknowledged in the meta-conversation. "If I promise to be open to learning from your reactions—and from the information you bring in—can you learn from me on this topic? Even though I'm white? Are we in this together?" If the class is mostly white while the teacher is black, the meta-conversation will be different but still needs to be held.

Depending on class composition, teachers might introduce the meta-conversation with, "Some people tell me that an all-white class does not have enough variety of experience to handle the subject of slavery." Better still might be a line I came up with when I was teaching an early morning

5th-grade class in Stamford, Connecticut. That middle school is very diverse, with European Americans, African Americans, Haitian immigrants, millionaire parents, and students on the free lunch program. My assignment was to teach every social studies section in turn, until at the day's end I had reached the entire 5th grade. Before that first class, the assistant principal, who had engaged me, asked me, "Now, Jim, what do you plan to do with these students?" I replied with enthusiasm, showing her some of the images I was going to use, including some of the illustrations in this book.[6] "Oh, Jim, do you have to?" was her immediate response. I *did* have to, especially after that response, but I had never taught 5th graders before. So before I showed the first class a thing, I said to them, "You know, some people tell me that 5th graders are not mature enough to handle the images I'm about to show you." They rose to the occasion and handled the discussion just fine. So I repeated the ploy throughout the day. Teachers can similarly challenge their classes: "Some people say that 9th graders are not mature enough to handle the subject of slavery." They, too, will rise to the occasion.

The introduction to a unit on slavery needs to cover at least one other topic. I call it "racial nationalism." Simply put, none of us is responsible for anything that went on before we were born. That's a simple enough idea, and uncontestable. Nevertheless, there is a tendency for white Americans to take pride of ownership in, say, American democracy, or perhaps the music of J. S. Bach, or the architecture of Frank Lloyd Wright. Conversely, whites can feel guilty or defensive about the injuries and inequities of slavery, especially whites who can trace their U.S. lineage back to before the Civil War. Positive or negative, these feelings are examples of racial nationalism.

African Americans are not immune to this kind of thinking. Years ago, before there was Black History Month, there was Negro History Week, the week in February that included Abraham Lincoln's birthday. At the black college where I then worked, posters went up in celebration, typically saying:

NEGRO HISTORY WEEK
We ain't what we oughta be
We ain't what we're gonna be
But thank God almighty
We ain't what we was

An uplifting slogan, I suppose. Yet what "we was" was slaves, of course. So the poster incorporated a bit of shame, as well. Elements of that thinking are embodied in the color gradations that still linger to some degree within the black community. The black poet Paul Laurence Dunbar supplied another example of this kind of thinking in his poem "The Colored Soldiers," which ends:

> And their deeds shall find record
> In the registry of Fame,
> For their blood has cleansed completely
> Every blot of Slavery's shame.[7]

Dunbar was right: the actions of United States Colored Troops during the Civil War were often heroic. The "registry of fame" that he describes, however, shows racial nationalism. So does the "blot of Slavery's shame."

I find it hard to get rid of racial nationalism in my own mind. I still take an "in-group" kind of pleasure in the architecture of Frank Lloyd Wright, as if his excellence somehow implies something good about me as a white person. So I am quick to excuse it among students—but I still point it out to them and ask them to examine it at arm's length.

Students need to understand that to hold anyone responsible, today, for having been a slave, a slaveowner, or for slavery in general, is anachronistic.[8] A unit on slavery isn't about proving a group bad. A white person is not bad because some other whites, many decades ago, enslaved people. A black person is not bad because some other blacks, many decades ago, were slaves. Indeed, if a white student teases a black student today—"Your people used to serve my people"—or if a black student rages at a white student today—"You people have always been racist"—they themselves are displaying vestiges of slavery unwilling to die. At the end of the introductory metaconversation, students should know to chorus "no" when asked, "Is anyone in this classroom responsible for enslaving?" "Is anyone in this classroom responsible for being enslaved?" Finally, they should have useful ideas about slavery's impact on our past and present in response to the question, "Why, then, must we learn about slavery?"

SLAVERY AND RACISM

The main reason why it can still be hard to discuss slavery is that the nation still struggles with its legacy today. That legacy, already noted, is racism. Students must make this connection. They need to see that racism began as a rationale for slavery. If this is not clear, then all kinds of dangerous misinformation can fill this void. I have heard serious adults—teachers, social scientists, historians—say that whites are racist by nature—that is, genetically. Nonsense. No one is born with the notion that the human race is subdivided by skin color, let alone that one group is or should be dominant over the others. Racism is a product of history, particularly of the history of slavery.

Slavery had not always been caught up with race. Europeans had enslaved one another for centuries. The word itself derives from "Slav," the group most often enslaved by other Europeans before 1400. Native Americans and Africans likewise enslaved their neighbors long before Europeans arrived. Ethnocentrism has long existed among human groups. Many—perhaps all—societies have been ethnocentric. Saying "we're better than they" can rationalize enslaving "them." But then the enslaved grow more like us, intermarry with us, have children, and speak our language. Now ethnocentrism can no longer rationalize enslaving them. Neither can ethnocentrism unify people from different societies across cultural differences. Indeed, Europeans did not think of themselves as a group before the slow increase of racially based slavery beginning around 1400.

As Europeans sailed down the west coast of Africa, however, they traded with coastal tribes for captives from the interior. Slaves came to be more and more identified as dark-skinned Africans, and vice versa. Increasingly, whites viewed enslavement of whites, especially Christian whites, as illegitimate, while enslavement of Africans was acceptable, maybe even "good for them." Unlike in earlier slaveries, children of African American slaves would be slaves forever. They could never achieve upward mobility through intermarriage with the owning class. The rationale for this differential treatment was racism. Racism arose around 1400 to justify this permanent form of slavery.[9] As Montesquieu ironically observed in 1748: "It is impossible for us to suppose these creatures to be men, because, allowing them to be men, a suspicion would follow that we ourselves are not Christian."[10] Therefore, racism gradually increased in Western culture. At first, Europeans considered Africans exotic but not necessarily inferior. Shakespeare's 1604 depiction of Othello, derived from a story written in 1565 by Giovanni Battista Giraldi, still fits this description.[11] As more and more European nations joined the slave trade, followed by the United States, whites came to characterize Africans as stupid, backward, and uncivilized. Concurrently, they came to see themselves as "white," as well as civilized and intelligent.

The slave system in America changed over time. We have already noted a tendency in American popular culture and history textbooks to assume that things always progress. Slavery was *not* getting easier or nicer as decades passed in the nineteenth century. In the Upper South—especially Maryland, Virginia, and Kentucky—owners were increasingly finding that their biggest source of profit was people. So they split up families and sent children and young adults hundreds of miles away, to slave markets in Natchez, New Orleans, and Mobile. In the Deep South, these young slaves would clear land and grow cotton or cane sugar, destined never to see their parents or friends again. Meanwhile, cotton was becoming so profitable that Natchez claims to have had more millionaires per capita in 1860 than anywhere else in America. Of course, "King Cotton," as it was called, was planted, cultivated, and picked by unpaid labor. Egypt and India could not compete.

Nothing in the development of American slavery suggested it was on its last legs or would come to an end in the foreseeable future. On the contrary, slavery was growing more rigid. Between 1820 and 1860, several slave states passed new laws interfering with the rights of owners to free their workers. Some made it impossible to free slaves without getting them out of state. At the same time, some nonslave states required African Americans or their former owners to post huge bonds before they could enter. The legal position of already-free African Americans became ever more precarious. In 1859, Arkansas passed a law requiring all "free Negroes" to leave the state within the year or be enslaved. Several other states considered following suit. In the North, too, African Americans found life getting harder every year. Increasingly they were barred from voting, except in New England, and faced growing threats from slave catchers, even if they had never been enslaved.

Racism as an ideology intensified in the period 1830–1860, as slave-owners labored to justify slavery's injustice. Chapter 10 will suggest ways students can investigate America's increasing and decreasing levels of racism over time. By the 1850s, many white Americans, including Northerners, claimed black people were so hopelessly inferior that slavery was a proper form of "education" for them. After all, it removed them physically from the alleged barbarism of the "dark continent." The rise of racism as an ideology is a perfect example of cognitive dissonance (see Chapter 3). At some point, every course in U.S. history needs to give an explanation for racism. Unfortunately, few textbooks even try.[12]

Although textbooks mostly avoid the "r word," they do tell how slavery increasingly dominated our political life between 1830 and 1860, how the cotton gin made slavery more profitable, and how its ideology grew harsher. By the 1850s, Southern politicians no longer apologized for slavery as a necessary evil, the way Jefferson had. To get elected, they now had to claim that slavery was "of positive value to the slaves themselves," to quote one textbook.

Racism is thus a product of history. It is not innate or necessary. Students must never be allowed to say that it is without being contradicted— preferably by other students. Of course, showing how racism developed to rationalize slavery does not mean that whites adopted it consciously and hypocritically to defend the otherwise indefensible unfairness of slavery. Whites sincerely believed it. Indeed, Chapter 9 will show that most white Southerners came to view the 4 million African Americans in their midst as a potential menace, were slavery ever to end. Slavery had given rise to white supremacy as an ideology; between 1855 and 1865, white supremacy prompted a fierce defense of slavery.

FOUR KEY PROBLEMS OF SLAVE LIFE

To understand slavery, students need to understand the four key problems it posed to men, women, and children in bondage. First and most obvious was their lack of freedom. One day while walking toward the Library of Congress, where I was researching slavery, I spotted a squirrel ahead of me on the sidewalk, eating an acorn. Seeing me coming, he carried the acorn off to the middle of the street. There he sat, munching.[13] I thought him stupid—after all, Second St., SE, complete with a Federal Express dropoff store, is a fairly busy thoroughfare. Then I realized, stupid or not, the squirrel had the capability of making his own decisions. Deciding what to do is the basic condition not only of humankind, but of all thinking creatures.[14] Depriving people of this freedom is the basic *in*humanity or *un*naturalness of slavery. Slaves could not decide whether to work, or where or how, what to eat or when or how to eat it, or simply what to do from moment to moment.

Students need to grasp this indignity. Not for a moment should they buy into the idea that it might be nice to have someone else take care of someone, make all the tough decisions. It might—if that was what slavery was about and if one had granted them that authority. But slavery first and foremost stripped from people their ability to act. That is what "seasoning" was all about. An owner or overseer could tell a slave to sit, or stand, or how to sit, or to stand on one leg, and the slave had to comply. Defiance would be punished, sometimes by death, if it came to that.

Related to the removal of freedom was slaves' lack of control over their own family relationships and lives. Slavery was not a matter of someone else taking care of a person. On the contrary, slavery often forced slaves to be on their own even as children. In narrative after narrative taken down by the WPA in the 1930s, elderly African Americans tell of having their parents sold away from them as children and being unable to plan for the future. On many plantations, this anxiety peaked every year around Christmas, when some slaves were rented for a year to off-site employers beginning January 1. It might be a year or even more before husband saw wife or child saw parent again.

Near the end of her life, one African American in Maryland, "Old Elizabeth," recalled the impact of such a relocation on her:

> In the eleventh year of my age, my master sent me to another farm, several miles from my parents, brothers, and sisters, which was a great trouble to me. At last I grew so lonely and sad I thought I should die, if I did not see my mother. I asked the overseer if I might go, but being positively denied, I concluded to go without his knowledge. When I reached home my mother was away. I set off and walked twenty miles before I found her. I stayed with her for several days, and we returned together. Next day I was sent back to my new place, which renewed my sorrow. . . . On reaching the farm, I found the overseer was displeased at me for going without his liberty. He tied me with a rope, and gave me some stripes of which I carried the marks for weeks.[15]

Many slave weddings were sham ceremonies, conducted to foster the production of a "crop"—enslaved children—and to let owners feel they were fostering moral behavior among their slaves. Owners were not bound by the vows and frequently sold couples to different owners, thus ending the marriages. Some marriage vows even included the phrase, "'til death or distance do us part," taking note of the problem. Selling children away from parents was also common. Many enslaved persons valued their family relationships greatly, of course. An adult might refuse to work or hide out in a nearby forest or swamp until the owner agreed to let him or her see and even live with their partner again. When the Civil War disrupted and ended slavery, many newly freed people went to great lengths to find their partners and children, reestablish family ties, and marry spouses again, this time for real.[16]

Before 1863, most slaves had no control over their destinies and no way out of slavery, even for their children, no matter how hard they worked. A way to help elementary children see the unfairness of slavery is to enlist a group to play Monopoly, but with a rule change: except for one player (the "Owner"), none of them can own real property. They will participate happily for a few minutes, happy to play during school hours, until gradually they realize there is no point. The winner is foreordained, despite their best efforts. No strategy or tactics are even useful—just like slavery, for most enslaved participants.

The third problem slaves faced was violence. Paul Escott studied over 2,000 slave narratives that were recorded during the 1930s. He found that when interviewers asked ex-slaves to assess their owners, whipping was the most important single attribute to which they referred. Whippings could be life-shattering experiences. Consider this old black man in Texas in the 1930s, remembering a whipping he had received as a young boy, 70 years earlier: "I just about half died. I lay in the bunk two days, getting over that whipping—getting over it in the body, but not the heart. No, sir, I have that in the heart 'till this day." Some overseers then rubbed salt in the wounds. Escott found that about 70% of the slave narratives told of being whipped as slaves—and these narratives came from people who averaged perhaps ten years old when slavery had ended. Women and girls faced the special problem of forced sex by their owner, overseer, or a slave chosen for them as a likely breeding partner.

Overt resistance was never prudent and often not possible. Another old man told of the whipping given to his young sister 70 years earlier, who had accidentally broken a clock:

> My old marster took her and tied a rope around her neck—just enough to keep it from choking her—and tied her up in the back yard and whipped her I don't know how long. There stood mother, there stood father, and there stood all the children and none could come to her rescue.[17]

Some students—usually boys—find it hard to grasp the nature of outright coercion. "I would have done *something*," they insist. Such youthful exuberance is often to be applauded, but here it amounts to inadequate verstehende of the situation. Teachers can head off such responses by stating the problem to the class before it occurs. Invite students to invent or imagine demonstrations that would convince such a student that constraint in slavery posed a problem that mere strength of character could not overcome.

For example, the teacher might ask for one student to volunteer to be the "slave." She should choose an agreeable person, but an "alpha male" who is popular with his peers. She then tells him to stand on one leg—except that this exercise should be done hypothetically, not in reality. Students will probably agree that the student, especially if the teacher has singled out an agreeable person, would probably do as asked at first. But after 5 minutes? After the class is no longer watching but has moved on to other things? After putting the other leg down and getting yelled at for so doing? After it hurts? Students can further discuss why even this rather mild simulation of slavery had best be done as a mental experiment engaged in by the class, rather than an actual demonstration, lest the teacher get in trouble. Students can continue the mental experiment, predicting what might happen if the teacher kept the student standing to the end of the period and even beyond. They will understand that the student has resources. Parents, other students, other teachers, the principal, even the American Civil Liberties Union might play a role. Slaves had resources, too, including other slaves and perhaps other masters, but far fewer. The power imbalance tilted greatly toward their owners.

"Gordon" had been whipped on Christmas day, 1862. He then escaped from his Louisiana plantation and made his way to the U.S. forces that held most of the Mississippi River. There, an army officer photographed him, stripped to the waist for his physical examination. This is what a whipping looks like in slavery, some five months afterward. Gordon of course moved on, rising to corporal in the U.S. Army.

The fourth key problem of slave life was the sense of racial inferiority that most whites believed and many blacks half-believed. Much of the slavery system expressed extraordinary inequality along racial lines. Consider the seemingly uncomplicated matter of eating. Earlier I mentioned that many slaves were not allowed to decide for themselves how to eat their food. Fanny Kemble, who was married to a South Carolina planter, wrote that their "slaves mostly ate with crude wooden spoons or by using their fingers, as the children did." Archaeologist Teresa Singleton says that crews excavating slavery plantations have recovered so few spoons or forks as to suggest that this was how slaves ate on most plantations. This was not by choice. Many African Americans interviewed in the WPA collection complained about such practices. "The slaves had to eat with mussel shells for spoons," related a Mississippi woman, "and we sopped our gravy with our bread." Children had it still worse. On some plantations, planters had slave children eat from troughs, with or without wooden paddles or spoons. One former slave remembered:

> There was a trough out in the yard where they poured in mush and milk, and us children and the dogs would all crowd 'round it and eat together. We children had homemade wooden paddles to eat with, and we sure had to be in a hurry about it, because the dogs would get it all if we didn't.

Even without dogs, children often competed with each other for basic sustenance.

While their slaves ate like animals, the richest planters and their children ate like gods. Today dining tables at many plantation homes still display the elaborate serving dishes, fine china place settings, silver tableware, and crystal glasses that impressed visitors before the Civil War. Such splendor encouraged everyone, then and now, slaves and tourists alike, to believe that no ordinary mortals inhabited these halls. No, these were impressive elegant people who are worthy of our respect. Conversely, visitors then—and even to a degree enslaved people themselves—witnessing slave children tussling over their morning or evening meal, might conclude, "They eat like animals!" The contrasting scenes could reinforce the notion that slavery was right.

Viewed another way, the comparison reinforces the opposite conviction: such astounding inequality was deeply unjust. No slaves thought slavery just. Students can research spirituals dating back to slavery time and sing them or read them aloud together: "*Nobody* knows the trouble I've seen"; "Got hard trials in my way; Heaven shall be my home."

Nevertheless, students should not conclude that slaves were only victims. While blacks did sometimes buy into the notion that whites were superior, at other times they knew better. Some escaped and hung out in the woods for weeks to repay an owner for unfair treatment and negotiate better terms for the future. Some even escaped to Mexico, Indian tribes, the North, or Canada. Most enslaved people never had a good opportunity to escape, but they helped each other, from giving birth to funeral ceremonies. They developed sly stories and jokes in which African Americans got the best of their "masters." They resisted slavery in subtle ways (like doing bad work that had to be repeated), stole extra food (but not enough to be noticed), or became indispensable (to win better treatment). Some learned to read and informed themselves of political affairs. They built a religious faith that promised a better life to come. Simply staying alive, remaining sane, and retaining the hope of eventual freedom, whether in this life or in an afterlife, was a form of resistance to enslavement.

Although no analysis of slavery should suggest that whites had it rough, too, slavery did have at least four major problematic effects upon white culture. First, it gave rise to an anti-work ethic that persists to this day among some social strata in the plantation South. Under plantation ideology, hard work, especially manual labor, was looked down upon as "nigger work."[18] Second, slavery caused the slave system to become defensive and fear ideas. As slavery tightened between 1800 and 1860, just to *receive* abolitionist literature became a crime. During the Nadir, political orthodoxy reigned in the South as an outgrowth of white supremacy; to be anything other than a Democrat prompted suspicion. Third, as we noted, slavery led to racism among whites. Finally, as the next chapter will discuss, slavery led to distorted history.

ADDITIONAL PROBLEMS IN TEACHING THE HISTORY OF SLAVERY

Some teachers believe it is wrong to separate slavery as a topic. After all, it infused Thomas Jefferson's foreign policy, Andrew Jackson's Indian policy, our war with Mexico, and many other aspects of U.S. history from the colonial period to today. They have a point. However, at some point teachers need to help students think about the institution itself—what it was like, for all participants, how it changed, how people coped, why there were few open revolts. That is why I think slavery should be one of the 30–50 topics teachers choose to teach.

The remainder of this short chapter cannot outline all the themes and topics students need to understand. All three segments of the international slave trade deserve attention, not just the Middle Passage. Students should understand the extraordinary profits slavery made possible and the political clout resulting from this wealth. How enslaved people reacted—from resisting to running away to building whatever community they could—must be part of the story. In the space that remains here, let me treat three general problems that afflict most treatments of slavery: biased choice of verbs as applied to owners and slaves, the racism inherent in "soft" treatments of slavery, and downplaying the opponents of racism.

A pervasive problem in the literature (and at antebellum plantation homes, too) has to do with who does the work. Too often, the owner does. At the Edmonston-Alston House in Charleston, South Carolina, Charles Edmonston "built his residence," for example. Then "Alston modified the appearance of the house." In reality, neither Edmonston nor Alston laid hammer to nail. About clothing, the children's book *If You Grew Up with George Washington*, part of a series by Scholastic, puts it this way:

> If you were a slave, you would wear the plainest and the poorest clothes of all. The planter who owned you would give you your clothes.
> Every year the planter would give you a few new things to wear. But mostly your clothes would be old and raggedy.[19]

Planters "gave" slaves nothing. Slaves either made everything on the plantation, including their own clothing, or it was bought with proceeds from the sale of other things slaves made.

If You Grew Up with George Washington exemplifies another problem with slavery that students need to understand. It sounds like an enigma: racist portrayals of slavery can make slavery itself seem less racist. The most basic fact about slavery—that slaves were held against their will—goes unmentioned. *Gone with the Wind* exemplifies this "soft" treatment of "the peculiar institution." Why would almost all slaves abandon Tara if slavery there had been so nice? Mitchell never seems to notice the contradiction.

Since textbooks mystify and underplay the role of racism in our past, they have no alternative but to mystify and underplay the role of *anti-racism*. From the beginning of European settlement in the Americas, some people, including some whites, always opposed slavery. Their opposition must be part of the story of slavery. Otherwise, children may imagine that all whites were racist. Then European American children who still harbor some racial nationalism within their minds may think that they have no one of "their race" with whom to identify. Besides, opposition to slavery provides some ripping good stories.

Bartolomé de Las Casas famously opposed enslaving Native Americans. Almost as infamous is his approval for using African slaves to replace American Indian slaves. Not so well known is his change of heart. Writing of his earlier advice in the third person, Las Casas recanted completely, concluding "that black slavery was as unjust as Indian slavery":

> This advice to give a license for the bringing of black slaves to those lands was first given by the priest Casas, who was unaware of the injustice with which the Portuguese take them and make slaves of them. Later, after falling into this snare, he regretted it, and would not have given that advice for all the world, for he always believed they were enslaved unjustly and tyrannically, because they have the same right to freedom as the Indians.[20]

Maybe the high point of Las Casas's life came in 1542, when he took part in perhaps the most important trial ever to take place on Earth. Held at Valladolid, Spain, the issue was, Are Indians human beings, or are they some subordinate species, appropriate for slavery? Amazingly, Las Casas won, if only temporarily. Although Spain reneged and allowed slavery to return to its colonies, centuries after his death Las Casas was still influencing history. Simon Bolivar used his writings to justify the revolutions between 1810 and 1830 that freed Latin America from Spanish domination. Even today, Las Casas inspires movements for justice in Mexico and South America.[21]

A class might take on the assignment to build a Hall of Fame honoring opponents of slavery. Each student can find and choose a hero. Among

The fact that slavery was a penal system eluded me for years. This photograph of the cells attached to the Franklin and Armfield slave trading firm in Alexandria, Virginia, helped me see the light. On their home plantations, few slaves had to be kept under lock and key. There they had family ties, friendships, and routines that were hard to break. Moreover, rural life afforded few options for escape. White patrollers would challenge any African American traveling without a pass as a potential runaway. Keeping African Americans in slavery was always more of a problem in cities. The anonymity of urban life made it harder for whites to know whether a black person was free, rented out, or absent from their owner without leave. Many Southern hotels had rooms with barred windows and externally locked doors to draw the trade of owners traveling with a valet or coachman. Owners could lock their slaves in for the night, then retire to their own quarters secure in the knowledge that none could run away. Franklin and Armfield also provided this service for slaveowners visiting Alexandria, advertising "safe keeping at 25¢ per day."

the interesting people they can unearth from closer to our time are participants in the Underground Railroad like Levi Coffin, John Rankin, Row-
land Robinson, or Harriet Tubman; the unnamed slaves who revolted
at Destrehan Plantation, near New Orleans;[22] Edward Coles, a Virginia
planter who brought his slaves to Illinois, freed them, and took the lead
in keeping Illinois from becoming a slave state; Harriet Jacobs, who wrote
Incidents in the Life of a Slave Girl; Osceola, Seminole leader; Elijah Lovejoy,
killed in Alton, Illinois; the Grimké sisters, banished from South Carolina
for their abolitionist views; U.S. spy Elizabeth Van Lew of Richmond; political leaders like Owen Lovejoy, Charles Sumner, and Thaddeus Stevens;
Cassius Clay (not the boxer!); and many others.

Many antiracists in our past lost. Andrew Jackson is on our $20 bill, while
the Whigs who opposed his forced removal of the Indians from the Southeast lie forgotten. Many opponents of slavery left a record, however. Students can bring them back to life. Above and below the Mason-Dixon Line,
families participated in the Underground Railroad. Students can tell their
stories, based on careful research.[23] Almost every community in the slave
states had Unionists during the Civil War. Their stories are important.

Every student needs to learn about white antislavery activists like
Coles and Van Lew. Then none can graduate thinking that all whites were
racist. All students—especially white Southerners—need to have anti-
Confederate and antiracist white Southerners available as role models.
Every student needs to learn about black antislavery activists like Jacobs
and the Destrehan slaves. Then none can graduate thinking blacks accepted slavery and did nothing about it.

To address the issue of racism in our time, Americans must acknowl-
edge the importance of slavery in our past. "Those plantations were not
some sideshow," says Edward Ball, author of *Slaves in the Family*. "This
was the trunk of American history, from which the current society has
grown."[24] The next two chapters show the lingering influence of slavery
even to our time.

FOCUSED BIBLIOGRAPHY

Julius Lester pulls no punches in *To Be a Slave* (NYC: Dial, 1968). Even
more valuable than the paragraphs he extracted from the WPA narratives
are his own italicized analytic comments.

George Rawick got the WPA narratives published. In 1972, before the
Web (where they are now available, at archives.gov), this was important.
In *From Sundown to Sunup* (Westport, CT: Greenwood, 1972), Rawick gives
a good introduction to slavery.

Ira Berlin, *Many Thousand Gone* (Cambridge: Harvard UP, 1998), offers a solid general overview of American slavery and how it changed over time.

In the first pages of *The Slave Community* (NYC: Oxford UP, 1979), John Blassingame tells of whites enslaved in northern Africa. This helps readers see that "slave behavior" is not racial.

Slavery Remembered by Paul Escott (Chapel Hill: U of NC P, 1979) is based on the WPA narratives. Escott mostly just applied simple arithmetic to them, as students could do, yet the result is a fine book.

In *My Bondage and My Freedom* (Google Books, books.google.com/books?id=QPNdgtQ1P64C&printsec=frontcover&dq=%22My+Bondage+and+My+Freedom%22&ei=Cd8ESYrqOqDKzQTE35SbAg#PPA78,M1, 10/2008 [1857]), Frederick Douglass offers a remarkably balanced account of life in bondage. Thoughtful students can see the erosion of the family, prohibition against meaningful conversation across racial lines, and other subtle aspects of slavery that dehumanize both parties.

The essay on Maryland in Loewen, *Lies Across America* (NYC: Simon & Schuster, 2000), is my best short statement on what is essential for teachers to know and teach about slavery.

Steven Mintz, "Digital History," digitalhistory.uh.edu/modules/slavery/index.cfm, 7/2008, offers information for teachers on many topics of U.S. history, including slavery. However, some information is wrong or misleading, so use with care.

CHAPTER 9

Why Did the South Secede?

BEFORE THE CIVIL WAR, REPUBLICANS TALKED about "the slave power." They noted that eleven of our first fifteen presidents were slaveholders or members of the pro-slavery wing of the Democratic Party. So were seven of nine members of the Supreme Court when it decided *Dred Scott*. They saw slavery's influence everywhere, and they had a point. Historian Steven Deyle points out that the monetary value of Southern slaves was more than twice that of all other economic investment in the entire United States. No other single interest in U.S. history has ever been so dominant economically or politically.[1] "The slave power," or rather its ideological and economic descendants, still wields considerable influence. One way to see this force in our culture, even today, is by asking students why the South seceded.

TEACHERS VOTE

During 2008, I led workshops for teachers of U.S. history and social studies in Florida, Maryland, Ohio, Michigan, Illinois, Colorado, California, and Oregon. During the workshops, I asked the teachers, "Why did we have a civil war?" All knew that the Civil War resulted from the secession of South Carolina, followed by other states, so the question became, "Why did South Carolina, followed by ten other Southern states, secede?" The teachers generated four answers:

1. slavery
2. states' rights
3. tariffs and taxes
4. the election of Lincoln

They agreed that those answers exhausted the likely alternatives. I then asked them to vote. "This is not Chicago," I said. "You may only vote once."

When the polls closed, 16% to 20% had voted for slavery, 2% to about 10% for the election of Lincoln, 60% to 78% for states' rights, and 5% to 18% for tariffs and taxes. Results were remarkably uniform across the country.

Then I asked, "What should we do now? What would be the best evidence to resolve the matter?" Individuals volunteered "diaries from the time" and "newspaper articles," a bit vague. I bantered with them: "The diary of an 1859 dairy farmer in Michigan?" Immediately they responded, "No, diaries or articles from Charleston"—better answers, but hardly the best sources. Eventually, in each audience, someone asked, "Wasn't there some sort of convention? Didn't it *say* why South Carolina was leaving the Union?"

Such a convention did meet, of course, in Charleston. In December of 1860, it voted to take South Carolina out of the United States. On Christmas Eve, its members signed a document to explain why, entitled "Declaration of the Immediate Causes Which Induce and Justify the Secession of South Carolina from the Federal Union." Based on its title alone, it sounded precisely on point, my teachers agreed.

This four-page document begins with a biased and incomplete history of the formation of the United States. Then it lists South Carolina's grievances against the North:

> We assert that fourteen of the States have deliberately refused, for years past, to fulfill their constitutional obligations, and we refer to their own Statutes for the proof.

The only constitutional obligation that concerned South Carolina in 1860 was the fugitive slave clause, the third clause of the second section of the fourth article. The declaration proceeds to quote it:

> No person held to service or labor in one State, under the laws thereof, escaping into another, shall, in consequence of any law or regulation therein, be discharged from such service or labor, but shall be delivered up, on claim of the party to whom such service or labor may be due.

The federal government "passed laws to carry into effect these stipulations of the States," the declaration then notes. "For many years these laws were executed. But an increasing hostility on the part of the non-slaveholding States to the institution of slavery, has led to a disregard of their obligations."

The document immediately lists the states and the rights they tried to exercise, which South Carolina opposes:

The States of Maine, New Hampshire, Vermont, Massachusetts, Connecticut, Rhode Island, New York, Pennsylvania, Illinois, Indiana, Michigan, Wisconsin and Iowa, have enacted laws which either nullify the Acts of Congress or render useless any attempt to execute them. In many of these States the fugitive is discharged from service or labor claimed, and in none of them has the State Government complied with the stipulation made in the Constitution.

New Jersey, the declaration goes on to complain, has done likewise.

Then the convention went on to list other state actions that it denounced. "In the State of New York even the right of transit for a slave has been denied by her tribunals," the document protests. This upset South Carolina's aristocrats, who had grown accustomed to vacationing on Manhattan or Long Island in the summer with their house slaves.

Other states infuriated South Carolina by "elevating to citizenship, persons who, by the supreme law of the land, are incapable of becoming citizens." That sentence, too, refers to African Americans, of course. States in New England let African Americans vote in 1860. For that matter, so had North Carolina until 1835, if they were free and owned enough property. Who was a citizen and therefore could vote was a state matter until the 14th and 15th amendments to the U.S. Constitution, adopted after the Civil War. Yet here South Carolina tells us that among its reasons for secession was states' definition of "citizen" to include African Americans.[2]

What gave South Carolina the right to feel outraged by black voting in New England? The phrase "by the supreme law of the land" offers a hint. In the 1857 *Dred Scott* decision, the U.S. Supreme Court had declared African Americans to be an "inferior class of beings, who had been subjugated by the dominant race, and, whether emancipated or not, yet remained subject to their authority. . . ." Indeed, the court went on, "they were so far inferior, that they had no rights which the white man was bound to respect." This language delighted South Carolina. But *Dred Scott* did not exactly take away states' rights to define voters and citizens:

> In discussing this question, we must not confound the rights of citizenship which a State may confer within its own limits, and the rights of citizenship as a member of the Union. It does not by any means follow, because he has all the rights and privileges of a citizen of a State, that he must be a citizen of the United States. He may have all of the rights and privileges of the citizen of a State, and yet not be entitled to the rights and privileges of a citizen in any other State. . . . The rights which he would acquire would be restricted to the State which gave them.

The State Seal of South Carolina expressed its view of the new nation in 1776. Its front shows twelve spears bound to a palmetto, representing the twelve other original states and South Carolina. The band binding them together bears the inscription "Quis Separabit," meaning "Who shall separate [us]?" Understandably, the Ordinance of Secession did not feature the state seal.

Thus *Dred Scott* did not restrict states' rights to determine citizenship within their own borders.[3] South Carolina's outrage at the states in New England that let blacks vote was not really justified by "the supreme law of the land." Like some other parts of the declaration, this claim by South Carolina distorts the facts. It does show South Carolina's opposition to states' rights whenever the states and the rights favored blacks or seemed to threaten slavery.[4]

South Carolina was further upset that Northern states "have permitted open establishment among them of [abolitionist] societies, whose avowed object is to disturb the peace and to eloign the property of the citizens of other States." Presumably Northern states do not have the right to let their citizens assemble and speak freely—not if what they say might threaten slavery or offend South Carolina. South Carolinians also gave as a reason for secession that Northerners "have denounced as sinful the institution of slavery." Thus, they contested the rights of residents of other states even to speak negatively about their "peculiar institution."

In short, South Carolina was not *for* states' rights, but *against* them. As these excerpts show, concern about slavery permeates the document. None of the teachers in my audiences who had voted for states' rights as a cause of the Civil War meant that South Carolina seceded *against* states' rights, indeed was *outraged* at states' rights. Yet that would be more accurate.

Those teachers who chose "the election of Lincoln" did not err. His victory was a trigger, not an underlying reason, but is correct as an immediate cause, and the South Carolina document says so. Of course, Lincoln triggered secession because he and his party opposed the extension of slavery into the territories, which in turn portended the decline and eventual end of the institution. Thus, this cause of secession too is all about slavery. The "Declaration of Immediate Causes" never refers to any issues about tariffs or taxes. In all, then, most K–12 teachers today—65% to 80%—do not know why the South seceded. This ignorance is not sectional but national, making this exercise worth doing anywhere in the U.S., not just in the Carolinas.[5]

The people who voted—and mostly voted wrong—are presenting this issue to the next generation of Americans. Even if we fixed this problem tomorrow morning, most of the people leading our government and other institutions in the year 2050 will have been miseducated on this point. But we have not fixed the problem. Paradoxically, the fact that most teachers still misteach secession shows the extraordinary reach of "the slave power," even today.[6]

TEACHING AGAINST THE MYTH

The silver lining is, the foregoing referendum makes for a gripping teaching activity for students. As they approach the Civil War, teachers can invite students to come up with all the reasons they can as to why South Carolina, followed by ten other states, seceded. Students who respond "I don't know" can be prodded with "What have you heard?" or "What do you think?" Then they might be set loose to research the matter—in their textbook, other textbooks, the web, and books in the library treating the Civil War and the steps leading to it. Eventually, the four alternatives will surface; probably no other suggestion will draw much support.

Once in a while, a student simply refuses to believe the document. Its title, timing, and adoption by the convention that took South Carolina out of the U.S. make it a "smoking gun." Nevertheless, the student (or their parents) is so disappointed that their choice of states' rights or tariffs and taxes was not correct that they cannot accept it. History teachers cannot accept this as a mere difference of opinion, any more than geography teachers could allow a student to maintain that the world is flat. Everyone has a right to his/her own opinion, to be sure, including every elementary student (and every parent). As the first chapter pointed out, however, people do not have the right to their own facts. They must back up their opinions with real evidence. Students who claim that South Carolina seceded over states' rights, disagreements over tariffs or taxes, or for that matter, anything else, must find some evidence from 1859–61 to back up those positions. They also must explain why South Carolina never mentioned such reasons in their primary document telling why they seceded.

Gentle prodding with two different questions can ease this problem. First, can students find a serious historian who has claimed that the South Carolina convention was lying? (No, they cannot.) "The secessionists knew why they seceded," wrote David Duncan Wallace, the dean of South Carolina historians, and a white supremacist as well. He pointed out that they always cited the threat to slavery, real or imagined, as the cause.[7] No significant South Carolina historian claims otherwise. Second, what plausible motive would prompt its members to censor all mention of their pro-states' rights feelings or their disagreement with some national tax or tariff? (None.)

Their error is not their fault. We shall see that it is historically determined and caused. Showing students that their thinking comes from 1900 rather than, say, 1860 or 2010, can also help prompt rethinking. Challenged to use actual evidence to mount arguments favoring one interpretation over another, students will gravitate toward the right answer.

They will, partly because the case does not rest on this one document. At least four other states, when seceding from the Union, incorporated passages and ideas from South Carolina's document in their statements telling why. The secession convention in Texas, for example, proclaimed:

> The States of Maine, Vermont, New Hampshire, Connecticut, Rhode Island, Massachusetts, New York, Pennsylvania, Ohio, Wisconsin, Michigan, and Iowa, by solemn legislative enactments, have deliberately, directly or indirectly violated the 3rd clause of the 2nd section of the 4th article of the federal constitution, and laws passed in pursuance thereof. . . .

Texas lists pretty much the same states, in pretty much the same order. The constitutional clause they are charged with violating is of course the same fugitive slave clause about which South Carolina complains.

Other states said the same thing in their own words. For example, concern over slavery permeates Mississippi's "Address Setting Forth the Declaration of the Immediate Causes Which Induce and Justify the Secession of Mississippi":

> Our position is thoroughly identified with the institution of slavery. . . . [A] blow at slavery is a blow at commerce and civilization. That blow has been long aimed at the institution, and was at the point of reaching its consummation. There was no choice left us but submission to the mandates of abolition, or a dissolution of the Union. . . .

As well, South Carolina and other Deep South states sent ambassadors to other states that allowed slavery, trying to persuade them to secede. These envoys used similar language, stressing slavery first, last, and foremost. Henry L. Benning, for instance, speaking to Virginia's secession convention on behalf of Georgia, said:

> What was the reason that induced Georgia to take the step of secession. That reason may be summed up in one single proposition. It was a conviction, a deep conviction on the part of Georgia, that a separation from the North was the only thing that could prevent the abolition of her slavery.

Confirmation also comes from the famous "Cornerstone Speech" by Alexander Stephens, vice president of the Confederacy. He spoke before a huge audience in Savannah, Georgia, on March 21, 1861, as the Confederacy was forming. After telling several ways that he deemed the new constitution for the Confederate States of America superior to the U.S. Constitution, Stephens reached the central point of his speech:

> The new constitution has put at rest, forever, all the agitating questions relating to our peculiar institution—African slavery as it exists amongst us—the proper status of the Negro in our form of civilization. This was the immediate cause of the late rupture and present revolution. Jefferson in his forecast, had anticipated this, as the "rock upon which the old Union would split."

Stephens then spoke at some length on how Jefferson and other founders believed that all men were created equal. He continued:

> Our new government is founded upon exactly the opposite idea; its foundations are laid, its cornerstone rests upon the great truth, that the Negro is not equal to the white man; that slavery—subordination to the superior race—is

his natural and normal condition. [Applause.] This, our new government, is the first, in the history of the world, based upon this great physical, philosophical, and moral truth.

Thus, the South was not just seceding over the issue of slavery, but over the issue of race as well. White Southerners could not imagine what to do with the four million African Americans in their midst if they were to be free. For that matter, neither could many white Northerners. White supremacy was not just an expedient adopted to rationalize the otherwise indefensible unfairness of slavery. Most whites sincerely believed it. Therefore, white Southerners came to see blacks as a menace, were slavery ever to end. Slavery had given rise to white supremacy as an ideology; now white supremacy prompted a fierce defense of slavery. Thus, to a considerable degree, secession was about white supremacy. In November 1864, the *Richmond Daily Enquirer* asked and answered the cause question: "What are we fighting for? We are fighting for the idea of race."[8]

No one contested any of this in the 1860s. When Abraham Lincoln said in his Second Inaugural, "All knew that this interest [slavery] was somehow the cause of the war," he was not trying to convince his audience. He was merely stating the obvious, en route to some searing statements about slavery, God, and justice.

What was common knowledge at the time became encrusted by myth during the Nadir of race relations, around 1900. In 1907, John Singleton Mosby, the "Gray Ghost of the Confederacy," grew so disgusted with the campaign of pettifoggery that Southern neo-Confederates (and some actual Confederates) were waging that he wrote:

> The South went to war on account of slavery. South Carolina went to war—as she said in her secession proclamation—because slavery would not be secure under Lincoln. South Carolina ought to know what was the cause for it seceding.[9]

In 1996, historian William C. Davis noted, "All peoples part with their myths reluctantly, and historians are at some risk when they try to dismantle those of the Confederacy."[10] K–12 teachers can be at greater risk from neo-Confederate white parents and school board members who believe that the South was right, that it seceded for states' rights and other unspecified constitutional principles, and therefore that secession should be celebrated, not inquired into. If, despite the statements above by Lincoln, Stephens, Benning, Mississippi, Texas, and South Carolina, a teacher feels the need for more evidence that the states' rights issues did not prompt secession, here are three additional suggestions:

- Look up, print, and have ready the reasons for secession given by each Confederate state as it left the Union.
- Read the secondary sources that make the case compactly and effectively, listed at the end of this chapter.
- Consider the Confederate Constitution. Note that Confederates built into it no right to secede and no chance for states to have their own say about slavery. Instead, it forbade states and territories from ever "impairing the right of property in Negro slaves," regardless of local sentiment. As always, slavery trumped any commitment to states' rights.

If the above steps do not stiffen a teacher's resolve to present secession accurately, s/he must teach math, not history or social studies! Americans are ignorant enough about the Civil War as it is. We cannot have another generation grow up believing falsehoods about a central event in our past.

EXAMINING TEXTBOOKS

Secession provides another opportunity for students to critique their textbook. Why does it say South Carolina seceded? I surveyed six high school history textbooks on this point, all published since 2000. Not one quoted any statement about why the South seceded.[11] *Holt American Nation*, for example, says, "Within days of the election, the South Carolina legislature called a convention and unanimously voted to leave the Union. Alabama, Florida, Georgia, Louisiana, Mississippi, and Texas soon passed similar acts of secession." Similar to what? *Holt* does not quote a single word from any of these documents. No textbook quotes Alexander Stephens. None quotes Jefferson Davis or Robert E. Lee or any other Confederate leader on the idea of race.

Not only do our textbooks avoid primary sources, the accounts they do provide sometimes contradict the historical record. *Holt* writes,

> The southern secessionists justified their position with the doctrine of states' rights. They asserted that since individual states had come together to form the Union, a state had the right to withdraw from the Union.

If read literally, in a certain circular sense *Holt* is right: secessionists seceded while asserting their right to secede.[12] This is hardly what people meant then by "states' rights," however. Nor is it what people mean today. Proponents of states' rights defend the power of individual states to make public policy, vis-à-vis the power of the central government. The secession documents show that Southern states were outraged by the rather feeble attempts by Northern states *to* exercise states' rights. They never mention any inability of their own to do so.

Some textbooks toss tariffs into the mix. *The American Pageant*, for instance, admits, "The low Tariff of 1857, passed largely by southern votes, was not in itself menacing." Nevertheless, it goes on to hypothesize, "But who could tell when the 'greedy' Republicans would win control of Congress and drive through their own oppressive protective tariff?" This might sound plausible, but it is "what if?" history, referring to some future possibility in some future year. Not one state mentioned concern about tariffs when seceding in 1860–61.

If students find that their textbook does a better job, they might send words of praise to the author(s) and publisher. If they conclude that their textbook is not better, they might send the author(s) and publisher a letter setting forth their complaint, backed by evidence, inviting them to respond.

Hopefully, students also have access to other textbooks. Chapter 1 suggested teachers might easily collect old textbooks in U.S. history. Older textbooks are even less clear. *Triumph of the American Nation* was the most popular textbook in the 1970s and '80s, when most of today's teachers went to high school. Its 1990 edition says:

> Why did the North and South go to war in 1861? What was the immediate cause of the tragic conflict? There is no easy way to answer these two questions. Historians have studied the issues for years and still reach different conclusions.
>
> Some historians have stressed the basic economic and social differences of the North and the South. Other historians have pointed to disagreements over tariffs, internal improvements at public expense, money and banking, the disposal of public lands, and slavery. Still other historians have emphasized the issue of states' rights.

This treatment sounds professional. It starts by saying this is a hard question. It is multicausal, complex, surely better than simplistic. Then it uses the tried-and-true device of saying "some historians say" while "others emphasize." Surely this is a defensible summary.

Only it isn't. From the start, this passage makes unclear things that are clear. It never even addresses the second of its two questions, which has an easy answer: the immediate cause of the conflict was the election of Lincoln. The South Carolina document could not be clearer. Historians have "studied this issue for years" and always reach the same conclusion. No historical controversy exists here. If students want other evidence, they can research when South Carolina leaders first suggested holding a convention—directly after Lincoln's election. Taking something that is plain and making it complex and beclouded amounts to obfuscation.

Assuming that the first question seeks deeper causes, again these paragraphs obfuscate. Slavery, clearly the cause according to South Carolina, is reduced to a single word, and that comes after four other alleged causes. States' rights then gets the final sentence all by itself. On what basis?[13] *Triumph of the American Nation* includes no primary sources, of course—textbooks rarely do. Indeed, it contains no sources of any kind. If historians really disagree, why are none named in support of any of these six positions? Why are there no footnotes? Like most textbooks, *Triumph* provides nothing but assertion. Students should not be gentle in their criticism of writing like this. If they are supposed to back their claims with evidence, they should condemn textbooks for not doing the same thing.

Students can then ask deeper questions. Why would textbooks get secession wrong? Why would their authors not quote the critical documents, easily available to them? Four basic reasons explain this failure. First, textbook authors have got into the habit of not quoting anything. One textbook even gives students two paragraphs *about* William Jennings Bryan's famous "Cross of Gold" speech while not quoting a single word of it, beyond its title. Authors drone on in an omniscient monotone, rather than letting the voices of the past speak.

Second, publishers don't want to offend. Flatly saying that slavery was why Southern states seceded might cause state textbook adoption boards across the South to reject a textbook. At least, so worry publishers' marketing departments.

Third, authors are too busy to write "their" textbooks. Most high school textbooks—especially as they age—aren't really by the scholars whose names grace their covers. Some of the people who actually write textbooks don't even have a B.A. in history. As one textbook editor put it, "They pick things up pretty quickly, and in a couple of days, they're up on the Civil War."[14] Only they're not. They don't know enough to question the popular culture, let alone challenge it, and the popular culture, as the teachers' poll showed, holds that the South seceded for states' rights.

Fourth, downplaying slavery as the chief reason for secession got set in our culture as well as our textbooks about a century ago. By now, the "states' rights" explanation has become a textbook tradition. It's hard for publishers to buck tradition, especially since the people who actually write their textbooks are often not the scholars whose names grace their title pages. Instead, publishers typically hire anonymous writers who lack the independence, credentials, and knowledge to start a new tradition.

GENESIS OF THE PROBLEM

During the Nadir of race relations, that terrible period from 1890 to 1940 when race relations deteriorated, Northerners found it embarrassing to think about the cause they had abandoned. They had fought for something, after all. At first, they'd gone to war to prevent the breakup of the United States. As the war ground on, it became a struggle to end slavery. By the summer of 1862, Union soldiers were going into battle singing "Battle Cry of Freedom" and "John Brown's Body." Getting students singing historical songs is an excellent way to make history come alive. It helps students have verstehende, too. No one can sing the words of these songs without perceiving that freedom *and* Union were both war aims of the United States and without feeling some of the power of that combination. At Gettysburg in the fall of 1863, Abraham Lincoln was already proclaiming "a new birth of freedom." The freedom to which he referred was black freedom, and again, everyone understood that at the time. Conversely, on their way to and from Gettysburg, Lee's troops seized scores of free black people in Maryland and Pennsylvania and sent them south into slavery. This was in keeping with Confederate national policy.

During the Nadir, however, black freedom turned out to have been stillborn, as the next chapter shows. In 1892 Grover Cleveland would win the presidency with a campaign that derided Republicans as "nigger lovers." Four years later, the U.S. Supreme Court would grant official approval to racial segregation in *Plessy v. Ferguson*. Around that time, racial segregation became required by custom if not law throughout the North. No longer were Americans "dedicated to the proposition that all men are created equal," as Lincoln had said we were at Gettysburg.

During those decades, our popular culture also celebrated the antebellum plantation South, from minstrel shows to movies like *Birth of a Nation* and *Gone with the Wind*. Now the South and North came to be considered morally equal during our "tragic" Civil War. As part of this program, textbooks had to downplay slavery as the cause of secession. This is also when authors started portraying Abraham Lincoln as being indifferent to slavery. His Emancipation Proclamation was only a political gesture, done to win support from England and France or abolitionist Republicans. (In reality, the Proclamation cost Republicans votes in the November 1862 elections, as Lincoln and his cabinet had predicted.)

Asked what speech, what address, what letter by Lincoln textbooks are most likely to include, students chorus "The Gettysburg Address." It's a good choice, partly because it's so short. The entire speech will fit in a little box in the corner of a page. Several textbooks put it there, too, isolated from the main narrative of the war, so it's not clear it should even "count." Students can survey various textbooks to see what words of Lincoln textbook authors quote as part of their main narrative. When I did so, the runaway winner was this paragraph, from his letter of August 22, 1862, to Horace Greeley's *New York Tribune*:

> I would save the Union. . . . If I could save the Union without freeing *any* slave, I would do it; and if I could save it by freeing *all* the slaves, I would do it; and if I could save it by freeing some and leaving others alone, I would also do that. What I do about slavery and the colored race I do because I believe it helps to save this Union; and what I forbear, I forbear because I do not believe it would help to save the Union. . . .

These sentences present a Lincoln who obviously did not care about slavery. In *Lies My Teacher Told Me*, I berate textbooks for claiming that these sentences show Lincoln's true war aims. Such misrepresentation again fits with the program of showing the North and South as moral equals.

Textbook portrayals of Lincoln before he became president concentrate on the Lincoln-Douglas debates. Textbooks devote much space to this series, as well they might. However, they never quote the blatant racism of Stephen A. Douglas. Instead, they leave his views of African Americans vague. Again, this downplays the key moral issue of the day.

The next chapter will explain why these distortions took over in our textbooks and our culture.

FOCUSED BIBLIOGRAPHY

James Oliver Horton gave a lecture, "Slavery and the Coming of the Civil War: A Matter for Interpretation" (nps.gov/history/history/online_ books/rthg/chap5.htm, 7/2008), to staff members of the National Park Service around 2001, when they faced the need to tell more than military history at Civil War battlefields.

Loewen, "South Carolina Defines the Civil War in 1965," 371–76 of *Lies Across America* (NYC: Simon & Schuster, 2000), explains why South

Carolina would emphasize states' rights when it put up its state memorial at Gettysburg. Like many other sources, the resulting monument tells more about when it was written (1965) than what it is about (1863).

David Duncan Wallace, *South Carolina: A Short History* (Columbia: U of SC P, 1951), especially 527; William C. Davis, *The Cause Lost: Myths and Realities of the Confederacy* (Lawrence: UP of KS, 1996), especially 177–82. Both are acclaimed Southern white historians.[15]

CHAPTER 10

The Nadir

AN IMPORTANT ERA IN AMERICAN HISTORY goes unnamed and unknown, except in historical monographs read only by graduate students. I refer to the "Nadir of race relations," which extended from 1890 to about 1940.[1] We apply inconsequential labels to parts of this period—Gay Nineties, Roaring Twenties—but except for professional historians, most Americans don't even learn the name of this much more important epoch.

During this time, race relations worsened for Native Americans, African Americans, Chinese Americans, and Mexican Americans. Lynchings peaked. African Americans got thrown out of the Major Leagues, the Kentucky Derby, and broader job categories such as mail carrier. In the South, they lost the right to vote. The "sundown town" movement swept the North, resulting in thousands of communities that kept out African Americans (and sometimes Jewish, Chinese, Japanese, Mexican, or Native Americans).

This chapter teaches teachers about the Nadir so they can teach their students. Doing so is important. Indeed, the Nadir is so important that I suggest it should be one of the 30–50 topics that every U.S. history teacher is excited to include. Without knowledge of the Nadir, nonblack students are likely to wonder, "Why are African Americans taking so long to get over slavery? After all, slavery ended in 1863–65. That's almost a century and a half ago!" Black students, too, may wonder, "Why are we taking so long to get over slavery? Is there something wrong with us?"

CONTEMPORARY RELEVANCE

A good hook to get students thinking about the Nadir is to ask, Who was the first black baseball player in the Major Leagues? The answer is *not* Jackie Robinson. Moses Fleetwood Walker was probably first, back in 1884. Then the Nadir set in, and "organized baseball" (major and minor league) banned African Americans by the mid-1890s. Robinson is the first "after the Nadir," or "in the modern era." Just dropping the name Moses

Fleetwood Walker intrigues students' curiosity, and they themselves can discover what happened to black players.

Then ask, "Who was the first jockey inducted into the Jockey Hall of Fame?" The answer, easy to find, is Isaac Murphy, who won the Kentucky Derby three times, in 1884, 1890, and 1891. Murphy was black. The last black jockey to win the Derby, Jimmy Winkfield, who won in both 1901 and 1902 and almost won the following year, is also in the Hall of Fame. One other African American jockey is in the Hall: Willie Simms, who raced between 1887 and 1901. As in baseball, although more gradually, horse racing closed to black jockeys as the Nadir set in. African Americans won 15 of the first 28 Kentucky Derbies, but after 1911, black jockeys were shut out.[2] Not just unusual or elite jobs like baseball player or jockey became closed to black people. During the Nadir, in the North as well as the South, whites forced African Americans from skilled occupations like carpenter, government jobs like postal carriers, and even unpleasant manual labor, like steam locomotive fireman.[3]

In addition, we shall see that the Nadir has two important legacies that still affect us today: distorted history and residential segregation. The three John Brown portraits in this book comprise an example of distorted history. Showing them to students can spark a discussion: What happened to this man after he died?

Another way to show what the Nadir did to how Americans live, by race, is to introduce the Index of Dissimilarity ("D"). D provides the most useful single measure of the degree of residential segregation within a metropolitan area.[4] When D = 0, integration is perfect: Every census tract has exactly the same racial composition as every other census tract. D of 100 represents complete apartheid: not one black in any white area, not one white in any black area. For values between 0 and 100, D tells the percentage of the smaller group—usually African Americans—that would have to move from disproportionately black areas to white areas to achieve a neutral distribution of both races.

In 1860, the average Northern city had a D of 45.7—only moderately segregated. If 45.7% of the African Americans in an average city moved to predominantly white neighborhoods, the city would be perfectly integrated. Until the Nadir set in, African Americans shared neighborhoods with working-class whites. Even in middle-class neighborhoods a few black families lived. Neighborhoods were also integrated by social class. Affluent residents wanted to have labor nearby—someone to stoke the coal furnace at 6 a.m. to warm the house for the day—a maid, and maybe a gardener.

During the Nadir of race relations, these patterns changed dramatically. Now maids and gardeners could take streetcars or buses to get to

Many people do not recognize this portrait of John Brown, taken in 1857.[5] He looks like a middle-aged businessman. That's because, when not engaged in a specific action against slavery or in defense of free settlers in Kansas, Brown *was* a middle-aged businessman. Students can compare this portrait with the illustrations of Brown presented in Chapter 3 (p. 72). John Brown went mad around 1890, as the portrait by John Steuart Curry shows. He was interred in 1859, of course. His madness was more ideological than psychological. After 1890, the United States became so racist that whites could not imagine that a sane white person might go south and ultimately give up his life on behalf of black rights.

what were becoming white neighborhoods. Now having a black family on the block, even an affluent black family, reflected badly on whites' status, implying they did not have the social power to keep out such "riff-raff." By 1940, cities averaged a D of 85. Twenty years later, the average D was an astonishing 88, close to total apartheid. Since 1968, segregation has slowly eased across much of the nation. By 2000, cities averaged 65, but many metropolitan areas still scored above 80, including Detroit and New York City.[6]

Also beginning in about 1890 and continuing to form until 1968, white Americans barred African Americans from thousands of towns across the United States, especially in the North. These are called "sundown towns," because some of them posted signs that typically read, "Nigger, Don't Let The Sun Go Down On You In [town name]." Some communities passed ordinances that barred African Americans after dark or kept them from owning or renting property. Still others used informal means, harassing and even killing African Americans who violated the rule. Some sundown towns kept out Jews, Chinese, Mexicans, Native Americans, and other groups.

The idea that entire cities could keep out African Americans amazes many people. Students can do research to confirm or disconfirm possible sundown towns in their area. Some communities remain all white even today. So do some neighborhoods. Another legacy of the Nadir is the belief, still held by many people today, that an all-white neighborhood is reason for status, not shame.

ONSET OF THE NADIR

Having established the importance of the Nadir, let us examine this period more closely. Some people mistakenly think that Republicans' commitment to racial justice ended with the formal end of Reconstruction. This was the so-called Compromise of 1877 that made Rutherford B. Hayes president, "in exchange for" his promise to remove U.S. troops from the South. Although here is not the place to remedy the problem, this analysis is too simple. Hayes did care about black rights in the South, but he knew that if Republicans did not retain the presidency, then black rights would be doomed. Well after Hayes, during the "Fusion era," from the end of Reconstruction to the 1890s, Republican administrations continued to show at least some concern for the rights of African Americans.

Three events late in 1890 prompt historians to date the onset of the Nadir precisely at that time. On November 1, 1890, a state convention in Mississippi passed a new constitution with clauses that effectively made it impossible for African Americans to vote or serve on juries. The key clause was that a prospective voter be able to give a "reasonable interpretation" of any clause in the state constitution. "Reasonable" would be left to the judgment of the registrar, invariably a white Democrat. Although not racist at face value, this clause was intended to eliminate black voting. As the president of the constitutional convention put it, "We came here to exclude the Negro. Nothing short of this will answer."[7] Although all this was in direct defiance of the 14th and 15th amendments to the Constitution, the U.S. did nothing. Seeing this, all other Southern states, including even Oklahoma, followed suit by 1907.

Second, on December 29, 1890, in what used to be called the Battle of Wounded Knee but is now known more accurately as the Wounded Knee Massacre, the U.S. Army opened fire on an encampment of Sioux or Dakota Indians at Wounded Knee, South Dakota. Here Native Americans lost the last shards of their independent nationhood and sank into their Nadir period for certain.

Third, throughout December and into January, Southern Democrats in the U.S. Senate filibustered to death a proposed federal elections bill. It was designed to give the federal government power to curb the "annual autumnal outbreaks"[8] of violence during Southern elections. Democrats had defeated civil rights measures in the past, of course, and when they did, they tried to tar Republicans as "nigger lovers." In past years, Republicans had responded that African Americans had a right to vote in peace. In 1891, however, made uncomfortable by the charge, Republicans replied by moving on to other issues. African Americans now found themselves without political allies for the first time since the Civil War.

By the way, the onset of the Nadir provides a fine opportunity to contrast historical contingency with chronological ethnocentrism. The Nadir was hardly foreordained. The House had already passed the voting bill, and if the Senate had followed suit, Republican president Benjamin Harrison would have signed it into law. Armed with this new law, federal marshals and judges would have been more able to preserve black voting rights across the South. Then Republicans would have won more congressional and statewide elections. Certainly they would have been less defensive about having supported this measure, since it would have been a success, at least in the Congress. In short, Republicans would not have abandoned African Americans, at least not in 1891, and would have had a triumph to point to, rather than a defeat, in the 1892 election. Thus, the Nadir itself need not and might not have occurred. Things might have turned out quite differently.

Writing after 1890, historians and sociologists treated the reimposition of white supremacy as "natural." In his famous book *Folkways*, published in 1906, sociologist William Graham Sumner wrote,

> The mores of the South were those of slavery in full and satisfactory operation. . . . Emancipation in the South was produced by outside force against the mores of the whites there. The consequence has been forty years of economic, social, and political discord.[9]

To Sumner, the disturbance of the racial hierarchy between 1864 and 1890 was the problem, not its reestablishment. Writing in 1964, historian John K. Bettersworth still echoed this thinking in his high school Mississippi history textbook:

> Slavery was gone, but the problem of the free former slaves was not. . . . Yet by 1875 the old political order had returned, and white and black people set about the task of getting along together in the "New South" as they had in the "Old."[10]

When historians and sociologists write as if the racial hierarchy set in 1890 (and to some degree in 1875) was natural, rather than something to be explained, this helps to maintain the status quo. Doing so implies that African Americans, not racism, were "the problem," as Bettersworth put it. Such faulty analysis then became part of the Nadir itself, bolstering the ideology of racism, along with eugenics, Social Darwinism, and other intellectual currents of the time.

HISTORICAL BACKGROUND

Antiracist idealism had largely been spawned by the Civil War. During the war, the United States found itself fighting not only to hold the country together, but also to end slavery. As early as 1862, U.S. troops were going into battle singing "Battle Cry of Freedom" and "John Brown's Body." Cognitive dissonance, our old friend from Chapter 3, helps explain why. On the ground, the U.S. armed forces effectively ended or threatened slavery everywhere they went, especially everywhere they won. After Lincoln announced the Emancipation Proclamation on September 22, 1862, ending slavery became a formal goal of the United States. It is hard to risk one's life doing a job that is ending slavery, without coming to the conclusion that ending slavery is a good thing. As racism was the ideological handmaiden of slavery, so antiracism was the ideological handmaiden of emancipation.

Moreover, especially in the western theater and then on Sherman's march through Georgia and up through the Carolinas, white soldiers found themselves relying upon black civilians for food and water, knowledge of the terrain, information about the Confederates, and support services like doing laundry and digging fortifications. Black soldiers soon entered the picture as well. Beginning in May 1863, at Port Hudson, Louisiana, they showed that they would fight at least as well as white soldiers. After that battle, a New York soldier wrote home:

They charged and re-charged and didn't know what retreat meant. They lost in their two regiments some 400 men as near as I can learn. This settles the question about niggers not fighting well. They, on the contrary, make splendid soldiers and are as good fighting men as any we have.[11]

The antiracism of this quotation, magnified by a million other reports home, led directly to the 13th, 14th, and 15th amendments. In 1866, Congress declared that "citizens of every race and color . . . shall have the same right . . . to inherit, purchase, lease, sell, hold, and convey real and personal property." When President Andrew Johnson and the Democrats tried to win the 1866 congressional elections by attacking Republicans for such measures, the result was a historic landslide for the Republicans.

UNDERLYING CAUSES OF THE NADIR OF RACE RELATIONS

What prompted the erosion of this antiracist majority? What caused race relations to deteriorate so badly after 1890? Of course, many white Northerners—especially Democrats—had never been persuaded that white supremacy was wrong. Moreover, by 1890, memories of the war had dimmed. Only one American in three was old enough even to have been alive when it started. Millions more had immigrated to the United States after the war's end and had played no role in it. The sheer passage of time took its toll on antiracist idealism. In addition, three underlying causes explain why racism triumphed at the end of 1890. I call these "the three I's."

First came the continuing Plains Indian Wars. Whites discovered gold on Indian land in Colorado, Dakota Territory, and elsewhere. If they had done so on white-owned land, or black-owned land (after the 14th Amendment passed in 1868), they would have had to talk with the owners—paid them, licensed it, made some deal. Not so on American Indian land. They just moved in and took it, and when the Ute or Dakota Indians attacked them, the army was called out to put down the Indians. To maintain that all people should enjoy equal rights without regard to race—except Native Americans—is not easy. As William Graham Sumner famously observed, "The mores tend toward consistency." If it is OK to take Indians' land because they aren't white, why isn't it OK to deny rights to African Americans, who aren't white, either?

Second, immigrants posed a continuing problem for Republican antiracists. The issue first surfaced in the West. There, white miners and fishers were competing with Chinese immigrants and hating them for it. Republicans tried to stand up for the immigrants' rights, but whites rioted and forced Chinese from jobs, neighborhoods, and entire towns in the 1870s. Republicans, who had controlled all three of California's congressional seats in 1870, barely held on to one of (now) four by 1874. So party leaders distanced themselves from Chinese rights. Again, if it is OK to take Chinese Americans' jobs because they aren't white, why isn't it OK to deny rights to African Americans, who aren't white either?

In the East, Republicans faced an immigrant problem that was both different and the same. Try as they might, they could not seem to win many votes from among the new immigrants from Italy, Poland, Russia, and other countries who were rapidly becoming naturalized citizens. There were two reasons for this. First, the Republicans were beginning to flirt with prohibition. You do not win the Italian American vote by coming out against wine, nor the Polish American vote by coming out against beer. Second, the Democrats' continued white supremacy appealed to new European immigrants who were competing with African Americans for jobs at the wharves, in the kitchens, on the railroads, and in the mines. Some Republicans converted to a more racist position to win these white ethnic votes. Others, including the Henry Cabot Lodge, the Massachusetts congressman who had sponsored the 1890 elections bill, grew disgusted with "ethnic Americans" and helped found the Immigration Restriction League. Again, if it is OK to keep out Southern and Eastern Europeans because they are considered inferior to WASPs, why isn't it OK to deny rights to African Americans, also considered inferior?[12]

The third "I" was not an American development. Imperialism as a modern ideology arose in Europe and England, but it washed over our shores around 1890. The United States bought into it. Between 1887 and 1897, the United States annexed Hawai'i; the process for it to go from independent kingdom to U.S. territory took a full decade. Underlying the transition was the claim that white Americans would govern those "brown" people better than they could govern themselves. Then, after winning the Spanish American War in 1898, the following year the U.S. turned against its allies, the Filipinos, who had done most of the work of removing the Spanish from the Philippines. The McKinley administration used the same rationale: our military governor over the islands, William Howard Taft, said "our little brown brothers" would require at least half a century of white supervision before they would be capable of democracy. Democrats responded, "What about our little brown brothers in Mississippi? In Alabama?" McKinley had no cogent reply. The United States also dominated Puerto Rico, Cuba, Nicaragua, Haiti, the Dominican Republic, and other Caribbean and Central American nations, always with the rationale that we, a white nation, could govern them better than they could govern themselves. Once more, if it is OK to dominate natives in other countries partly because they aren't exactly white, why isn't it OK to do the same to African Americans at home?

There were still other causes of the decline of Republican antiracism. During what some historians call the Gilded Age, some capitalists, mostly Republicans, amassed huge fortunes. Doing likewise became the dream of many Republicans, a goal that was hard to reconcile with the party's former talk of social justice. This increasing stratification sapped America's historic belief that "all men are created equal." To justify the quest for wealth, a substitute ideology was created, Social Darwinism—the notion that the fittest rise to the top in society. It provided a potent rationale not only for class privilege but for racial superiority as well.

Once the fatal events of 1890 took place, whites across the country had to rationalize them. Again, cognitive dissonance played a key role. Americans, even as far from Mississippi as New England, had to explain to themselves that state's removal of African Americans from effective citizenship. They could hardly say, "I am an American; I believe in freedom and democracy and equal rights for all," since they had acquiesced in Mississippi's action. So they had to say, "I believe in freedom and democracy and equal rights for all—except nonwhites." They told themselves that African Americans—and Native Americans, too—just "weren't ready" for equal rights. White Southerners knew best what to do, after all.

Thus, theories of racial inferiority again became important, as during slavery, to rationalize the discriminatory treatment of black people. Now these theories came with the imprimatur of science, "eugenics"— improving the human race by discouraging reproduction by undesirable groups. The leader of the eugenics movement, Madison Grant, wrote in *The Passing of the Great Race* in 1916, "[I]t has taken us fifty years to learn that speaking English, wearing good clothes, and going to school and to church do not transform a Negro into a white man."[13] The fact that African Americans lagged in income and status owing to discrimination now provided reason to discriminate further.

STUDENTS CAN REVEAL THE NADIR THEMSELVES

Students can see the Nadir at work by counting the representation of African Americans in Congress from 1868, when the 15th amendment began to take effect, to 1890, and from then until 1940. They will find that the rather sturdy representation of the race who took their seats in, say, 1877, dwindled to a single person—George White of North Carolina—by 1900. White's valediction to the House of Representatives, delivered January 29, 1901, provides a concise summary of the fair treatment that African

Americans were *not* getting during the Nadir. Underlying the elimination of African Americans from Congress was their removal from voting. If their county has a substantial black population, students may be able to see what happened to black voting where they live, thus showing a local manifestation of a national trend.

Students can also research the "racial history" of the National Football League. They will learn that from its founding in 1920, its teams played in small Midwestern cities like Decatur and Rock Island, Illinois; Canton and Akron, Ohio; and Green Bay, Wisconsin. (Only Green Bay survives from this era.) They will also discover that African Americans played until 1933. As the Nadir continued to shut down opportunities for African Americans, whites found it hard to justify employing blacks when white athletes were out of work during the Great Depression. So for a dozen years, football joined baseball and became lily-white.

Leola Bergmann analyzed the treatment of African Americans in Iowa newspapers from 1865 to the end of the century. At first, she found that newspapers reported reasonably well about the organized activities and individual stories within the black community. Gradually, however, "as the emotions of the Civil War era cooled," newspapers started doing terrible jobs. By the 1890s, almost every story about African Americans that saw print concerned crime. Even when Republican President Benjamin Harrison named a black Iowan ambassador to Liberia in 1890, not one Iowa newspaper reported it.[14] Students can carry out similar content analyses of their local paper, the leading newspaper in their state, or a national source like the *New York Times*. Many newspapers are online and can be searched for words like "negro," "black," "colored," and "nigger." Students can also characterize each story as "positive" (+1), "neutral" (0), or "negative" (-1), and put this rating into a spreadsheet. Then it's easy to calculate the total number of stories in each decade, compute the mean rating for each decade, and see if trends appear. A simple bar graph will clarify trends and help students become proficient at reading and understanding graphs and tables.

Students who can gain access to American histories published between 1866 and 1880 can compare their portrayal of the Civil War to that in books published later, between 1895 and 1940.[15] Things to look for include why the South seceded, the role of black troops, whether Andrew Johnson is seen as a persecuted martyr or a bad president, and use of the terms "carpetbagger" and "scalawag." They should also look to see if the Civil War came to be called the "War Between the States" as time passed. As the Nadir deepened, textbook expositions of Lincoln's war aims may say less and less about ending slavery.

Another way students can see the Nadir is in this ad for Cream of Wheat depicting a five-year-old white boy whipping his elderly black babysitter. The man is not the boy's uncle, of course. Rather, whites called older and more senior African Americans "uncle" and "aunt" or "auntie" as terms of quasi-respect during the Nadir; "Mister," "sir," or "ma'am" would imply they were fully human. In conjunction with the photo of Gordon, who had been whipped (p. 168), this illustration makes its point, especially when we consider that in 1914, Cream of Wheat thought it would convey a warm glow to most Americans, prompting them to buy their breakfast cereal.

"GIDDAP, UNCLE!"

The Nadir of race relations happened across the entire United States. Therefore, students can look for it almost everywhere, including in their own neighborhood. Within their county, African Americans may have held elective office before the Nadir, or after the Civil Rights Movement, but not between. Students can use the manuscript census for 1860 through 1930 to map where African Americans lived.[16] Probably they will see increasing concentration. They can also compute D for their town over time.[17] Students can also look for sundown towns in their area.[18]

Many Americans do not realize that formal racial segregation afflicted not just the South, but half of all states in the early 1950s. In addition to the eleven former Confederate states, Delaware; Maryland; West Virginia; the southern third of Ohio, Indiana, and Illinois; Kentucky; Missouri; much of Kansas; Oklahoma; Arizona; and some communities in California kept African Americans out of white schools. Even farther north, many communities barred African Americans from swimming pools, theaters, parks, and other spaces used by the public. Private companies were often worse. Breweries in Milwaukee started to hire African Americans only in 1950. The city of Milwaukee did not employ a single black teacher until 1951. No major department store in that city hired a single African American as a full-time sales clerk until 1952. Across the North, most jobs in construction were reserved for whites until the 1970s.[19] Student research can reveal what schools, pools, theaters, hotels, and other institutions in their community operated without regard to race, and which places barred African Americans (and sometimes Jews and others) during the Nadir. They can also learn which jobs were open and which were closed to African Americans.

DURING THE NADIR, WHITES BECAME WHITE

Before the Nadir, whites weren't sure that the world contains three races of mankind. Often, they thought there were many more. The main building of the Library of Congress was built in 1897. Its embellishments included 33 "ethnological heads," carved in stone, placed above its windows. They symbolize the 33 races of mankind, according to Otis Mason, who was curator of the Department of Ethnology at the Smithsonian at the time. Herbert Small wrote the *Handbook of the New Library of Congress* to coincide with the building's dedication. Modified and retitled, it is still in print. He tells of the ethnological heads:

> The list of the races . . . is as follows . . . : 1, Russian Slav; 2, Blonde European; 3, Brunette European; 4, Modern Greek; 5, Persian (Iranian); 6, Circassian; 7, Hindoo; 8, Hungarian (Magyar); 9, Semite, or Jew; 10, Arab (Bedouin); 11, Turk; 12, Modern Egyptian (Hamite); 13, Abyssinian [Ethiopian]; 14, Malay; 15, Polynesian; 16, Australian; 17, Negrito (from Indian Archipelago); 18, Zulu (Bantu); 19, Papuan (New Guinea); 20, Sudan Negro; 21, Akka (Dwarf African Negro); 22, Fuegian; 23, Botocudo (from South America); 24, Pueblo Indian (as the Zuñis of New Mexico); 25, Eskimo; 26, Plains Indian (Sioux, Cheyenne, Comanche); 27, Samoyete (Finnish inhabitant of Northern Russia [Lapp]); 28, Korean; 29, Japanese; 30, Ainu (from Northern Japan); 31, Burmese; 32, Tibetan; 33, Chinese.[20]

Small goes on to boast, "The series is unique in that it is the first instance of a comprehensive attempt to make ethnological science contribute to the architectural decoration of an important public building." In the 1990s, old-timers at the Smithsonian claimed that the sculptors worked from real heads, pickled in brine, that still existed in barrels deep in the bowels of the National Museum of Natural History! Small implicitly confirms that tale:

> The large collection of authentic, life-size models, chiefly of savage and barbarous peoples . . . is the most extensive in the country, and many of the heads on the Library keystones are taken directly from these.

Small concludes that, given the difficulty of working in granite, the result "is one of the most scientifically accurate series of racial models ever made." Each head is intended to "exemplify all the average physical characteristics of his race."[21]

The heads are presented in a sequence that embodies Social Darwinism. Eugenics rears its ugly head here, although some of the carved heads are in fact quite beautiful. Closest to Congress and nearest to the main entrance are the winners—the "highest" types, such as "Blonde European [of] the educated German type, dolichocephalic, or long headed," followed by "Brunette European [of] the Roman type, brachycephalic, or broad-headed," in Small's words. On the right but still facing Congress are "Chinese" and "Japanese" and the like. Relegated to the back are the really bad races, the losers, "savage and barbarous peoples" such as "Australian," "Negrito," "Zulu," "Papuan," and "Akka (Dwarf African Negro)." However, some African Americans note that this allots black peoples the position of honor on the east, facing the rising sun.

Today people scoff at this entire enterprise. Egyptian race? Greek race? Nonsense! It seems obvious now that there are only three races of humankind.

What are the three races? Black, white, and "yellow," of course, but somehow that last term sounds disrespectful. Caucasoid, Negroid, and Mongoloid? The last word sounds like slang for Down syndrome. There are other problems with this scheme as well. For example, what about Australian Aborigines? They are hardly "Negroes." What about Native Americans? They are hardly "Mongolians." What of Malays? Somalis and Ethiopians in northeastern Africa? Pygmies or Mbuti people in central Africa? Some of those last peoples, though classed "Negroid," may be genetically closer to "Caucasians" or "Mongolians." I'm getting confused!

Besides, the "Caucasian" group turns out to have been invented by two Germans, notably J. F. Blumenbach (1752–1840), who got his history and geography all wrong. He believed that Caucasians were the first and most beautiful race of mankind and originated in the Caucasus Mountains, between the Black and Caspian seas. Now we know that all humans originated in Africa. Nevertheless, his classification scheme not only lives on but strikes many people as somehow more scientific than using mere colors.

All "races of mankind," whether 3 or 33, are social constructs, set up and agreed to by Western opinion leaders. The only defensible statement of biological race is this: We are all one race, the human race. Depending upon environmental conditions and the degree of isolation from others, after leaving the part of Africa where humans first originated, people started to grow more different from one another. Then, beginning around 200 BC, developments in transportation and the nation-state began to put people around the world back into contact with one another. It follows that no "racial" differences are qualitative. All are matters of degree. Besides, some differences among groups may not have conveyed any survival value but just happened to be linked genetically to

Today we snicker at the last line under this bust of Christopher Columbus. We "know" Italians are not a race. Obviously this was not Italian Americans' understanding in 1920, however, when they erected this bust at the Indiana State Capitol.

differences that did. Other differences resulted from genetic drift, having neither positive nor negative implications. In sum, the racial hierarchy and categories that developed over the last 500 years are products of history, not biology.

We must conclude that the notion of three races is hardly carved in stone. Our "modern" way of viewing the world, so far as race is concerned, is largely a product of the Nadir. Between 1890 and 1940, such immigrant groups as Greeks, Italians, and Slavs achieved reclassification as "white." Irish Americans had attained this label somewhat earlier, as Noel Ignatiev explains in his wonderfully titled book, *How the Irish Became White*. Jews reached it a bit later, as Karen Brodkin tells in *How Jews Became White Folks and What That Says About Race in America*.[22] Armenians, Turks, Egyptians, and Arabs took just a little longer, but they, too, have now found room under the "white" umbrella (although reactions to the attacks of 9/11/2001 may be pushing Arabs back toward "other" status). Without these additions, "whites" would have been outnumbered long ago.

One way to increase the solidarity of an in-group is by creating an out-group, an "other." Jews and Rom people played this role during the Third Reich. African Americans (and in the West, Native Americans and Asian Americans) played this role in the U.S. This process is shown in operation in Granite City, Illinois. Between 1900 and 1970, this St. Louis suburb grew from 3,122 to 40,440, owing to skyrocketing employment. Meanwhile, its black population fell from 154 to 6. Between 1900 and 1910, hundreds of new immigrants, mostly from Macedonia and Bulgaria, poured into Granite City. "Poorly paid, they lived in pathetic squalor, ignorant of American institutions," according to a 1971 history of the community. Nevertheless, Granite City at least tolerated and sometimes even welcomed these white ethnic group members. They may not have been American, but at least they were not black. Meanwhile, the town was busy expelling its African Americans. The Macedonians had started at the bottom, in competition with African Americans, but when Anglo, Irish, Polish, Greek, Italian, and now Macedonian and Bulgarian Americans joined to expel Granite City's African Americans around 1903, "whites" were now united. By 1971, Macedonian and Bulgarian American children were fully accepted. African Americans were still totally excluded. Granite City was still a sundown town.[23]

Today, "white America" seems to be incorporating Latinos and Asian Americans. Increasingly, Japanese and Korean Americans marry outside their group, mostly marrying whites. Most sundown towns have long admitted Asian and Latino Americans. In 1960, Dearborn, a sundown suburb of Detroit, called Arabs from the Middle East "white population born in

Asia" and Mexicans "white population born in Mexico" in official documents, thus remaining "all white" as a city. Sundown town policy now seems to be: all groups are fine except African Americans.[24]

Students can uncover for themselves the relative position of various ethnic and racial groups in their community over time. Tombstones, the manuscript census, city directories, and school yearbooks supply useful data sources. Often smaller towns have only one cemetery. Since tombstones record burial dates and names often reveal ethnic group membership, students can map the location of an ethnic group's dead over time. They may be absent entirely, early in the Nadir; then graves appear at one edge; more recent burials occur throughout the cemetery. Similarly, students can use the manuscript census to map where ethnic groups lived from 1900 through 1930. City directories or old phone directories can supply this information for later years. Again, students may find considerable residential concentration at first, followed by dispersal. Students can visit that part of town and see how it looks today. They can map other groups, such as African Americans, over time, and see if similar dispersal took place. Students can also assess the state of civil rights in their communities today, decades after the Civil Rights Movement began to undo the effects of the Nadir. Have schools resegregated owing to white flight, withdrawal to private schools, or tracking within schools? Do governments and private employers hire without regard to race, or do whites still run things while blacks and Latinos clean up?

Many school yearbooks show photos of their graduating seniors accompanied by a list of activities and honors after each name. If they do not supply such lists, they do include photographs of student organizations, from science club to cheerleader. Students can enter the number of organizational memberships for each student, the student's race, ethnic group, and other information into a spreadsheet. Then they can look for trends by decade. It may be helpful to categorize minor activities like Latin Club or Prom Decoration Committee from more important posts like Student Council Vice President or lead in the class play. Members of an ethnic group may list no activities at all in early yearbooks. Then they can be found in the academic clubs and the band, and still later in athletic organizations. Finally they get chosen as cheerleader, class president, or prom king or queen.

END OF THE NADIR

After about 1940, race relations started to improve. Racism as an ideology started to decrease. Again, three underlying factors were involved.

First came the "Great Migration" of African Americans from the South to the North. Blacks didn't move everywhere in the North, however. Sundown practices closed many potential communities, channeling migrants toward the larger cities. Within these cities, increasing levels of residential segregation—shown by the higher D's mentioned previously—meant that African Americans were restricted to just a few neighborhoods. Northern states never chased African Americans from voter rolls, however. Therefore, black residential concentration during the Nadir, unfortunate as it was from a race relations standpoint, carried with it one reward: African Americans were able to elect members of their race to city councils and state legislatures. In 1928, Chicago's South Side elected Oscar De Priest to the U.S. Congress, the first African American since George White.

Second, imperialism as an ideology became a spent force after World War I. That hapless war taught the "undeveloped" nations that Western nations weren't so smart. Nationalist movements arose in India, Ghana, and other nations. During World War II, the question of India's independence, and that of such nations as Indonesia, Ghana, and the Philippines plainly became not "whether" but "when." Whites were no longer seen as necessary or appropriate to rule nations of color. Also, when World War II ended, the United States found itself locked in a contest for world supremacy with the U.S.S.R., which boasted an explicitly egalitarian racial ideology. Segregation and exclusion on racial grounds now became an embarrassment, especially when African and Asian diplomats to the United Nations in New York and ambassadors in Washington embassies could not find places to sleep or even to eat in trips outside those cities.

Adolf Hitler provided the third and most important factor. The U.S. has always demonized its opponents in war; all nations do. But Germany made it easy. As Americans learned more about Nazi policies of extermination regarding Jews and "Gypsies" (Rom people), they recoiled. In addition, the connection of those policies to our own practices of exclusion (sundown towns), reserves (Native Americans), concentration camps (Japanese Americans), racial segregation, and forced sterilization (of "mental defectives," mixed-race people, and paupers) during the Nadir became all too clear. Germans took those practices to their logical extreme. Moreover, shockingly, they did it to people who were becoming defined in the U.S. as "white." In sum, Hitler gave a bad name to eugenics, Social Darwinism, and racial discrimination in general. As a result, just as the Civil War had led to whites becoming antiracist, so, to a lesser extent, did World War II.

After the war, the old order began to crack. Jackie Robinson, President Truman's order desegregating the armed forces, and the *Brown* decision both presaged and helped to cause the Civil Rights Movement. In turn, the Civil Rights Movement helped white Americans to question the underlying premise of the Nadir—that African Americans are on the bottom because they are inferior. As soon as that premise got questioned, then historians could see that the Nadir was unfair—indeed, now they could see that it existed.

Students can see the effects of the Nadir in old newspapers, simply by counting their use of terms like "uncle" and "Mrs." During the Nadir, whites rarely called African Americans "sir" or "ma'am" or used courtesy titles like "Mr." or "Mrs." (See the figure caption on p. 199.) Instead, whites called older and more senior African Americans "uncle" or "aunt." Relics of this system include Uncle Ben's rice and Aunt Jemima's pancake syrup today. Students can also count the number of stories about black weddings, church happenings, and other social events over time.

History textbooks usually lag social change by a few years. To see the gradual end of the Nadir, students can compare textbooks over time. They can count the number of photographs that include African Americans (or Native Americans or women). More subtle investigations—such as assessing the sanity level of John Brown—will also prove interesting.

Students can use the same data sources discussed above—tombstones, the manuscript census, city directories, school yearbooks—to show improvement in race relations in their community after 1940. Newspaper articles and school district files can help students write the history of the two or more high schools that merged to form one, if the school district desegregated. Students can also interview members of the generation that first broke these barriers. In many communities, the first black children to attend interracial schools and the white children who welcomed or did not welcome them have never told their stories. Now they are aging, and these important historical resources may be lost forever.

IMPLICATIONS FOR TODAY

We have mentioned that the Nadir of race relations has left us with two important legacies today. Chapter 3 tells that the Nadir distorted the way textbooks present John Brown, Reconstruction, and other topics, including their omission of the Nadir itself. This chapter has introduced sundown towns and residential segregation as a second legacy of the Nadir, along with the curious claim by some residents that an all-white community or neighborhood is cause for status rather than shame. Students can do research to learn if all-white neighborhoods and communities near them are all-white on purpose. Students can also investigate other inequalities that linger from the Nadir period. For example, more computers may be available in elementary schools that have whiter student bodies. The number of library books per student in each high school may be higher in whiter high schools. This is especially likely across district lines in metropolitan areas. Students can find out such facts and then take steps to change them.

After researching the Nadir, students may feel that their textbook should give the topic more attention. If so, they can construct an account of the Nadir, summarizing their local research and what they have learned nationally about the period. They might even put this into textbook style, complete with illustrations and study questions, as a resource for next year's students. Also, they can write a class letter to the author(s) and publisher of their textbook, pointing out the problem. They might attach their research as an appendix. Earlier chapters told of a class that wrote such a letter about slave-owning presidents. Unfortunately, they got back a mindless reply from the publisher and none at all from the author. Even such a result has its benefits: at the least, it cautions students not to take textbooks too seriously.

The lower overall status today of African Americans and Native Americans (and to a degree Hispanics) is not simply "their fault" but has historical roots. Even in this age of Obama, textbooks must recognize racism as a continuing force in our national life. Otherwise they discourage students from using history to address our most persistent and historically embedded national problem. Textbooks must tell how racism has increased and decreased over time. Otherwise, they prevent students from asking (and then discovering) what causes and what eases racism. The Nadir must be part of such exegesis.

Inserting the Nadir into discussions of affirmative action changes those discussions. Now students no longer talk about atavisms lingering from slavery. It isn't slavery that holds back African Americans today. Moreover, while it's true that many white families suffered in the conflict that ended slavery, white families only enjoyed unfair advantage during the swelling discrimination of the Nadir. When students understand that overt discrimination continued into the recent past and even to the present, then they see that the Nadir and its legacies still haunt us today. Getting students to make this connection between the past and present is exciting. So is helping them make the connection between something they learned and actions they take in the public arena.

FOCUSED BIBLIOGRAPHY

Teachers (or students) who need to know more about Reconstruction should read Lerone Bennett, *Black Power U.S.A.: The Human Side of Reconstruction* (Baltimore: Penguin, 1969 [1967]) or Eric Foner, *Reconstruction*

(NYC: Harper & Row, 1988). Unfortunately, both stop at 1877; no good survey treats the Fusion period, circa 1875–1895 (varying by state).

Loewen, "The Nadir," Chapter 2 of *Sundown Towns* (NYC: New P, 2005), is the best short introduction to this neglected era nationally.

C. Vann Woodward's classic short book, *The Strange Career of Jim Crow* (NYC: Oxford UP, 1965 [1957]), tells of the Nadir in the South.

Students have done good work on the waning of the Nadir and the end of segregation. See *In Relentless Pursuit of an Education, Keeping the Struggle Alive, Minds Stayed on Freedom,* and "The First Black Students at Virginia Tech," cited at the end of Chapter 4.

Still More Ways
to Teach History

W E HAVE REACHED THE END OF THIS BOOK, but not the end
of a course in U.S. history. Chapters 1 through 10 have suggested various ways to get students interested in learning about the
past, beginning with coming to their own conclusions about how people
first got to the Americas. Teachers need not cover every one of their 30–50
topics via world-class, once-in-a-lifetime student projects, however. Chapter 1 pointed out that simply reading and discussing the textbook might
cover some topics effectively.

A teacher may have learned a given subject from an impressive lecturer in college and may have saved her lecture notes or developed new
ones. Now she believes that by the old-fashioned lecture method she can
teach that subject well. Fine! She can tell her charges that they have advanced to college level in their abilities and are now ready to learn the
way most college students do—listening to lecture and taking notes. The
teacher can follow up by asking students to be sure they understand their
notes by pairing with another student to discuss the lecture and agree on
its main points. Followed by a quiz—to give feedback to students and the
teacher about what was learned well and what was not—such a unit can
impart knowledge effectively. It can also help students anticipate that college courses are unlikely to be as varied in form as they are in K–12.

Although they may be the best methods for certain topics, these traditional techniques still present knowledge for students to "learn." Therefore,
they run the risk that students will learn, only to forget, because they have
not really invested psychic energy in the topic. "I read, I forget," goes the
first third of a saying about teaching. My first-year college students prove
that adage correct. "I see, I remember," continues the saying, and finally, "I
teach, I understand." So why not invite students to teach a topic? The first
topic of the year—how and when people arrived in the Americas—offers
a good site, as each group tries to convince the class that its choice of date
and route is correct. Or, when learning about the diverse Native American
societies in North America, each student might choose a tribe or nation to

explore, taking care to bring their story into the present. Each student gets ten minutes and is expected to make up a one-page handout or develop a PowerPoint or website display that other students can access. Then the presentations can be tested upon and get taken seriously.[1]

Various other subjects during the year lend themselves to student teaching. These include explorers before and after Columbus, immigrant groups and Americanization, as suggested in Chapter 4; or different facets of the rise of urban and suburban America. Almost any recent topic will also work, from the Korean War through the women's movement to the present, because sources are readily available, including newspaper stories and people to interview. Since classes typically reach recent topics near the end of the school year, this means that student teaching can fill that lame duck session after the APUSH exam, statewide exams, or, for seniors, after graduation lists have been turned in. Whenever they do it, teaching their peers will cement facts and ideas in students' heads. With guidance from their teacher, students will also understand that they have to have a storyline—indeed, that history is, in large part, the creation of a storyline.

Another year-end project derives from the teacher's list of 30–50 topics: Ask each student to suggest an item that should have been on that list. They should defend their choice to the class, explaining its importance and its relevance to the present. If the class agrees, then the student prepares a handout (or PowerPoint or website) and takes the class over for ten minutes to teach about their topic.

Another way to get students teaching their peers is to assign parts of a book to different members of the class. While a graduate student, leading a seminar of college sophomores, I happened upon this method by accident. I had just finished my doctoral dissertation, now published as *The Mississippi Chinese: Between Black and White*.[2] Near the end of the semester, aware that I had been writing it all year, my students asked if they might read it. I realized it would be good for them to read a sociological monograph, but it was not reasonable for each to read 300 pages in the last week of class. So I gave each student a chapter, winding up with two or three students assigned to each. In the last class meeting, diffident about teaching my own work, I said, gruffly, "You people don't want to discuss this, do you?" "Well, yes," they replied. Those who had read early chapters wanted to know how the saga turned out. Those who had read the last chapter, telling that Chinese Americans were now reasonably well off in the social structure of the Mississippi Delta, wanted to know how they had risen in status and wealth. Readers of middle chapters wondered why Chinese Mississippians lived only in the Delta, that flat plantation land between Memphis and Vicksburg. All I had to do was keep the discussion on track chronologically; students kept it going by asking questions for more than an hour.

Many books might spark discussion, so long as they are narrative (telling a story) or faceted (each chapter presenting part of an interlocking analysis). The novel *Okla Hannali* offers a rich and factual account of the nineteenth century from the viewpoint of an (imaginary) Choctaw leader.[3] Another novel, *Jubilee*, the "antidote" to *Gone with the Wind*, tells how a black family experienced slavery, the Civil War, and Reconstruction in Georgia.[4] Many nonfiction books can also be used.

Teachers or the class might also end the year by choosing a current national or world problem and have students trace its roots back in time. Doing so is another good way to engage student interest, since they can see history not only as a past event but also as a part of our present.

Chapter 3 argued that understanding historiography is one of the great gifts a history course can impart to students. Teachers can engage them with this idea once more at the end of the year. With historiography securely in their minds, students can engage in an interesting thought experiment: What will historians write 50 years hence about a given topic? That question takes them out of the present and can help reveal limitations in our vision today.[5]

The course should end as it began: with the recognition that history is important and students in the class are important. In the introduction I argued—hoped?—for a reciprocal relationship between truth about the past and justice in the present. Students can make this connection come to pass. They can make a difference, even before they leave school, as examples cited in Chapter 4 show. Conversely, students will make a difference—and not for the better—if they choose to do nothing in their job as Americans for the rest of their lives. That job, as the introduction suggested, is to bring into being the America of the future. At the end of the course, teachers can turn students loose to start doing that job. On what topic do they want to work? What defect in our society do they want to remedy? What policy—public or private—needs reversal? What issue do Americans need to rethink, aided by new information? How is history relevant to this topic? Again, each student might present his or her topic to the class. Then all students can suggest steps the individual can take to make a difference. And then they can all get started.

Notes

Introduction (pp. 1–18)

1. I don't fully grasp the distinction between history and social studies. According to the National Council for the Social Studies, "Social studies is the integrated study of the social sciences and humanities to promote civic competence." (National Council for the Social Studies 1972 statement, reprinted in "Curriculum Standards for Social Studies: I. Introduction," socialstudies.org/standards/introduction/, 7/2005.) Seems vague, but otherwise, who can argue with it? To be competent, historians, too, must use the insights and methods of the social sciences. They must know how to construct a table, read the census, and employ theoretical ideas like social structure or cognitive dissonance. Moreover, when competently taught, history provides marvelous preparation for "civic competence."

In some districts, social studies is taught in middle school, history in high school. Some college professors routinely put down social studies as more concerned with building students' self-image than imparting knowledge. At a conference for K–12 teachers organized by the National Council for History Education, I listened to a famous history professor extol history and denounce social studies. He may not have known that more than half of his audience actually taught "social studies" and were interested in teaching it better, which was why they were attending his lecture. All he did was make them feel bad. He did not help them teach better.

I shall use "history" and "social studies" interchangeably.

Notes will use postal abbreviations for states, "NYC" for New York City; "DC" for Washington, DC; "U" for "University"; and "P" for Press. Dates after website URLs tell when they were retrieved.

2. The National Commission on Excellence in Education came out with the most influential jeremiad of all, *A Nation At Risk*, in 1983 (DC: GPO, 1983).

3. Later in 2007, a second edition came out, completely revised in light of six new U.S. history textbooks published between 2000 and 2007. It also contained a new chapter analyzing what textbooks do and do not say about 9/11 and Iraq.

4. John K. Bettersworth, *Mississippi: Yesterday and Today* (Austin: Steck Vaughn, 1964). These were two "Old South" images: a drawing of a white mistress reading from the Bible to a group of slaves and a painting by a white artist showing cotton pickers. In addition, an illustration of boys on the deck of a steamboat may include

a black boy dancing a jig; since he is just 3/8" tall, we cannot be sure. Robert B. Moore, *Two History Texts: A Study in Contrast* (NYC: Center for Interracial Books, 1974), compared his book and ours systematically.

5. John Bettersworth, "After the War Was Won," *NY Times Book Review*, 7/25/1971.

6. There are about 250 items because some counties have more than one county seat.

7. Actually, nothing in our book was new to historians. It was controversial only in the context of Mississippi's educational climate of the time.

8. *Loewen et al. v. Turnipseed et al.*, 488 F. Supp. 1138.

9. Between about 2004 and 2007 an uptick occurred, with slightly fewer students falling below "basic" on the American history test of the National Assessment of Educational Progress, for example. Can we credit the 'No Child Left Behind' Act? The widespread use of *Lies My Teacher Told Me* in teacher education programs? Improvements in textbooks? (The 2007 edition of *Lies* argues that textbooks have not materially improved.) Increased viewing of the History Channel?

10. Caren Benjamin, "College Seniors Flunk History Test," *Chicago Sun Times*, 6/28/2000; National Assessment of Educational Progress (NAEP) results discussed in Richard Rothstein, "We Are Not Ready to Assess History Performance," *Journal of American History*, 3/2004, 1389.

11. In workshops, I deliver these lines deadpan, and audiences crack up, so I hope readers grasp that I'm trying to be comical. I don't really believe for a moment that soclexia is genetic. But then, neither is the difficulty poor and minority children have, when they try to learn history from the usual textbook approach.

12. Mean incomes are always pulled up by very rich families; median is therefore a better measure. Data from U.S. Census Bureau, "Current Population Survey, 2005 Annual Social and Economic Supplement," pubdb3.census.gov/macro/032005/hhinc/new06_000.htm.

13. Charlotte Crabtree and David O'Shea, "Teachers' Academic Preparation in History," *Newsletter* (National Center for History in the Schools), *1*, #3 (11/1991), 4, 10. I don't know that this statistic has improved more recently.

14. George Santayana, *Life of Reason* (NYC: Scribner's, 1905), 284.

15. G. W. F. Hegel, "Introduction," *Philosophy of History*, widely quoted, e.g., EpistemeLinks, epistemelinks.com/Main/Quotations.aspx?PhilCode=Hege, 8/2008.

16. Nothing wrong with a good cliché now and then!

17. Unfortunately, textbook authors are too timid to use it. "History as power" implies that some people are not amicable, that they may lie or cover up, and that ideas matter and are worth battling over. Santayana's maxim sounds so much nicer.

18. Chapter 10 will show how the lives of some potential role models were distorted or removed from view altogether during the "Nadir of race relations."

19. Specifically, from African American culture.

20. Wikipedia, "American exceptionalism," en.wikipedia.org/wiki/American_exceptionalism, 6/2007.

21. Daniel Boorstin and Brooks Mather Kelley, *A History of the United States* (Needham, MA: Pearson/Prentice Hall, 2005), xix.

22. Paul Gagnon, *Democracy's Untold Story* (DC: American Federation of Teachers, 1987), 19.

23. Thomas A. Bailey, *The American Pageant* (Boston: Little, Brown, 1961), summarized by Mark Selden in "Confronting World War II: The Atomic Bombing and the Internment of Japanese-Americans in U.S. History Textbooks," in Andrew Horvat and Gebhard Hielscher, eds., *Sharing the Burden of the Past: Legacies of War in Europe, America, and Asia* (Tokyo: Asia Foundation and F. E. Stiftung, 2003); Bailey, *Pageant* (Boston: Little, Brown, 1966), 881; David M. Kennedy, Lizabeth Cohen, and Bailey, *Pageant* (Boston: Houghton Mifflin, 2006), 822–25.

24. Kathleen Hulser, NY Historical Society, talk at Organization of American Historians, 4/2002.

25. What of the dragging death of James Byrd Jr. in Jasper, Texas, in 1998? That was horrific, to be sure, and a hate crime, but not a lynching. Byrd was killed after midnight on a deserted road, and when the community found out, the perpetrators were arrested, tried, convicted, and harshly punished.

26. Sundown towns are communities that for decades were all-white on purpose (and some still exist). See Loewen, *Sundown Towns* (NYC: New P, 2005).

Chapter 1 (pp. 19–41)

1. The average of 1,150 pages derives from these six books: Joyce Appleby, Alan Brinkley, and James McPherson, *The American Journey* (NYC: Glencoe McGraw-Hill, 2000); Daniel Boorstin and Brooks Mather Kelley, *A History of the United States* (Needham, MA: Pearson Prentice-Hall, 2005); Paul Boyer, *Holt American Nation* (Austin: Holt, Rinehart & Winston [Harcourt], 2003); Andrew Cayton, Elisabeth Perry, Linda Reed, and Allan Winkler, *America: Pathways to the Present* (Needham, MA: Pearson Prentice Hall, 2005); Gerald A. Danzer, et al., *The Americans* (Boston: McDougal Littell [Houghton Mifflin], 2007); David M. Kennedy, Lizabeth Cohen, and Thomas A. Bailey, *The American Pageant* (Boston: Houghton Mifflin, 2006).

2. College textbooks are much better than high school textbooks. I know, because among the first twelve American history textbooks upon which I based *Lies My Teacher Told Me* was a college textbook, *America: Past and Present*, unbeknownst to me. As I analyzed how the twelve treated various topics—Columbus, John Brown, and so on—it kept on coming out on top. Finally I called the senior author, Robert Divine, and told him his book surpassed the other high school textbooks I was surveying. "Hold it," he stopped me, "that book is intended for college students." I had gotten my copy from a high school where students were using it and had too quickly concluded it was a high school book. I replaced it with a high school textbook, but my error provided a natural experiment that showed college books to be better, especially since *Past and Present* is hardly the best college textbook available.

3. H. Lynn Erickson, *Concept-Based Curriculum and Instruction* (Thousand Oaks, CA: Sage Corwin, 2002), 5–6, 15–16, 63–64; R. J. Marzano and J. S. Kendall, "Awash in

a Sea of Standards" (Aurora, CO: Mid-Continent Research for Education and Learning, 1998), mcrel.org/PDF/Standards/5982IR_AwashInASea.pdf, 2008.

4. In turn, teaching 30–50 topics requires a manageable class size. Helping 30 students complete term papers is hard. Involving 30 students in a mock court is even harder, and assigning 10 to audience roles won't do. This need for classes smaller than 24, hopefully smaller than 20, is not unique to history. Nor does it amount to an argument for relying on studying the textbook when class size is large.

5. Near the end of the year, teachers might assemble students into groups of two or three and ask them to apply as many themes as they can to the 30–50 topics covered during the year. Make a contest of it. Call out the first topic and ask the first group for a theme they applied to it and for their reasoning. If their selection obviously fits, ask how many groups chose that theme and have them award themselves a point. Then go to the next group, ask what additional theme (if any) they applied, and repeat. If a theme's applicability does not seem apparent, ask the group to justify their choice. If you are convinced, award a point to them (and to others who chose likewise). If not, invite a class vote on the matter. This exercise not only reviews all the topics taught, but also provides a final shot at telling their importance.

6. Interviews at Williamsburg, 1993; Irving J. Sloan, *Blacks in America, 1492–1970* (Dobbs Ferry, NY: Oceana, 1971), 2; Howard Zinn, *The Politics of History* (Boston: Beacon, 1970), 67.

7. Whether Bush drew appropriate conclusions from the Vietnam War is not at issue here. Indeed, to the degree that his conclusions were *not* appropriate, accurate knowledge and interpretations of the Vietnam War would be *more* important.

8. Occasionally, transitions can be awkward. On my list, for example, "Wilson's interventions abroad, including WWI," is followed by "Women's rights, culminating in suffrage," followed by "the Depression and FDR," and "WWII." Still, chronology is the teacher's friend. As well, teachers can come up with a transitional paragraph, such as—"As Wilson left office, suffragists finally got the 19th Amendment passed, giving women the right to vote. Deep down, Wilson and his wife opposed women's suffrage, but they didn't make an issue of it, because women's suffrage was an idea whose time had come."—and the class is off and running on the next topic.

9. Cf. Marc Stengel, "The Diffusionists Have Landed" (*Atlantic Monthly* 1/1/2000, 35–48, at theatlantic.com/issues/2000/01/001stengel.htm; Steve Olson, "The Genetic Archaeology of Race," (*Atlantic Monthly* 4/2001, 70–71ff).

10. An interesting graphic summary of a historical topic is Kim Love's portrayal of my talk to the Annie E. Casey Foundation about "Sundown Towns" (uvm.edu/~jloewen/content/sundown_poster_two.jpg).

11. The introductions to the tenth anniversary edition of *Lies My Teacher Told Me* (NYC: New Press, 2005), xxv–xxvi, and the 2nd edition (NYC: Simon & Schuster, 2007), xviii, supply anecdotal evidence on this point.

12. Personal communication, 3/2000.

13. Personal communication, 1/2001.

14. That statistic should amaze. A high school math teacher who never took a single math course in college is unimaginable. The same for a chemistry teacher. A high school English teacher who never took a single English course in college is impossible—most colleges require at least a semester of English to graduate.

Only in history/social studies might teachers teach with *no* college preparation to guide them.

15. Teachers must avoid routinely turning questions back to the students who asked them. That can have the unfortunate result of quelling future questions, lest they result in more work.

16. Widely quoted, including on the inside cover, of Robert Moore, *Reconstruction: The Promise and Betrayal of Democracy* (New York: CIBC, 1983). Today Douglass, who was a leading feminist, would doubtless rephrase to include women, implicitly incorporated in "he."

17. Some shops won't even carry them, because there is so little demand. In others, they cost $.50 each. Some districts retain old books and may let teachers have single copies for free.

18. Chapter 3 shows how studying different editions of the same textbook can be even more valuable.

19. Students might also choose to make different lists: the list of a scientist, doctor, feminist, Native American, or transportation engineer.

Chapter 2 (pp. 42–67)

1. Richard L. Sawyer, "College Student Profiles: Norms for the ACT Assessment, 1980–81" (Iowa City: ACT, 1980), shows larger differences by race and income in social studies than in English, mathematics, or the natural sciences. Subsequent research shows this gap growing still wider since 1980. This is partly due to the establishment bias of most U.S. history textbooks and of courses built upon them, which especially alienates have-not students.

2. Sometimes they *don't*, though, and sometimes their teachers don't really notice, inferring instead that these students *are* doing the work, and doing it very well, when in fact they may be doing only an average job.

3. Harvey and Slatin had started with a much larger bank of photos. They discarded images that provoked disagreement among the teacher-judges.

4. That takes care of the minority of respondents who agree with almost anything (called "yeasayers" by social scientists) or agree with almost nothing ("naysayers").

5. This is not a complete exposition of their work, but it does summarize their most important results. For the complete study, see Dale Harvey and Gerald Slatin, "The Relationship Between Child's SES and Teacher Expectations," *Social Forces*, 54 #1 (9/1975), 140–59.

6. Admittedly, teachers were just following instructions. Absent the request, some teachers might not categorize students that way. However, the normal course of business in many school systems implicitly asks teachers to categorize students in similar ways. Even in 1st grade, a teacher may be expected to form his or her class into reading groups, recommend students for "gifted and talented" programs, and otherwise classify them as superior, average, or remedial in performance and ability. Classes with more than 20 students make hasty grouping more likely, since teachers don't have time to evoke and learn each student's abilities.

7. Harvey and Slatin, *Ibid.*, 141.

8. John Ogbu, *Black American Students in an Affluent Suburb* (Mahwah, NJ: Erlbaum, 2003), 133–35.

9. Barbara J. Fields, "Of Rogues and Geldings," *American Historical Review*, 108 #5 (12/2002), 1401.

10. I am not arguing that black English is just fine. Teachers should teach students standard English and expect from them papers written in standard English. Every student—African American, Mexican American, Native American, recent Hmong immigrant—needs to be able to handle and perform in standard English. One reason why students need this ability is precisely so no one will pigeonhole them as incapable. And there are other reasons. Standard English is a marvelous tool, understood by more and more people around the world. Linguistic acrobats like Amiri Baraka, Michael Eric Dyson, and Nikki Giovanni show us the power and glory of black English partly by their ability to frame their use of it in standard English.

11. Most children's names, whatever their racial or class background, were not identifiable as black, white, working class, or upper class, so a student with a "black" name often had siblings with nonblack names, for example. To minimize the chance that major changes had taken place in the family's life situation, he used siblings born within two years of each other.

12. David N. Figlio, "Names, Expectations and the Black-White Test Score Gap," bear.cba.ufl.edu/figlio/blacknames1.pdf, 2004, *Journal of Human Resources*, forthcoming.

13. Loewen, *The Mississippi Chinese* (Prospect Heights, IL: Waveland, 1988), 145.

14. Colleges said to discriminate based on skin color include Loyola of New Orleans and Howard University. Dark-skinned students did attend and graduate from both schools, of course, but in numbers not nearly commensurate with their share of the black population.

15. Sally Zepeda, "Leadership to Build Learning Communities," *Educational Forum*, Winter 2004, findarticles.com/p/articles/mi_qa4013/is_200401/ai_n9389284; research summarized by Gilah Leder, "Teacher Student Interaction: A Case Study," *Educational Studies in Mathematics*, 18 #3 (8/1987), 255–60; Rhona Weinstein, "Student Perceptions of Schooling," *Elementary School Journal*, 83 #4 (3/1983), 292–94.

16. Robert Rosenthal and Lenore Jacobson, "Teacher Expectations for the Disadvantaged," *Scientific American*, 248 #4 (4/1968), 21–25. See also these authors' *Pygmalion in the Classroom* (NYC: Holt, 1968). While this work resonated with the classroom experience of other educational researchers and teachers, it proved controversial statistically and led to more than a thousand subsequent studies. Some researchers questioned the findings, but enough studies confirmed them to give reason to believe in their generality. For a partial review of this literature, see Robert Rosenthal, "Covert Communication in Classrooms, Clinics, and Courtrooms," *Eye on Psi Chi*, 3 #1 (1998), 18–22, at psichi.org/pubs/articles/article_121.asp, 4/2008.

17. Jere Brophy and Thomas Good, *Teacher-Student Relationships* (NYC: Holt, 1974), 10.

18. I don't know that he had taken a coaching class, and they were less widespread then than now, but he probably had, given his low scores, wealth, and suburban metropolitan location.

19. Harcourt Assessment website, harcourtassessment.com/haiweb/Cultures /en-US/Harcourt/Community/PostSecondary/Products/MAT/mathome.htm, 10/2007.

20. ETS has institutional relationships with scores of colleges and universities that might provide such data.

21. Dinesh D'Souza attacked this reasoning in his book *Illiberal Education* (NYC: Free P, 1991, 45). He seized upon an item using black slang in my "Collegiate IQ Test," a teaching tool sometimes entitled "Loewen Low-Aptitude Test" (see "Introductory Sociology: Four Classroom Exercises," *Teaching Sociology*, 6 #3 [April 1979], 237). "Why a familiarity with this vocabulary is a good preparation for college," D'Souza wrote, "Loewen does not say."

D'Souza missed my point, surely deliberately. I make no claim that knowing the word "dashiki" is good preparation for college. But neither is knowing the word "sake" good preparation for graduate school.

For that matter, the reasoning employed by an analogy using dashiki might be more complex than the simple "A"—"A" thinking in the sake item. Compared to shirts, dashikis are handmade, more expensive, more individual, more colorful, and of course African. There are additional differences: dashikis are put on differently and are less sexist, particularly since in the 1970s women's shirts always buttoned right over left while men's buttoned left over right. Item writers might use any of these differences or a combination to construct an interesting analogy and attractive distractors. So the rejected dashiki item would be more useful than the sake item in measuring reasoning abilities, presumably related, in turn, to college success.

The newest SATs have abandoned analogies, but that revision does not alter the main point. The exam maintains its built-in bias against African, Native, and Latino Americans, the working class, and rural Americans, for reasons this paragraph in the main text explains.

22. See Loewen, "Statement," in Eileen Rudert, ed., *The Validity of Testing in Education and Employment* (DC: U.S. Commission on Civil Rights, 1993), 42–43; cf. Loewen, "A Sociological View of Aptitude Tests," *Ibid.*, 73–89.

23. Alicia P. Schmitt, Paul W. Holland, and Neil J. Dorans, "Evaluating Hypotheses About Differential Item Functioning" (Princeton, NJ: ETS Research Report 92–98, 1992), 16.

24. James W. Loewen, Phyllis Rosser, and John Katzman, "Gender Bias on SAT Items," American Educational Research Association, 4/1988, New Orleans; ERIC ED294915.

25. Again, the new SAT no longer uses analogy items, but differential knowledge of vocabulary remains a major component of test bias. Analogy items illustrate this problem compactly.

26. For that matter, even among students from elite backgrounds, those few who have learned the words and get the item right might be more retentive, as well as good reasoners, and hence do better in college.

27. One answer to this problem is to rely less on multiple-choice items when making prescriptive decisions about individuals, such as to put them in "advanced" or "slow" classes or admit them to college. Some colleges are making less use of SAT and ACT scores in their admissions process.

28. "Discussion," in Rudert, ed., *The Validity of Testing in Education and Employment*, 58–59; cf. Loewen, "A Sociological View of Aptitude Tests," *Ibid.*, 73.

29. collegeboard.com/student/testing/sat/about.html, 12/2007.

30. As a general rule, if a course demands more than 125% as much as other comparable courses, students will resist those demands.

31. Susan Eaton, *The Children in Room E4* (Chapel Hill: Algonquin Books, 2006), 257.

32. This was the mantra of Ernst Borinski, longtime sociologist at Tougaloo College and a subject of the movie *From Swastika to Jim Crow*.

33. Betty Hart and Todd Risley, *Meaningful Differences in the Everyday Experience of Young American Children* (Baltimore: Brookes, 1995), 30, 62–70, 123–48, 159–68.

34. In *The Blind Side*, Michael Lewis showed the difference that intense intervention coupled with expectations can make. The subject of the book, Michael Oher, basically raised himself, homeless on the streets of Memphis. A rich white family took him in, partly because his athletic prowess might make him an asset to the football program at Ole Miss, their alma mater. Tutoring and private school helped Oher realize his academic potential. As of this writing (2/2008), Oher has just decided to return to Ole Miss for his senior year, foregoing an early draft to the NFL. More importantly, he has succeeded academically, with an A- GPA, majoring in journalism. (Michael Lewis, *The Blind Side* [NYC: W.W. Norton, 2006]; Scott Cacciola, "Oher says he's not entering NFL draft," Memphis *Commercial Appeal*, 1/17/2008, commercialappeal.com/news/2008/jan/17/oher-says-hes-not-entering-nfl-draft/, 2/2008.) My point isn't to suggest that every rich family in America adopt a street kid—although that would be interesting—but to suggest that poverty and ignorance can make capability hard to spot.

35. James Rosenbaum, *Making Inequality* (NYC: Wiley, 1976), 33–34.

36. See Jay Mathews, *Class Struggle* (NYC: Times Books, 1998), 234–35; Linda Darling-Hammond, "Inequality and Access to Knowledge," in James A. Banks, ed., *Handbook of Research on Multicultural Education* (NYC: Macmillan, 1995), 474; and Anne Wheelock, *Crossing the Tracks* (NYC: New P, 1992), 57–58, 92–117.

37. Louanne Johnson, "They're All My Children," *Reader's Digest* (May 1995), 155–63 ff, based on experiences described in *The Girls in the Back of the Class* (NYC: St. Martin's, 1995).

38. Postings to APUSH discussion list, 3/2004.

39. The AVID program—Advancement Via Individual Determination—helps "average" students develop skills to succeed in "advanced" courses. See avidonline.org.

40. James Agee, *Let Us Now Praise Famous Men* (Boston: Houghton Mifflin, 1939–41), 289.

41. For the record, the right answer is A.

42. Yes, they're small states. Don't be fooled. Larger states have larger tax bases, too. States rely upon multiple-choice twig tests because they're cheap. Too often states then let out-of-state testing agencies recycle old questions, graded by machine, thus reaping windfall profits. If a topic is worth testing—history/social studies is—then it is worth testing well.

Chapter 3 (pp. 68–82)

1. John Unruh Jr., *The Plains Across* (Urbana: U of IL P, 1979), 156, 176, 185.

2. Brigham Madsen, "The 'Almo Massacre' Revisited," *ID Yesterdays*, 37 #3 (Fall 1993), 59.

3. Larry McMurtry, "Broken Promises," *NY Review of Books*, 10/23/97, 16.

4. See Loewen, *Lies Across America* (NYC: Simon & Schuster, 2000), 92–93.

5. Leon Festinger, "Cognitive Consequences of Forced Compliance," *Journal of Abnormal and Social Psychology, 58* (1959), 203–10.

6. For decades the federal government acquiesced in Southern states' denial of citizenship and equal treatment to their black residents.

7. Adam Goodheart, "Change of Heart," *AARP Magazine*, 5/2004, 45–47.

8. *Ibid.*

9. Bernard Weisberger, "The Dark and Bloody Ground of Reconstruction Historiography," *Journal of Southern History*, 25 #4 (11/1959), 427–47; Eric Foner, "Reconstruction Revisited," *Reviews in American History*, 10 #4 (12/1982), 82–88.

10. My hope is that this relationship is indeed reciprocal: that telling the truth about the past helps bring about justice in the present.

11. Some students may have learned a somewhat similar checklist from speech or English courses, based on the acronym SOAPS, which stands for Subject, Occasion, Audience, Purpose, and Speaker. SOAP provides a checklist for speakers planning a talk; modified with a final S, "Speaker," it offers another way to teach historiography and critical reading.

12. That one was John A. Garraty with Aaron Singer and Michael Gallagher, *American History* (New York: Harcourt Brace Jovanovich, 1982).

13. Actually, he did not. "Landslide" is defined as 60% to 40%. Pierce won 1,601,274 votes, or 51%; Whig Winfield Scott got 1,386,580, or 44.1%. Of votes cast for the two major candidates, Pierce won 53.6%. He did win the electoral college by 254 to 42.

14. Paul Boyer, *Holt American Nation* (Austin: Holt, Rinehart and Winston, 2003), 350.

15. The civil rights era is a watershed event in our historiography, even more than in our history. Students should be cautioned to look at when books were written—before or after the struggle for civil rights. Of course, historians wrote good books before 1956. Certainly, historians wrote bad books after 1972. But regarding not just black-white race relations, the Civil War, slavery, and Reconstruction, but also women's history, American Indian history, social class, and various other topics, as the struggle for civil rights reverberated through American culture, it changed the assumptions underlying historians' thinking.

Chapter 4 (pp. 83–102)

1. For most presidents, they didn't have to dig very deeply, to be sure. The web sufficed.

2. I'm not suggesting chiselling off the letters on one side and putting on new ones. Most markers aren't made that way. Students might attach temporary marker text, maybe on foam board, with permission and with media coverage, thus making public the problems with the original. Various states are rewording bad markers (Kansas, Virginia), tearing them down (Mississippi), or putting up corrective plaques nearby (Wisconsin, Wyoming).

3. To be sure, the census is now on the web. Even the "manuscript census" is on the Web. Increasingly, newspapers show up on the web and can even be searched electronically. Sources like the census or old newspapers are usually as accurate on the web as they are on microfilm or hard copy. Even traditionalists have no quarrel with such information. By inveighing against "the web," they mean to challenge websites with unvetted pages by unqualified authors, like the Pierce page just discussed, and also such collaborative efforts as Wikipedia. Articles in Wikipedia vary wildly in quality, so traditionalists are right not to accept them thoughtlessly, but many articles show care, erudition, and a level of detail not readily available elsewhere. Books, newspaper articles, and the like can certainly be biased or wrong. Indeed, my book *Lies My Teacher Told Me* demonstrates errors in history textbooks. Nevertheless, several people have usually reviewed a book or article by the time it appears in a library.

4. Adrian Turner, *A Celebration of 'Gone with the Wind'* (NYC: W. H. Smith, 1992), 166. It is also the most widely viewed movie in Great Britain, according to the British Film Institute ("*Gone with the Wind* tops film list," BBC News, 11/28/2004, news.bbc.co.uk/1/hi/entertainment/film/4049645.stm, 2/2008).

5. *Books in Print* online, bowker.com/brands/bip.htm, 2/2008; "A Favorite Still," *Burlington Free Press*, 1/24/1988.

6. Darden A. Pyron, *Southern Daughter: The Life of Margaret Mitchell* (NYC: Oxford UP, 1991), 19–29, 84–85.

7. Mitchell, *Gone with the Wind* (NYC: Avon, 1973 [1936], 645.

8. Olivia de Havilland quoted in Thomas K. Arnold, "'Wind' still blows even co-star away," *USA Today*, 11/2/2004. De Havilland, of course, had no idea what *black* cast members thought.

9. Because Reconstruction was so poorly taught throughout the Nadir of race relations, and because inertia so afflicts the textbook industry and the teaching profession, teachers need to read a "modern" interpretation of that important period. (Bear in mind that modern interpretations are similar to those made at the time.) Here are three, the first fictional: Margaret Walker, *Jubilee* (NYC: Bantam, 1967); Eric Foner, *Reconstruction* (NYC: Harper & Row, 1988); Lerone Bennett, *Black Power U.S.A.: The Human Side of Reconstruction* (Baltimore: Penguin, 1969).

10. To be sure, some professors have grown so pessimistic about the quality of the results that they no longer ask students to write anything substantive in college, either. Thus, we progress.

11. Teachers may choose to make the reasoning behind a group explicit to its members or may imply that the groupings are more or less random. This is a delicate decision best made in the light of knowledge about the students involved.

12. Daniel Boorstin and Brooks Kelley, *A History of the United States* (Needham, MA: Prentice-Hall, 2005), 6–10, 15–16, 23–24.

13. Jules Benjamin, *A Student's Guide to History* (NYC: St. Martin's, 2000), bedfordstmartins.com/history/benjamin/con_index.htm?wri, 2/2008.

14. I prefer "storyline" because "thesis" can imply that the work can be summarized in one hypothesis. For an experiment in rat psychology this may be true, although some sociologists of science deny that science works this way. It is definitely too limiting for most history papers, which are often more open and more exploratory. In everyday usage, "argument" implies disagreement. While historians use the term to refer to a position taken vis-à-vis other scholars, this does not resonate well with high school students.

15. They do have underlying story lines, such as the archetype of unrelenting progress, but these are rarely made explicit. So far as students can infer, they just present one thing after another.

16. Once in a while, a student will footnote *too* often. See the discussion of "common knowledge" in the next paragraph.

17. Previously the teacher will have read the proposal to ensure it is neither embarrassingly bad nor above criticism.

18. Some parents will miss both sessions. Don't judge them, and don't let their child feel that their absence will hinder him/her.

19. Included should be email and phone contact information for the teacher, the name of the school librarian (who has been alerted to the project), the name of a staff member at the community library (who has also been alerted) along with its address and hours, a website or two that will likely prove helpful, and how students can access that website without a computer or internet connection at home.

20. Elaine W. Reed, *Helping Your Child Learn History* (DC: U.S. Dept. of Education, 1993), at ed.gov/pubs/parents/History/index.html, 2/2008.

21. *One Hundred Years of Progress: The Centennial History of Anna, Illinois* (Cape Girardeau: Missourian Printing, 1954).

22. I write "perhaps" because the size and destructiveness of the Chicago fire may not merit the attention it gets in our national narrative. After all, on the same day, fire destroyed Peshtigo, in northeast Wisconsin, and went on to consume 1,875 square miles of forest, an area almost as large as Delaware. The Peshtigo fire destroyed 17 towns, killed between 1,200 and 2,500 people (at least five times as many as died in Chicago), and remains the deadliest fire in U.S. history. The Peshtigo fire was the first conflagration in history to be understood as a firestorm; hence it was studied by U.S. armed forces planners before bombing cities in Germany and Japan in World War II. See Denise Gess and William Lutz, *Firestorm at Peshtigo* (NYC: Holt, 2002), 205–12. Students might enjoy researching the Peshtigo fire, making the case that it dwarfed the Chicago fire, and analyzing why Chicago got more news coverage, both then and later.

23. See Loewen et al., *Mississippi: Conflict and Change* (NYC: Pantheon, 1980), 214–17, for a summary.

24. "The First Black Student at Virginia Tech" and *In Relentless Pursuit of an Education* in the bibliography provide examples.

25. For an example of this kind of history, see Charles Bright, "It was as if we were never there," *Journal of American History*, 3/2002, 1440.

26. Admittedly, one Illinois town's local history collection consists of a single book!

27. The educational research literature is too vast to cite here. James Rosenbaum's *Making Inequality* (NYC: Wiley, 1976) deserves mention, however, not only as an exemplary piece of research but also as a good read (for teachers). He studied "the hidden curriculum of high school tracking" in a Massachusetts city where students varied very little in social class, yet got tracked as if they did.

28. The 1990 and 2000 censuses are fairly easily used. For earlier years, selecting the year of interest yields a morass of pdf files. The census of population is in there, usually including the specific tables a student needs, but digging around is required to find them. The printed census in a community library or nearby university can be less frustrating.

29. The manuscript census is available for a fee at ancestry.com. For individual states, it is usually available for free somewhere, sometimes at the state historical society's website. Many libraries and genealogical collections also have it on microfilm.

30. I do not advocate documentary and performance competitions. Shooting a documentary seems alluring and, when done in the service of a local history topic, can be important and compelling. Unfortunately, most historical research, including local research, is not telegenic, since the event itself is past. Poring over the manuscript census or looking through old newspapers does not make for good video. At best, research may include an interesting interview on an important topic, but that interview may flow better if it is *not* filmed. Besides, students know that "head and shoulder" interviews are considered boring video. So they pick a telegenic topic—usually something copied from the History Channel or its clones. This often means military history. While there is nothing wrong with military history, the resulting student documentary rarely adds much to the original. Most students focus on the basics of what happened rather than developing storylines of their own. Since students already watch enough television, they gain little by being encouraged to watch more. Furthermore, we have not agreed upon a method for footnoting videos. That last problem also besets the performance competition. Students also wind up sinking too much time into costumes and props, rather than the history they are telling. Moreover, that history again emphasizes the basics—what happened—rather than why, or any storyline developed by the students.

31. In his transcribed interviews he had actually created important historical materials for the future, so I suggested that he ask Mrs. Robinson where her husband's papers are and to deposit his transcriptions there for future researchers.

32. Lindsay Harney and Amanda Staab, letter to Mayor Ossie Langfelder and petition to city council, 3/21/1991; Bernard Schoenburg, "A Day to Remember," *IL*

State Journal-Register, 5/27/1991; Harney, "It Started Small, It Grew," talk at Eastern Illinois University, 10/27/2000; *Springfield Had No Shame* (Springfield: Inst. for Public Affairs, U of IL, video, n.d.).

Chapter 5 (pp. 103–22)

1. Before the Present. Archaeologists often use "BP" rather than "BC" or "BCE." Because dates for long-ago remains and artifacts are ranges, not intended to be accurate within several hundred years, the passage of a few years as a published source ages does not invalidate such estimates.

Scholars increasingly use "BCE" ("Before the Common Era") rather than "BC" ("Before Christ"). Maybe teachers should, too, but they must decide for themselves whether this windmill merits a tilt. After all, 50 years before the common era was also about 50 years before Christ, and neither phrase necessarily has a religious content. AD (Anno Domini, or In the Year of the Lord) is harder to defend (versus CE), since it refers to the Christian God. "AD" grew more secular, however, as usage shifted from "AD 1492" to "1492 AD." The former was grammatically correct: Columbus indeed sailed "in the year of the Lord 1492." The latter has no similarly succinct translation, but none is required, because to most people "1492 AD" merely signifies 1,492 years after the division point from BC to AD.

2. Loewen, *Lies My Teacher Told Me* (NYC: Simon & Schuster, 2007), 95–97.

3. I will later argue that peer review can sometimes be a limitation.

4. Loewen, *Lies My Teacher Told Me*, 96–100, shows how textbooks portray the first settlers as dullards.

5. Homo erectus, an intermediate species between homo sapiens and apes, left stone tools on the island of Flores, in southeastern Indonesia, 750,000 BP. So humans had boats even before humans were fully human! See Boris Weintraub, "A Seagoing Human Ancestor?" *National Geographic*. 11/98, unpaginated front matter.

6. Walking might have been easier then than now, however, depending on the topography of the coast (now flooded). If a shore route was used, however, boats would have been required to cross rivers. Also, the alleged ice-free corridor went inland.

7. Genetic research summarized by science reporter Steve Olson shows that all male American Indians at one point shared a distinctive Y chromosome found in no other group, stemming from one person, implying that a small number of men made the trip from Siberia. (See Olson, "The Genetic Archaeology of Race," *Atlantic Monthly, 287* #4 (4/2001), 70–71.) Their genetic similarity is an additional reason why so many Native Americans succumbed to the diseases introduced after 1492. Cf. "Gene study suggests Native Americans came from Siberia," at Yahoo. com, 11/27/2007, news.yahoo.com/s/afp/20071127/ts_alt_afp/usamericasrussiaanthropologymigration, reporting a study in *PLoS Genetics*; and Malcolm Ritter, "Indian DNA Links to 6 'Founding Mothers,'" AP, 3/13/2008, news.wired.com/dynamic/stories/N/NATIVE_AMERICAN_DNA?SITE=WIRE&SECTION=HOME&TEMPLATE=DEFAULT&CTIME=2008-03-13-10-33-33.

8. Erich von Däniken, *Chariots of the Gods* (NYC: Putnam, 1970).

9. Most archaeologists are not well equipped to judge diffusion claims because they are expert only on American cultures. If they can readily dismiss claims of diffusion, then they need not become conversant with the cultures, plants, and technologies of the culture(s) alleged to have influenced the Americas.

10. Jack Forbes, *Black Africans and Native Americans* (NYC: Blackwell, 1988).

11. Inuit people have been making round trips across the Bering Strait at least since 1000 AD, of course.

12. Andrew Murr, "Who Got Here First?" *Newsweek*, 11/15/99.

13. "Comet theory collides with Clovis research, may explain disappearance of ancient people," U of SC website, uscnews.sc.edu/ARCH190.html, 6/28/2007; Colin Nickerson, "Cosmic blast may have killed off megafauna," *Boston Globe*, 9/25/2007, boston.com/news/nation/articles/2007/09/25/cosmic_blast_may_have_killed_off_megafauna/

14. Charles C. Mann, "The Pristine Myth," *Atlantic Monthly* (3/2002), theatlantic.com/doc/200203u/int2002-03-07; Clark Erickson, sas.upenn.edu/~cerickso/, 5/2008.

15. Egypt was construed as "white," even part of Mediterranean Europe in a way, overlooking its "mixed-race" people and the elements of its culture that came down the Nile from Sudan.

16. Simon G. Southerton, "How DNA Divides LDS Apologists," Signature Books, signaturebooks.com/dna.htm, 5/2008.

17. By not disclosing my current religious membership or theology, I am modeling how I suggest teachers should handle this query.

18. Walt Whitman, "Song of Myself," in *Leaves of Grass* (NYC: Doubleday, Page, 1927), 50. Another Whitman poem, "When I Heard the Learn'd Astronomer," 230–31, specifically addresses the issue of two very different ways of perceiving and understanding the world.

19. Psychologist Steven Pinker asserts, "Today no honest and informed person can maintain that the universe came into being a few thousand years ago and assumed its current form in six days." He is right. His statement does not negate religious ways of explaining and understanding the world, however. The John Templeton Foundation, which solicited Pinker's comment, offers many views on the relationship between science and religion at templeton.org/belief.

20. Las Casas is justly criticized for suggesting African slaves be brought in to replace Indian slaves. See Chapter 8 regarding how he recanted this proposal. Of course, no Native American had a chance to be the first historian, since the Spaniards destroyed almost every Mayan book they found in the Americas.

21. At this point, a note on these three terms may be helpful. Presentism is letting our present time's concerns and ways of thought distort our understanding of the past. Whig history and chronological ethnocentrism are near synonyms. They are examples of presentism, a larger category. (Other examples include some religious beliefs, assumptions built into capitalism, white supremacy, and the desire not to be racist or condescending toward Native Americans.) Whig history portrays the past so as to make the present seem foreordained, legitimate, even "natural." Chronological ethnocentrism views today's society and culture as better than

past ones. By their very nature, Whig history and chronological ethnocentrism build allegiance to society, whether deserved or not.

22. Sarah Palin would be an exception.

23. Loewen, *Lies Across America* (NYC: Simon & Schuster, 2000).

24. Robin Clarke and Geoffrey Hindley, *The Challenge of the Primitives* (London, J. Cape, 1975), especially 9–22.

25. Hobbs, *Leviathan*, Part I, "Of Man," Ch. 13 at bartleby.xcom/34/5/13.html

26. I did not put quotation marks around "primitive" because I meant it in its anthropological sense: rudimentary division of labor.

27. Colin Turnbull, *The Human Cycle* (NYC: Simon & Schuster, 1983), 34–35.

28. Geoffrey M. Anderson, "Making Sense of Rising Caesarean Section Rates: Time to Change Our Goals," *British Medical Journal*, 9/25/2004, at bmj.bmjjournals. com/cgi/content/full/329/7468/696, 5/2008.

29. Since about 1970, "natural childbirth" has gained adherents in the U.S. Such births are still very artificial compared to "primitive" societies but do let fathers be present and let babies stay with their mothers rather than in a large nursery. At the same time, Caesareans continue to increase.

30. Colin Turnbull, *The Human Cycle* (New York: Simon & Schuster, 1983), 21; cf. Richard Louv, *Last Child in the Woods* (Chapel Hill: Algonquin Books, 2005).

31. Richard Lee and Irven DeVore, "Problems in the Study of Hunters and Gatherers," in Lee, DeVore, and J. Nash, eds., *Man the Hunter* (Chicago: Aldine, 1968), 3.

32. Russell Means, "Fighting Words on the Future of the Earth," *Mother Jones* (12/1980), 24–32.

33. Louis H. Sullivan, *Kindergarten Chats and Other Writings* (NYC: Dover, 1979 [1918]), 151.

Chapter 6 (pp. 123–40)

1. It is interesting to ask students for the exceptions. Many will say "China," but China was controlled by France, the United Kingdom, Germany, Japan, and to a degree, the United States. Japan, Thailand, and Ethiopia governed themselves in 1892. So did two small kingdoms high in the Himalayas, Nepal and Bhutan, although both were close allies of the United Kingdom, which might have subordinated them had they not been. Morocco and fragmented forerunners of Saudi Arabia also governed themselves, though with European interventions.

2. At least, they had *better* be secular. If teachers give sacred answers, then they are imposing their religious beliefs in the classroom.

3. Actually, this conflict is not so deep as the clash between religious and scientific views of evolution, human origins, and the spread of people around the globe, as discussed in the last chapter. Parents and students can retain their belief that Christianity (or Islam, for that matter) is right, and that it spread (and continues to spread) because God (or Allah) willed (and wills) it. The teacher is merely teaching the worldly reasons why (and how) it "won."

4. Whether Christianity is right or wrong is by definition a religious, not historical, question. Whether, how, and why it is winning are historical questions.

Allowing the notion that Christianity is winning because it is right to go unchallenged amounts to religious teaching. Such thinking is religious partly because it is nonempirical. That is, God's will can be invoked to explain anything, not just the happy (to most Christians) fact that Christianity is expanding. Some Fundamentalist Christian ministers claim that God sent Hurricane Katrina to devastate New Orleans because of that city's notorious red light district, tolerance of gays, and other alleged sins. Other ministers have even explained the Holocaust as part of God's plan, since it resulted in the concentration of many surviving Jews in Palestine, in line with one interpretation of Biblical prophecies. Muslims are another group that can claim their religion is still spreading in influence. (Perhaps Buddhists can also make that claim.) Most Americans would not tolerate a public school that taught or implied that Islam is winning because it is right. The same must hold about Christianity.

5. R. R. Palmer, *A History of the Modern World* (NYC: Knopf, 1957), 3.

6. Felipe Fernandez-Armesto, *Millennium* (NYC: Scribner, 1995), 35.

7. Hugh Trevor-Roper, "Foreword," in Marcel Dunan, ed., *Larousse Encyclopedia of Modern History* (NYC: Crescent, 1987 [1964]), 10. Trevor-Roper was perhaps too Eurasian-centric to mention any civilization in Africa or the Americas.

8. Palmer, *A History of the Modern World*, 13.

9. Jared Diamond, *Guns, Germs, and Steel* (NYC: Norton, 1997), 16.

10. This item was emailed to me in 2005 by a person who chooses to remain anonymous.

11. Loewen, *Lies My Teacher Told Me About Christopher Columbus*, originally *The Truth About Columbus* (NYC: New P, 1992), especially 20–21.

12. Two examples are on my website, http://sundown.afro/illinois.edu/

13. A video of a recent total lunar eclipse seen from Spain shows Earth's shadow. It is readily available on the web, such as at video.aol.com/video-detail/total-lunar-eclipse-february-21-2008/1372835070 and video.yahoo.com/watch/2082035/6536743.

14. Loewen, *Lies My Teacher Told Me About Christopher Columbus*, 20–21.

15. Loewen, *Lies My Teacher Told Me About Christopher Columbus,* and Chapter 2 of *Lies My Teacher Told Me* (NYC: Simon & Schuster, 2007) can help students spot which other items on their inventory of Columbus's accomplishments may also be problematic.

16. To be sure, conquering had happened before, but not empires on the other side of the world.

17. See the Columbus chapter of *Lies My Teacher Told Me* for details.

18. The Columbus chapter of *Lies My Teacher Told Me* goes into greater detail.

19. "New," of course, depends on the item. Horses were new to the Americas. Potatoes were new to Europe. Also, note that these instructions are meant in the context of post-Columbian trade. For example, gold and silver came from many places, going far back in time; the enormous riches of Mexico, Peru, and Bolivia are the point in this exercise.

20. That short sentence does not do full justice to those two examples. Neither Irish nor Hebrew had quite died out, although very few children were learning either language when the revival efforts began. Nor has the revival of Irish

completely succeeded.

21. Jack Weatherford, *Indian Givers* (New York: Fawcett, 1988), gives a good account of some of the ways American Indian cultures have enriched our society and culture.

22. Note that the North did not initially participate in order to end slavery, but rather to hold the nation together. The South did secede primarily on behalf of slavery, as Chapter 9 shows. By mid-1862, ending slavery was becoming a major Union war aim.

23. David Wallechinsky, "Is America Still No. 1?" *Parade*, 1/14/2007, 4.

24. Marilyn Vos Savant, column, *Parade*, 6/8/2008.

25. Wallechinsky, "Is America Still No. 1?," 5.

26. The *CIA World Factbook* ranks nations on many interesting dimensions; see cia.gov/library/publications/the-world-factbook/index.html, 7/2008. Other sources include NationMaster, at nationmaster.com/index.php, and various published reference books. Sources often disagree, which is cautionary.

27. Wallechinsky, "Is America Still No. 1?", 5.

28. Cecil Adams, "Does the United States Lead the World in Prison Population?" The Straight Dope column and website, straightdope.com/columns/040206.html 2/6/2004, 8/2008.

29. Wallechinsky, "Is America Still No. 1?", 5.

Chapter 7 (pp. 141–54)

1. That proportion also includes a few immigrants from Guatemala, El Salvador, and other Central American nations.

2. Dorris, quoted in Calvin Martin, ed., *The American Indian and the Problem of History* (NYC: Oxford UP, 1987), 102. Dorris taught mostly non-Native undergraduates for years at Dartmouth.

3. Quoted in Francis Haines, "How the Indian Got the Horse," *American Heritage*, 15 #2 (2/1964), americanheritage.com/articles/magazine/ah/1964/2/1964_2_16.shtml, 6/2008.

4. Russell Shorto, *The Island at the Center of the World* (NYC: Doubleday, 2004), 55–57. Thanks to Jan J. Toof for bringing Shorto to my attention.

5. Lincoln Home National Historic Site, Abraham Lincoln Online, showcase, netins.net/web/creative/lincoln/sites/home.htm, 6/2008.

6. Although many writers call the Indians who lived on Manhattan Weckquaesgeeks, like most Indians in the East before Europeans arrived, they lived in villages only loosely organized into tribes. Some were called "Manahattans," variously spelled. Some may have been members of still smaller groups, such as the Reckgawawancs who were tributaries of the Weckquaesgeeks. The latter also lived in what is now the Bronx and Westchester County. No Indians may have been living on the southern tip of the island, for the Dutch moved in with no difficulty and lived there for a year with no treaty with anyone.

7. Absent primary sources, I rely on these secondary sources: Irving Wallace, David Wallechinsky, and Amy Wallace, *Significa* (NYC: Dutton, 1983), 326; Robert S. Grumet, "American Indians," in Kenneth T. Jackson, *Encyclopedia of NY City* (New Haven: Yale UP, 1995), 25–28; Reginald Pelham Bolton, *NYC in Indian*

Possession (NYC: Heye Foundation, 1920), 240–45; Bolton, *Indian Life of Long Ago in the City of NY* (NYC: Joseph Graham, 1934), 127; Peter Francis Jr., "The Beads That Did *Not* Buy Manhattan Island," *NY History, 67* #1 (1/1986): 5–20; Robert S. Grumet, *Historic Contact* (Norman: U of OK P, 1995), 219; James Finch, "Aboriginal Remains on Manhattan Island" (NYC: American Museum of Natural History, 1909 Anthropological Papers, 3), 72; E. M. Ruttenber, *History of Indian Tribes of Hudson's River* (Saugerties, NY: Hope Farm P, 1992 [1872]), 71–78; Russell Shorto, *The Island at the Center of the World* (NYC: Doubleday, 2004), 54–60, 112, 123–127; and Donna Merwick, *The Shame and the Sorrow* (Philadelphia: U of PA P, 2006).

8. Here is one source, as of 6/2008: vcdh.virginia.edu/encounter/projects/ monacans/Reconstructed_Village/jwhite.html. Part of another White illustration is in *Lies My Teacher Told Me* (NYC: Simon & Schuster, 2007), 105.

9. Sources for such maps include the website of the American Studies University of Groningen, Netherlands, let.rug.nl/usa/images/nadam2.gif, and hollandamericahistoricalsociety.org/

10. This map is available at Wikipedia in extraordinary detail at upload. wikimedia.org/wikipedia/commons/6/6c/Map_of_Lewis_and_Clark%27s_ Track%2C_Across_the_Western_Portion_of_North_America%2C_published _1814.jpg

In passing, we might note that the original "Corps of Discovery" was undertaken on an appropriation of $2,500 and eventually cost a total of $38,000. Between 2003–05, the National Park Service sent a repeat expedition, setting up tents with exhibits about the bicentennial of the journey. Even though it minimized costs by using interstate highways, the total cost of "Corps II," as it was called, came to just under $13 million (Stephen Adams, Supt., Lewis and Clark National Historic Trail, personal communication, 6/2008). This is another demonstration of inflation, of course. Teaching students that $2,500 or $38,000 was the cost of the Lewis and Clark Expedition would be silly—but not as silly as having them learn $24 as the price "we" paid for Manhattan.

11. Helpful resources include Gordon R. Young, *The Army Almanac* (Harrisburg: Stackpole, 1959), 496–99, 704–07; Robert M. Utley and Wilcomb E. Washburn, *American Heritage History of the Indian Wars* (NYC: Bonanza, 1982); Utley, *The Indian Frontier of the American West, 1846–1890* (Albuquerque: U of NM P, 1984).

12. Of course, Miss Elliot was not trained as a historian and surely never thought about the myth she was passing on.

13. Nevertheless, Europeans often then accused them of trespassing and jailed and sometimes killed them for the offense.

14. Mitchell, *Gone with the Wind* (NYC: Avon, 1973 [1936], 25.

15. Darden A. Pyron, *Southern Daughter* (NYC: Oxford UP), 64–85.

16. Lizabeth Cohen, *A Consumers' Republic* (NYC: Knopf, 2003), 217; Kenneth T. Jackson, *Crabgrass Frontier* (NYC: Oxford UP, 1985), 241; Levitt & Sons, ad taken out after murder of Martin Luther King Jr., 4/1968, in exhibit, "Levittown," Pennsylvania State Museum, 11/2002; Geoffrey Mohan writing in *Newsday*, quoted by Kevin Schultz, personal communication, 6/2002.

17. Maya Angelou, "On the Pulse of Morning," poem for the inauguration of President Clinton, 1/20/1993.

18. In 1995, two high school students in northern Minnesota began a movement that eventually convinced the Minnesota Legislature to eliminate the word "squaw" from geographic and place names in the state. Since then, sometimes again with prodding from students, several other states have followed suit.

19. Fifteen essays in Loewen, *Lies Across America* (NYC: Simon & Schuster, 2000), discuss problems in the way that historic sites treat Native Americans.

Chapter 8 (pp. 155–74)

1. This issue—did they or didn't they—continues to get undue attention. Whether Jefferson had sexual intercourse with Hemings is not nearly as important as how he allowed slavery to interfere with his foreign policy as president, for example. Ironically, defenders of Jefferson gave the matter its importance. Even before he became president, detractors of Jefferson used his sexual liaisons with Hemings against him. Several later biographers, absent good evidence that anyone else fathered her children, claimed it simply could not have been Jefferson; to do so was "inconsistent with his character." Aside from the fact that this claim hardly constituted evidence, it magnified the issue, for if Jefferson's character was a defense against the charge, then proof of the charge ipso facto amounts to a stain on his character. Good overviews of the matter are supplied by Annette Gordon-Reed, *Thomas Jefferson and Sally Hemings* (Charlottesville: U of VA P, 1998), and *Science in Dispute*, scienceclarified.com/dispute/Vol-2/Has-DNA-testing-proved-that-ThomasJefferson-fathered-at-least-one-child-with-one-of-his-slaves-Sally-Hemings.html, 6/2008.

2. Dalton Conley, "Forty Acres and a Mule Isn't Enough," en.monde-diplomatique.fr/2001/09/08richconley, *Le Monde Diplomatique* (Paris), 9/2001.

3. Loewen, *Sundown Towns* (NYC: New P, 2005), 81, 119, 144–45.

4. Kain research summarized in W. A. Low and V. A. Clift, eds., *Encyclopedia of Black America* (NYC: McGraw-Hill, 1981), 447–48; Michelle Singletary, "Helping Blacks Overcome Barriers to Homeownership," *Washington Post*, 10/14/01.

5. Douglas opinion, *Jones et us v. Alfred H. Mayer Co*, 392 US 409, 445–47 (1968).

6. Included were the photo of a lynching (p. 6), John Brown (p. 72), Gordon (p. 191), and other illustrations in Loewen, *Lies My Teacher Told Me* (NYC: Simon & Schuster, 2007), or on my website.

7. Quoted in *The Shaw Memorial* (Conshohocken, PA: Eastern National, 1997), 56.

8. I don't intend this sentence as a comment on the issue of reparations for slavery. My stand on reparations for slavery might depend upon what kind of reparations, paid to whom, by what governments or corporations.

9. A little later, racism also arose to justify the taking of Indians' land. Chapter 7 described one example.

10. Montesquieu, *The Spirit of the Laws* (Cincinnati: R. Clarke, 1873), 274–75, quoted in Felix Okoye, *The American Image of Africa: Myth and Reality* (Buffalo, NY: Black Academy P, 1971), 37.

11. William Harris and Judith Levey, eds., *The New Columbia Encyclopedia* (NYC: Columbia UP, 1975), 1088.

12. See Loewen, *Lies My Teacher Told Me*, 144–46; see also Leon Festinger, *A Theory of Cognitive Dissonance* (Evanston: Row, Peterson, 1957).

13. In truth I don't know the sex of the squirrel, nor how to tell at a distance.

14. Major exceptions would be captive animals: livestock, pets, animals in zoos, and so on. Some of these do have considerable autonomy from moment to moment, however.

15. *Six Women's Slave Narratives* (NYC: Oxford UP, 1988 [1863]), "Memoir of Old Elizabeth," 3–4.

16. Ira Berlin, *Many Thousand Gone*, listed at the end of this chapter, 130. In *My Bondage and My Freedom*, however, also listed at chapter's end, Frederick Douglass explains how slavery could rend family ties so thoroughly that they could not be reconnected.

17. George Rawick, ed., *The American Slave*, 18 (Westport, CT: Greenwood, 1972 [1941]), 43–44.

18. Loewen, *The Mississippi Chinese* (Prospect Heights, IL: Waveland, 1988), 51–52.; cf. David Bertelson, *The Lazy South* (NYC: Oxford UP, 1967).

19. Ruth B. Gross, *If You Grew Up with George Washington* (NYC: Scholastic, 1993).

20. Las Casas, *History of the Indies* (NYC: Harper & Row, 1971), 257; Las Casas quoted in Marcel Bataillon, "The Clerigo Casas," in Juan Friede and Benjamin Keen, *Bartolomé de Las Casas in History* (DeKalb: Northern IL UP, 1971), 415–16. Las Casas went on to say that he has prayed to God to have mercy on his soul for giving the pro-slavery advice in the first place, but "he does not know if God will do so." See also Loewen, *Lies My Teacher Told Me About Christopher Columbus*, originally *The Truth About Columbus* (NYC: New P, 1992), 34; "Antonio de Montesinos," Virtual American Biographies website, famousamericans.net/antoniodemontesinos/, 5/2008.

21. Loewen, *Lies My Teacher Told Me About Christopher Columbus*, 34–35; Thomas Benjamin, "A Time of Reconquest: History, the Maya Revival, and the Zapatista Rebellion in Chiapas," *American Historical Review* 4/2000, 424–27.

22. That we do not recall the name of their leader is an important part of the story, because they seem not to have had one leader. This revolt, therefore, shows a general readiness to resist slavery, at least in Louisiana, not a movement dependent upon a single charismatic leader.

23. Over time, every last root cellar in Vermont has become a stop on the Underground Railroad. While it's wonderful that so many Americans *wish* their property or their ancestors had played a role in opposing slavery, good history requires that only those properties and ancestors that *did* play a role get honored for it today. The National Park Service is completing a list of valid sites. Send results to them via nps.gov/history/ugrr/.

24. Ball quoted in Lynne Duke, "This Harrowed Ground," *Washington Post Magazine* (8/24/1994), 22.

Chapter 9 (pp. 175–88)

1. Steven Deyle, "Competing Ideologies in the Old South," presented at the American Historical Association, 1/99. As I write in 2008, gasoline prices are at an all-time high. Oil companies rejoice while auto manufacturers and airlines sink into debt. Slaveowners shared several fundamental interests, however, whether their slaves grew cotton or rice or made nails.

2. The "Declaration of Immediate Causes" is available in many places on the web, such as extlab7.entnem.ufl.edu/Olustee/related/sc.htm.

3. Moreover, if a citizen of a New England state who was denied citizenship in a slave state actually brought a case against that state, they might yet have prevailed on Constitutional grounds. Here Taney contradicts Article IV, Section 2: "The citizens of each state shall be entitled to all privileges and immunities of citizens in the several states." In such a case, Taney's language in this part of *Dred Scott* might be considered *obiter dictum*. Also, *Dred Scott* was wrong in its facts. When the U.S. formed, African Americans voted more widely than they did decades later, when Taney wrote his decision. To claim they had "no rights which the white man was bound to respect" overstated the matter, as Justice Curtis pointed out at the time in his dissent.

4. Secessionists also denounced the idea of local sovereignty in the territories, although South Carolina did not do so in this document. In the Missouri Compromise, Congress had closed territories north of the Arkansas-Missouri line to slavery, except Missouri itself. That was fine with most slaveowners in 1820. By the 1850s, however, they wanted more. Stephen A. Douglas wanted territorial governments in Kansas and Nebraska, until then Indian land, mainly to further his railroad interests. Slaveowners agreed to support the new territories only if Douglas included language opening them to slavery. Douglas capitulated and incorporated what he called "popular sovereignty" in the bill. This meant Kansas could become a slave state if it chose to, even though it lay north of the Missouri Compromise line. So, for that matter, could Nebraska. The notion was in accord with states' rights.

Within a year or two, this breakthrough was no longer enough for Southern extremists. One reason was, settlers in Kansas did not want slavery. At first, pro-slavery forces responded by trying to hijack the Kansas territorial government. "Border ruffians" from Missouri crossed over and voted, while intimidating some "Free Soil" settlers from voting. The Pierce and Buchanan administrations, controlled by the pro-slavery wing of the Democratic Party, went along. Eventually, pro-slavery leaders realized they could not prevail in Kansas, so they looked to federal protection of slavery, regardless of local sentiment. The pro-slavery Supreme Court majority granted this wish in *Dred Scott*. Indeed, Chief Justice Taney even denied that a legally constituted territorial government *could* pass laws restricting slavery.

5. Three other factors possibly underlay secession. Southern political discourse grew ever more extreme. By the late 1850s, Southerners were demanding that the federal government pass a slave code guaranteeing slavery in all federal territories. This was not politically feasible, but the internal dynamics of political rhetoric in the South made it hard to be reasonable. Just to admit that insisting upon guarantees for slavery in parts of the United States where slavery would never succeed made no sense caused politicians to get labeled "unsound on slavery." Then, having demanded slavery throughout the territories, having put their "honor" on the line and that of their state or section, politicians could not back down when, for example, Democrats nominated an opponent of a territorial slave code (Stephen A. Douglas), so they had to secede from the Democratic Party. Similarly, having stated that the election of "the black Republican" would threaten slavery in the South, they had to secede from the nation when Lincoln won.

Second, some participants claimed that white Southerners seceded simply to have power, to rule their own country. John A. Logan of Illinois advanced this argument in *The Great Conspiracy* (NYC: A. R. Hart, 1886, especially Chapter 11). To a degree, the argument is circular: Southerners formed their own government to form their own government.

Third, some slaveowners feared that Republican ideology might eventually make headway in slave states. They may have been right. Certainly most whites in east Tennessee, west Virginia, western North Carolina, northwest Arkansas, north Texas, and scattered other subregions in the South opposed secession, some because they opposed slavery. Pro-slavery leaders worried that if they did not secede on the occasion of Lincoln's election, they might not have another chance later. Then slavery might find itself threatened from within the South.

As causes of secession, these factors are more nebulous than slavery and the election of Lincoln. Necessarily they could never have been announced publicly—hence Logan's book title. Nor do they conflict with slavery and the election of Lincoln. I think they are nuances, too advanced for high school classes to consider.

Finally, near its end, the South Carolina document does predict that after Lincoln takes over, "a war must be waged against slavery until it shall cease throughout the United States." Then "the equal rights of the States will be lost. The slaveholding States will no longer have the power of self-government, or self protection. . . ." A diehard proponent of the claim that the South seceded for states' rights might exclaim, "Aha!", for here at last is a mention of "the equal rights of the States." The context is all slavery, however—worry about a federal war against slavery, a war that Lincoln had denied any intention to wage.

6. I do not suggest the literal continuation of the slave power. The next chapter shows that the same social and ideological elements in Southern society that welcomed *Dred Scott* and then forced secession won their point around 1890. During the Nadir of race relations (1890–1940), they minimized the role of slavery in causing secession. We still do.

7. David Duncan Wallace, *South Carolina: A Short History* (Columbia: U of SC P, 1951), 527.

8. *Richmond Daily Enquirer*, 11/2/1864, quoted in Drew Gilpin Faust, *The Creation of Confederate Nationalism* (Baton Rouge: LA State UP, 1988), 60.

9. John Mosby, "Letter to Sam Chapman, 6/4/1907" (NYC: Gilder Lehrman Institute of American History, GLC3921.21).

10. William C. Davis, *The Cause Lost: Myths and Realities of the Confederacy* (Lawrence: UP of KS, 1996), 177.

11. The books included Joyce Appleby, Alan Brinkley, and James McPherson, *The American Journey* (NYC: Glencoe McGraw-Hill, 2000); Daniel J. Boorstin and Brooks Mather Kelley, *A History of the United States* (Needham, MA: Pearson Prentice Hall, 2005); Paul Boyer, *Holt American Nation* (NYC: Holt, Rinehart, & Winston, 2003); Andrew Cayton et al., *America: Pathways to the Present* (Needham, MA: Pearson Prentice Hall, 2005); Gerald A. Danzer et al., *The Americans* (Boston: McDougal Littell [Houghton Mifflin], 2007); and David Kennedy, Lizabeth Cohen, and Thomas A. Bailey, *The American Pageant* (Boston: Houghton Mifflin, 2006). The last does quote from the South Carolina document but manages to avoid any

actual cause by the adroit use of ellipses. I suspect that Houghton Mifflin simply did not want to mention slavery, imagining that some Southern state textbook adoption board might take offense.

12. Holt does go on without delay to mention slavery: "The issue went beyond states' rights, however. Also at stake was the determination of the southerners to protect slavery...." Nevertheless, most readers would perceive states' rights as the primary reason, slavery second.

13. Alert readers will notice that I do not attack "the basic economic and social differences of the North and the South" as a cause of secession, because that phrase can be a euphemism for slavery.

14. Textbook editor, personal communication, 7/2006.

15. Well, Davis was born in Missouri, but he now teaches at Virginia Tech and has thrice won the Jefferson Davis Award, given by the Museum of the Confederacy.

Chapter 10 (pp. 189–208)

1. Historian Rayford Logan established the term in his *The Negro in American Life and Thought: The Nadir*. I use somewhat different dates but have been influenced by Logan's fine work, reprinted as *The Betrayal of the Negro* (NYC: Macmillan Collier, 1965 [1954]).

2. Robert A. Frister, "Forgotten heroes: Black winners of the Kentucky Derby," *Ebony*, 5/1989, at findarticles.com/p/articles/mi_m1077/is_n7_v44/ai_7568349, 7/2008.

3. Robert Azug and Stephen Maizlish, eds., *New Perspectives on Race and Slavery in America* (Lexington: UP of KY, 1986), 118–21, 125.

4. D is particularly useful because it is not affected by the overall proportion of African Americans in the metropolitan area. Thus we can compare the level of residential segregation in Atlanta (56% black in 2000) to Seattle (8% black), or Detroit in 2000 (83% black) to Detroit in 1890 (<2% black). D works for two groups at a time, here blacks and nonblacks.

5. This photo was taken in early 1857 or perhaps late 1856. (Thanks to Jean Libby for close scholarship on the date.) Within two years, Brown did grow a beard, perhaps in a modest attempt at a disguise. There was a price on his head after he helped eleven African Americans escape bondage in Missouri late in 1858 and get to Canada.

6. John Logan, Brian Stults, and Reynolds Farley, "Segregation of Minorities in the Metropolis: Two Decades of Change," *Demography*, 41 #1 (2/2004), Table 2.

7. James Loewen and Charles Sallis, *Mississippi: Conflict and Change* (NYC: Pantheon, 1974), 188.

8. I quote President Grant, writing much earlier, who was in the process of washing his hands of federal responsibility for dealing with the problem.

9. William Graham Sumner, *Folkways* (NYC: Mentor, 1960 [1906]), 91.

10. John K. Bettersworth, *Mississippi: Yesterday and Today* (Austin: Steck-Vaughn, 1964), 222.

11. Noah Andre Trudeau, *Like Men of War* (Boston: Little, Brown, 1998), 44.

12. Kenneth M. Stampp, "The Tragic Legend of Reconstruction," in Stampp and Leon Litwack, eds., *Reconstruction* (Baton Rouge: LA State UP, 1969), 17–20.

13. Madison Grant, *The Passing of the Great Race* (NYC: Scribner's, 1922 [1916]), 16.

14. Leola Bergmann, "The Negro in Iowa," *Iowa Journal of History and Politics*, 1969 [1948], 44–45.

15. Places to look for old textbooks include used bookstores and the main library and education library of the nearest state university. A few school districts keep copies of old textbooks or donate them to community libraries. The state textbook boards of those states that adopt textbooks statewide—about half of all states—may have kept copies of all books they adopted. These boards mostly date only to the Depression, however, so they will not have textbooks older than that. Local history rooms in community and college libraries will have state histories; while not textbooks, they, too, provide fascinating comparisons over time.

16. The entire manuscript census is available online at Ancestry.com. State historical societies and other libraries make it available for their state. The 1890 census was destroyed in a fire.

17. Chapter 11 of Loewen, *Social Science in the Courtroom* (Lexington: D.C. Heath, 1982), tells how to compute D and what D means.

18. My website, http://sundown.afro.illinois.edu/, provides a short article telling how to do this research.

19. Jerry Poling, *A Summer Up North* (Madison: U of WI P, 2002), 10.

20. Herbert Small, *Handbook of the New Library of Congress* (Boston: Curtis & Cameron, 1897), 15. I changed some spelling to match modern usage.

21. *Ibid.*, 13–15.

22. Noel Ignatiev, *How the Irish Became White* (NYC: Routledge, 1996); Karen Brodkin, *How Jews Became White Folks and What That Says About Race in America* (New Brunswick, NJ: Rutgers UP, 1998).

23. Granite City Public Library, *75th Year Celebration of the City of Granite City, IL* (Granite City, no publisher listed, 1971), 24. In *Whiteness of a Different Color*, Matthew Jacobson showed how whites unified racially nationwide during this period (Cambridge, MA: Harvard UP, 1998). Cf. *Sundown Towns* (NYC: New P, 2005), 95, 119, 157, 411.

24. David M. P. Freund, *Making It Home* (Ann Arbor: U of MI Ph.D., 1999), 515.

Afterword (pp. 209–11)

1. Indeed, the class can be asked, "Are you ready to be quizzed about the Mohawks? If not, tell [the student presenter] what more you need to know." Self-interest then leads students to give good critiques.

2. Loewen, *The Mississippi Chinese: Between Black and White* (Prospect Heights, IL: Waveland, 1988 [1971]).

3. R. A. Lafferty, *Okla Hannali* (Norman: U of OK P, 1991 [1972]).

4. Margaret Walker, *Jubilee* (NYC: Bantam, 1967 [1966]).

5. This question can also be asked throughout the year, perhaps as part of a recurring "fun with history" day.

Index

About the Author

James W. Loewen taught race relations for twenty years at the University of Vermont. Previously he taught at predominantly black Tougaloo College in Mississippi. He now lives in Washington, DC, continuing his research on how Americans remember their past, and gives workshops for teacher groups around the United States.

His gripping retelling of American history as it should and could be taught, *Lies My Teacher Told Me*, has sold more than 1,100,000 copies and continues to inspire K–16 teachers to get students to challenge, rather than memorize, their textbooks. It won the American Book Award and the Oliver Cromwell Cox Award for Distinguished Anti-Racist Scholarship. *Lies Across America: What Our Historic Sites Get Wrong* came out in 1999. The Gustavus Myers Foundation named his new book, *Sundown Towns*, a "Distinguished Book of 2005."

His other books include *Mississippi: Conflict and Change* (coauthored), which won the Lillian Smith Award for Best Southern Nonfiction but was rejected for public school text use by the State of Mississippi, leading to the path-breaking First Amendment lawsuit, *Loewen et al. v. Turnipseed et al.* He also wrote *The Mississippi Chinese: Between Black and White*, *Social Science in the Courtroom*, and *The Truth About Columbus*.

He has been an expert witness in more than 50 civil rights, voting rights, and employment cases. His awards include the First Annual Spivack Award of the American Sociological Association for "sociological research applied to the field of intergroup relations" and Fulbright and Smithsonian fellowships. He is also Distinguished Lecturer for the Organization of American Historians.